*Barnes & Noble Critical Studies*

---

*General Editor: Anne Smith*

# The Art of Jonathan Swift

# THE ART OF JONATHAN SWIFT

edited by

## Clive T. Probyn

BARNES & NOBLE
BOOKS
10 East 53d St., New York 10022
(a division of Harper & Row Publishers, Inc.)

Barnes & Noble Books
Harper & Row, Publishers, Inc.
10 East 53rd Street
New York

ISBN 0-06-495737-3

First published in the U.S.A. 1978


Printed and bound in Great Britain
MCMLXXVIII

# Contents

# Preface: Swift and the Reader's Role

> I profess to *Your Highness*, in the Integrity of my Heart, that what I am going to say is literally true this Minute I am writing: What Revolutions may happen before it shall be ready for your Perusal, I can by no means warrant.[1]

Here, in the dedication to Prince Posterity, in Swift's first book, *A Tale of a Tub*, is a key to Swift's complexity as a satirist and a reason for his continuing fascination. In the very moment of communication with his reader Swift's narrator reveals a startling awareness: meaning is not determined, least of all controlled, by the author but by the world of his readers. Swift's hack realises that the privileged, Renaissance intimacy between writer and patron has collapsed in the face of the indeterminable and heterogeneous demands of a new mass readership. The meanings we intend to convey through language are the victims of imprecision because language itself belongs in the public domain, common property with an infinite number of claimants. Swift is unique in his time, among literary artists, in exploiting this cultural realisation in satire. Critical interpretation of his satire is seen, at source, to be a sophisticated game subject to an infinite number of rules and procedures. As creator, Swift disappears behind substitute images, and we are each invited to replace the narrator as determiners of a 'fixed' textual meaning. The reader, via the book, becomes the target of Swift's satirical strategies.

It is characteristic of Swift's dramatic and self-regarding rhetoric that his own brief biography is written in the third person,[2] as though holding himself at arm's length might provide the required detachment from the bewildering personalities of authorship which he created elsewhere in his work. But Swift's ultimate elusiveness is remarkable. On the face of it there are so many portraits: the oblique intimacies of the *Journal to Stella*; the apparently autobiographical poems such as 'Verses on the Death of Dr. Swift' and 'Cadenus and Vanessa'; the magnificently detailed correspondence; and the secondary re-creations of his many biographers. Few authors have found themselves so endlessly interesting as literary subjects, and none have created so many images of the artistic self. But what we have left to us are crypto-Swifts; the playful confidant in the *Journal* is a narrative 'I', but in *Gulliver's Travels* the narrative 'I' is a front-man only, whereas in poems like 'The Day of Judgement' and 'The Place of the Damn'd' the 'Swiftian' element is no more than a raging tone of voice. Swift's harlequin disguises are adopted to divert the populace, to tease the perceptive readers into a narrative game which shocks them by a limitless talent for moral discovery through imitation of the familiar modes and commonplaces, and a re-creation of them in radically new guises. If to Swift the act of writing was the art of self-projection, as Pope realised in his *Dunciad* dedication to 'Dean, Drapier, Bickerstaff, or Gulliver', then the art of reading Swift is like entering a contest with an opponent who not only keeps changing the rules but who also eventually changes place with his opponent in order to enjoy the anarchy of his own absence.

In a famous article written in 1938 George Sherburn coolly observed that 'Of the making of many books about Jonathan Swift there is no end, and the reason is perhaps obvious: each admirer feels that he alone really understands Swift'.[3] The reason may be obvious, but it underrates Swift's own part in the reader's feeling. A more recent critic digs deeper. Henry W. Sams noted that 'more reputations survive encrusted in Swiftian commentary than were punctured by his satire', rather like maggots living on the corpse of one dead lion. The reason for this is that Swift is not only himself, but also 'the long story of numerous more or less adept virtuosi, who at times seem to seek themselves to be the amber and to make Swift the grub.' But Swift ultimately escapes from his critics, to stand apart as 'a sort of accidental absolute, a complex and irreducible fact of the language that we inhabit.'[4] In all of his 'situational comedies' (to use Quintana's phrase), Swift holds himself in reserve, entering the game only rarely *in propria persona*, and usually concentrates our narrative expectations on an intermediary narrative 'I', a created presence who invites the reader to react to him, though not necessarily to Swift. Thus if 'Swift' is the creation of his readers, it is also true that Swift has anticipated the role which they have adopted.

But the satirical energy in Swift's work drives a paradox. It not only invites and involves the reader, it disorganizes him once he is involved. The energy is entropic:[5] it frustrates the expected system of any particular genre. As Bertrand Bronson puts it, 'The world of print was made to order for Swift . . . How much confidence does he inspire in us that we have read him as he meant?'[6] The travel-narrative of *Gulliver's Travels*, the economic procedures of *A Modest Proposal*, the very physical form of the printed book in *A Tale of A Tub*, are each inverted, turned into a self-parodying feast. In each case it is Swift who turns the created author's *self-conscious* act of communication with the reader into an *involuntary* act of self-indictment and a revelation of private obsession. Again, the reader's role is to discriminate the overt intention of the *persona* from the covert intention of the creator-Swift. Whereas Richardson or Defoe denied the fictional rules by pretending that their books were images of a primary egocentric reality (arranged by an editor, but not written by an 'artist'), Swift always lets his representative voices acknowledge the *mode* of writing as an artefact, with public rules and procedures, but only to expose their inadequacies and errors.[7]

The central vehicle for this conversion is parody, a parasitic device which draws its life-blood from a parent model in order to create a hybrid offspring. Swift thus innovates from the rules of conventional forms and expectations. A passage from Thomas Mann's *Doctor Faustus* poignantly describes the motives for parody as 'intellectual mockery of art . . . the proud expedient of a great gift threatened with sterility by a combination of scepticism, intellectual reserve, and a sense of the deadly extension of the kingdom of the banal.'[8] Most readers of Swift would perhaps agree that his work shows, at the very least, an obsessive desire to free itself from the demands of a culturally degraded present, and that it does so by destructive means. But there is nothing effete about Swift's response to the dulness of his time. He confronts the present with a catastrophically *energetic* image of its own cultural disorders. The prodigal allusiveness of *A Tale of a Tub* makes the past a quarry and a graveyard for pedants, poetasters and preachers alike. It is an 'encyclopaedia of the follies of the seventeenth century.' But it is also uniquely prophetic of something quite new, a parody of the novel form nearly a generation before the first novel actually appeared.[9] The interpretative dilemma is tragically concentrated in Swift's image of the hack, desperately aware of the fragmentation of his own mind, his book, his audience, and of the language itself. Mouthpiece as well as satiric target, the hack uses the old forms of flattering address to a patron, with all the assumptions of agreed meaning, in a context of polysemic *dis*integration which destroys meaning in the act of creating it:

> where I am not understood, it shall be concluded that something very useful or profound is coucht underneath: And again, that whatever word or Sentence is Printed in a different Character, shall be judged to contain something extraordinary either of *Wit* or *Sublime*.[10]

The medium itself becomes the message, and the reader is asked to assume the role of interpretation left vacant by the author's dereliction. Words themselves must sink or swim according to the pleasure (or intellectual pride) of the individual reader. Like the hero of Sterne's *Tristram Shandy* the author has been defeated by the act of writing the book, and Swift underlines the status of the narrator as victim rather than hero by gaps in the manuscript at crucial points of 'deep meaning.' The narrator's mad scramble after intelligible form is dissipated by a doomed attempt to universalize atomizing truths: 'if the Audience be well compact, every one carries home a Share, and little or nothing is lost.' The reader is left with the crumbs of a chaotic feast.

The narrator of the *Tale* is, like Gulliver and the modest proposer, Swift's victim and proxy voice. This does not mean, however, that Swift's own values are simply ascertained by reversing the satire. Doubtless Swift did believe in the 'positives' which Ehrenpreis adduces from his work, and which include 'the Established Church, limited monarchy, classical literary standards, and rational judgements . . . the cultivation of Graeco-Roman antiquity, improved by Christian ethics and a cheering hope of salvation . . .

the monuments of unageing intellect';[11] but what Swift writes about most vividly are the antagonists and obstacles to such values. The distinction between such positives and their negative images is not easy to define in satire, but a valid distinction arises from what has been said already, i.e. the separable worlds of public and private conduct. A clue is provided in a letter Swift wrote in 1714 to his friend the Earl of Oxford: 'For in your publick Capacity [Lord Treasurer in Queen Anne's reign and Swift's political patron] you have often angred me to the Heart, but, as a private man, never once. So that if I only looktd towards my self I could wish you a private Man to morrow.'[12] The satirist's concern is always for the gap between the potential and the performance, between the ideal and the reality, and between what is desirable and what is practicable. Satire loses its efficacy if it suggests that there are grey areas in between where accommodation, compromise, and concessions are necessary. Even in his non-satirical programmes for moral reform Swift is radical, even extremist. His *Project for the Advancement of Religion, and the Reformation of Manners*[13] (published in 1709, the year of Swift's 'Apology' for the *Tale*), is a moral defence of the realm act, recommending reform through censorship, a spy network, early closing of taverns, leadership from the top in court, church, army, the universities, theatre and law. In making a public duty out of private self-interest it consciously recommends hypocrisy as the preferred alternative to open vice and infidelity. Its cynical and totalitarian quality seems to fly in the face of Swift's whole satiric career. Yet it does not. In the Aeolist section of *A Tale* man's learning is seen as no more than a skin, a suit of changeable clothes worn for the occasion, an accident of his essentially corrupt and ugly inner being. In the *Project* this 'satire' becomes an assumed premise, a truth. A habit, whether good or bad, may become the inner essence simply by the process of time and the pressures of social convention: 'a long continued Disguise is too great a Constraint upon Human Nature, especially an English Disposition . . . it is often with Religion as it is with Love; which, by much Dissembling, at last grows real.' It is not simply that some kinds of hypocrisy, in a fallen world, are less bad than others, but that hypocrisy *per se* is the pragmatic ground rule for vast areas of social and spiritual organization. If consensus demands the suppression of individualism, then stability and order may have a chance of survival. For the individual there *is* a choice, but it is a choice of evils:

> This is the sublime and refined Point of Felicity, called *the Possession of being well deceived*; The Serene Peaceful State of being a Fool among Knaves.

Swift's knaves are legion: disputing theologians, prying philosophers, self-advertising hack writers, carping critics, corrupt politicians. The fools are those naïve enough to allow any of the former group to persuade them into fellow-travelling. The wise man, like Swift's image of the Bee, is an independent eclectic, of no sect or persuasion, independently exercising his God-given powers of reasoned judgement, attempting the hardest task of all, in fact, which is making up his own mind in a world of patent stupidity and corruption.

As readers of Swift we belong in the outside world, subject to the strategies which he evolved to cross the void between private integrity and public compromise. Above all else Swift's real target is any sense in the reader that he alone is comfortably above and beyond implication. 'Reason itself', he wrote in his sermon on the Trinity, 'is true and just, but the Reason of every particular Man is weak and wavering, perpetually swayed and turned by his Interests, his Passions, and his Vices.' We see the better course, and approve it, but we follow the worse. Similarly, what we 'see' when we read Swift is not Swift himself, not the screenwork of his many personae, all of whom buttonhole us so vehemently, but something much more subversive: an image of our own involvement not only as readers of texts but also as actors or puppets in the human comedy of life itself.

Swift's critics are maggots in Sams' precise sense, 'devices for reducing dead lions to fertile soil, from which all manner of new life may spring'. Life continues to spring from Swift's perceptions, and it is therefore appropriate that this new collection of critical essays includes an examination, by David Woolley, of the earliest textual origins of Swift's most famous book, *Gulliver's Travels*. Angus Ross and J. A. Downie both reinterpret Swift's political writing (respectively, the Irish tracts and *The Conduct of the Allies*) in the light of biographical influences; two essays, one by David Nokes, and the other by the editor, concentrate on Swift's extraordinarily fertile use of linguistic ambiguity; two essays (by Jenny Mezciems and Pat Rogers) examine aspects of *Gulliver's Travels*; and the collection opens with W. B. Carnochan's essay on the private and public motivations of Swift's satire, drawing on the poetry for much of its evidence.

For help in the production of the illustrations to David Woolley's essay, which were photographed by Rodney Wright-Watson, I would like to thank Colin McKelvie and Joe Thompson, A.R.P.S.

C.T.P.

NOTES

1 *A Tale of a Tub To which is added The Battle of the Books and the Mechanical Operation of the Spirit*, ed. A. C. Guthkelch and D. Nichol Smith, second edition (Oxford, 1958), p. 36. All references throughout this book are to this edition, except where stated.

2 'Family of Swift', *The Prose Works of Jonathan Swift*, ed. Herbert Davis and others, 14 vols. (Oxford, 1939–68), V, 187–95, an unfinished sketch probably written 1727–9 and published after Stella's death, (1755). All subsequent references to Swift's *Prose Works* (except where stated) are to this edition.

3 George Sherburn, 'Methods in Books about Swift', *Studies in Philology*, XXXV (1938), 635–656, p. 635.

4 Henry W. Sams, 'An End to Writing about Swift', *Essays in Criticism*, XXIV (July, 1974), 3, 275–85.

5 Robert Alter uses this term, in another context, in *Partial Magic: The Novel as a Self-Conscious Genre* (Berkeley, 1975), p. 143, and also cites the passage from *Doctor Faustus* quoted below.

6 'The Writer', in *Man versus Society in 18th Century Britain*, ed. J. L. Clifford (Cambridge, 1968), pp. 117–18.

7 Claude Rawson remarks on *Gulliver's Travels* that 'Swift's whole ironic programme depends on our not being taken in by the travel book element, but it does require us to be infected with a residual uncertainty about it; and these instances of an over-successful hoax fulfil, extremely, a potential in the work to which all readers must uneasily respond.' See *Gulliver and the Gentle Reader: Studies in Swift and Our Time* (London and Boston, 1973), p. 9. On p. 12 Rawson writes of a 'quarrelsome intimacy' as the hallmark of Swift's satire.

8 Thomas Mann, *Doctor Faustus*, translated by H. T. Lowe-Porter (London, 1949), p. 154.

9 Cf. Gabriel Josipovici, *The World and the Book: A Study of Modern Fiction* (London, 1971), p. 154.

10 *Tale, ed. cit.*, pp. 46–7.

11 Irvin Ehrenpreis, *Swift The Man, his Works and the Age*, 2 vols. to date (London, 1962, 1967), I, 202–3.

12 *Correspondence of Jonathan Swift*, ed. Harold Williams, 5 vols. (Oxford, 1963–5), II, 44–5. All subsequent references to Swift's letters are to this edition.

13 *Prose Works*, II, 41–63. See Ehrenpreis, *op. cit.*, II, 276–297 for a discussion of the strategies involved in this piece.

# Brief Chronology of Swift's Life and Works

| | |
|---|---|
| 1667 | Jonathan Swift born in Dublin, 30 November, of English parents. |
| 1673–81 | Attends Kilkenny Grammar School. |
| 1682–86 | Trinity College Dublin; B.A. in 1686. |
| 1689 | Goes to Leicester after violence in Ireland following Revolution in England; secretary to Sir William Temple at Moor Park, Surrey; meets Esther Johnson ('Stella'). |
| 1690 | Returns to Ireland. |
| 1691 | Returns to his former employment at Moor Park. |
| 1692 | M.A. from Oxford; 'Ode to the Athenian Society'. |
| 1694 | Returns to Ireland and is ordained in the Anglican Church. |
| 1695 | Appointed prebendary of Kilroot. |
| 1696–99 | *A Tale of a Tub*, etc. written; chaplain to Berkeley, Lord Justice of Ireland; Temple dies in January 1699. |
| 1700 | Vicar of Laracor. |
| 1701 | Doctor of Divinity degree from Trinity College; writes *Contests and Dissensions* (the *Tale* was to be dedicated to one of the Whig lords, Somers, defended in this tract). |
| 1702–4 | Resident in England; *Tale* published in 1704. |
| 1707–9 | Represented Irish clergy seeking remission of the clerical taxes ('first fruits'); rejected by Whig government. |
| 1708 | *Sentiments of a Church of England Man.* |
| 1709 | Returns to England. |
| 1710–13 | *Miscellanies in Verse and Prose: Argument Against Abolishing Christianity;* returns to London for four years, shifts his allegiance from Whigs to Tories; *The Examiner* papers; *The Conduct of the Allies*; friendship with Harley and Bolingbroke. |
| 1713 | Dean of St. Patrick's Cathedral, Dublin; *The Publick Spirit of the Whigs*; 'Cadenus and Vanessa' (Esther Vanhomrigh). |
| 1714 | Swift and others found the Scriblerus Club; Swift returns to permanent residence in Ireland after death of Queen Anne and fall of the Tory government. |
| 1718 | Begins to write Irish tracts. |
| 1720 | *A Proposal for the Universal Use of Irish Manufacture*; begins to write *Gulliver's Travels.* |

| | |
|---|---|
| 1724 | *Drapier's Letters*, I–IV. |
| 1726 | *Gulliver's Travels* published, 28 October, Swift having left for Ireland two months previously. |
| 1727 | Last trip to England, April. |
| 1729 | *A Modest Proposal;* Swift given Freedom of the City of Dublin. |
| 1731 | 'Verses on the Death of Dr. Swift' (published 1739). |
| 1735 | First collected edition of Swift's works, in four volumes, published by George Faulkner, Dublin. |
| 1742 | His health failing, Swift was committed to the care of guardians. |
| 1745 | 19 October, Swift dies; buried in St. Patrick's Cathedral. |
| 1758 | *History of the Four Last years of the Queen* published. |

# I

# THE LANGUAGE AND MOTIVES OF SATIRE

# 1

# The Consolations of Satire

by W. B. CARNOCHAN

*1*

Swift threw up ramparts against pain and loss. One of these was an uncertain faith. Another was an art that inflicted pain and asserted power only to deny the pain and disavow the power. His satire murdered—not only to dissect but, ironically, to heal the wound of life itself. A riddle that I am convinced is Swift's own defines the processes of his satire:[1]

Most Things by me do rise and fall,
And as I please they're great and small;
Invading Foes, without Resistance,
With Ease I make to keep their Distance;
Again, as I'm dispos'd, the Foe
Will come, tho' not a Foot they go.
Both Mountains, Woods, and Hills, and Rocks,
And gaming Goats, and fleecy Flocks,
And lowing Herds, and piping Swains,
Come dancing to me o'er the Plains.
The greatest Whale, that swims the Sea
Does distantly my Pow'r obey.
In vain from me the Sailor flies,
The quickest Ship I can surprize,
And turn it as I have a Mind,
And move it against Tyde and Wind.
Nay, bring me here the tallest Man,
I'll squeeze him to a little Span,
Or bring a tender Child and pliant,
You'll see me stretch him to a Giant;
Nor shall they in the least complain,
Because my Magick gives no Pain.

this riddle of the mirror not be by Swift? Not only reflections of the *Tale* ('The greatest Whale, that swims Sea / Does distantly my Pow'r obey'), of *Gulliver's Travels* ('Nay . . . Giant') and of the *Modest Proposal* ('a tender Child and pliant'), but the autocratic power of the mirror is fair compensation for the Dean of St. Patrick's disappointed hopes for a life of power and place. The manipulations of distance in the last three couplets have the true Swiftian feeling to them. The divine but remote monarch of the opening lines becomes more and more petulant and threatening, summoning some unnamed bailiff-at-arms to fetch the tallest man in the kingdom for summary torture or a child to be put to the rack; yet there is a counterpoint to the tone of threat, an offhandedness of manner that transforms threat into casual gesture and the imperative 'bring' into amiable speculation: if you'll bring me the tallest man or a tender child, I will do terrible things to them that aren't really terrible at all. What's more, they won't mind, not in the least:

> Nor shall they in the least complain,
> Because my Magick gives no Pain.

This is less than straightforward, with its characteristic play on the forms of negation. Swift was forever amusing himself with the ambiguous 'in the least', and the more one dwells on the negatives in this couplet, the more precarious the sense becomes. For one thing, the syntax is two-edged; the victims of the mirror's power do not in the least (or, therefore, do) complain for either one of two reasons: 'Because' can be taken not only as pointing to the reason for their not complaining but also in the sense of 'that', in which case one ironic meaning is that, since they are not really victims at all, they cry out masochistically for something worse. But it is reasonable to settle for the most available of Swift's meanings: the victims don't complain because they aren't hurt. That is to say, they are like many of the victims in, and of, his satire.

*2*

It may not be sentimental to feel that Swift had more than his share of losses. The father who died before he was born, the mother who left him to the care of a nurse, the sister from whom he was separated, the substitute father (Temple) whose death left him without a patron, his hopes for preferment that were never fulfilled, his yearnings for absent friends while he suffered the frustrations of life in Ireland—the catalog of deprivations is a long one. To be sure, disappointment provides the theme of many a life and is hardly quantifiable. What is certain, however, is that Swift, even if he had to endure no more than some others, had the strong inclination to define his life by its disappointments:

> I remember when I was a little boy, I felt a great fish at the end of my line which I drew up almost on the ground, but it dropt in, and the disappointment vexeth me to this very day, and I believe it was the type of all my future disappointments.[2]

Phyllis Greenacre calls this a 'screen memory'—a minor incident of childhood to which special emotional importance is attached.[3] In the fish that got away from young Jonathan Swift we feel the tug of his grand hopes as well as his grand disappointments. Things he wanted slipped off his line just as he thought he had landed them, like the bishopric he hoped for. Of course those who don't get what they want sometimes don't really want it. In the case of his attachment to Jane Waring, Swift decided he didn't want to land his catch and engaged in strategies of letting go while pretending still to be hanging on.[4] But whatever the exact psychic truth of Swift's case, the tale of the fish that was the type of his future disappointments shows him acting out in his mind a disastrous parody: where the Old Testament foreshadowed, was a type of, the fulfillment to come, Swift's boyhood frustration foreshadows the later frustrations of his life. And, as a typological sign, it implies not only the frustration of specific losses but the vanity of human things.

Another of Swift's riddles is called '*The* Gulph *of all* human Possessions'.[5] It is full of cloacal joking about loss, some of it mainly satirical—

> This Gulph insatiable imbibes
> The Lawyer's Fees, the Statesman's Bribes.
> Here, in their proper Shape and Mein,
> Fraud, Perjury, and Guilt are seen.
> (ll. 19–22)

But some of it lies on the line between pun and elegy. It begins:

> Come hither and behold the Fruits,
> Vain Man, of all thy vain Pursuits.
> Take wise Advice, and *look behind*,
> Bring all *past* Actions to thy Mind.
> Here you may see, as in a Glass,
> How soon all human Pleasures pass.
> (ll. 1–6)

The italics are a fine and calculated affront to decency, but the claim that human endeavours are just excremental outpourings of a life, all of them signifying not gain but loss, strengthens the *vanitas* theme by grounding it in the realities of the body. Not only are human endeavours vain excrement, but excreting is a vain endeavour, practised daily. In '*The* Gulph *of all* human Possessions', in the scatological poems, and in still another of the riddles, to which the answer is 'Time'[6]—

> Ever eating, never cloying,
> All devouring, all destroying,
> Never finding full Repast,
> Till I eat the World at last—

the cycle of experience is a vicious cycle of the body, eating and evacuating, no sooner gaining than losing.

At the same time, Swift was adept at compensatory denials. One of these was to see this cycle as not only destructive but generative. Once Time has eaten the world 'at last', the waste matter of the world is still to be accounted for and, out of the dung of the world, may not gaudy tulips and other works in time arise?[7] When, at the end of the *Tale of a Tub*, life stirs from the nothingness that the author has been reduced to writing about, the ironic vision becomes affirmative and the pulse of the world starts up again. Out of the gulph of human possessions, 'a new Creation springs':

> Yet from this *mingled Mass* of Things,
> In Time a new Creation springs.
> These *crude* Materials once shall rise,
> To fill the Earth, and Air, and Skies:
> In various Forms appear agen
> Of Vegetables, Brutes, and Men.

*So Jove* pronounc'd among the Gods,
*Olympus* trembling as he nods.
(ll. 89–96)

The desolation of the outhouse leads to resurrection and even plenitude: earth, air, and sky will be filled again.[8]

But I have gotten ahead of myself. Swift's most successful compensations were public, not private; in his art rather than his life. Faced with the finality of human loss and the reality of pain, he was hard put to maintain composure and was often far less than stoical himself. He was uneasy in the presence of others' pain, especially when mingled with fear of social disgrace. The disturbing situation of his friend, Knightley Chetwode, about to separate from his wife, inspired some characteristic hedging. A letter to Chetwode in 1724 opens with customary complaints about Swift's state of health—complaints that serve a useful purpose here because they put him at a remove from the unpleasant business ahead. 'I am now relapsed into my old disease of deafness, which so confounds my head, that I am ill qualified for writing or thinking.' It is almost as if he were saying to Chetwode: 'I can't hear you.' But he cannot avoid the issue, and the surprising thing is that the suggestion to separate may have come from Swift: 'As to what you mention of my proposal at the Deanery, as far as a confused head will give me leave to think, I was always of opinion that those who are sure they cannot live well together, could not do a better thing than part.' If the suggestion was Swift's, he shields himself from it by recourse to his state of mind: he is an old deaf man with a muddled head. Still he owns up to being 'always of opinion' that those who can't live well together ought to part, and his advice to Chetwode is deeply revealing: 'I am likewise of opinion', he says, 'that such a thing as parting, if it be agreed on, may be done without noise, as if it were only going to visit a friend, and the absence may continue by degrees, and little notice taken.'[9] Much of this has to do with the fear of social shame, but the appeal to social values—the avoidance of 'noise' and notice—conceals deeper stratagems. Parting is just going to visit a friend—the public excuse, that is, becoming an act of psychic self-protection. Pain is lightened that way. If parting is going to visit a friend, maybe death is going to sleep. These stratagems are rooted in the fear of loss.

Hurt pride, Antonia Wenkart has said, 'erects a defensive wall against pain and on it is written *noli me tangere*'. At the same time, 'absence of pain is itself painful', and when the struggle to deny pain is successful, 'yet there lingers regret because an important event or a person has been made light of, skipped over, bypassed.'[10] In Swift's advice to Chetwode, the struggle is in its way successful—but at the price of skipping over an important person. Reasons of social discretion have something to do with the way Swift speaks of Mrs. Chetwode—but not everything: 'I am of opinion that this [a settlement] might best be done by knowing fairly, what the person herself would think the lowest that would be sufficient for what you propose . . .'[11] Chetwode's wife has turned into a non-person. Talk of 'the person herself' and of 'the lowest that would be sufficient for what you propose' anaesthetizes the mind. Behind the impersonal economics of a potential settlement lies the unacknowledged wound. The regret lingers on.

As partings mimic death, so did the presence of death call up Swift's urgent feelings. A 1727 letter to Mrs. Moore, on the death of her favourite daughter, blends piety with disquieting efforts at palliation. This much is unexceptionable: 'The dear Person you lament, is by no Means an Object of Pity, either in a moral or religious Sense. Philosophy always taught Men to despise Life, as a most contemptible thing in itself, and Religion regards it only as a Preparation for a better.' It was not Swift's way, however, to let the matter go at that. What (one wonders) did Mrs. Moore think of the proposition that 'Self-love, as it is the Motive to all our Actions, so it is the sole Cause of our Grief'? Or the proposition that it is more reasonable 'to reflect rather upon what is left, than what is lost'; and that the dead girl 'was neither an only Child, nor an only Daughter. You have three Children left, one of them of an Age to be Useful to his Family, and the two others as promising as can be expected from their Age'? Or of Swift's reflections on the perils of being a favourite child, 'Common Observation shewing us, that such favourite Children are either spoiled by their Parent's Indulgence, or soon taken out of the World; which last is, generally speaking, the lighter Punishment of the two'? If all our actions stem from self-love, the mother's love for her child is self-serving. The counting up of Mrs. Moore's remaining children and their attributes depends on a view of love as quantitative and self-serving. And the moralizing about parents who spoil a favorite child is alarming on any rational account: should Mrs. Moore conclude that the death of her child makes a better bargain than if she had lived and grown up under an indulgent hand? But rational accounts are not to the point. Mind is near the edge of its resources here; it is not the coherence or incoherence of Swift's response that counts most but its intensity. In the long run, intensity burns itself out in something like true resignation: the sufferings and losses of 'our declining Years' are 'intended by the Author of our Being, to wean us gradually from our Fondness of Life, the nearer we approach towards the End of it.' This is measured, believable. But Swift has reached this point at a price. The weaning of our affections seems gradual only in retrospect, over an interval of time. Wisdom comes with weariness as trauma succeeds trauma. Small wonder that Swift ends his letter with an apology: 'I fear my present ill Disposition both of Health and Mind has made me but a sorry Comforter.'[12]

In truth Swift was never cut out to be a comforter, at least not in the usual way, and he was especially bad at it when guilt colored the attempt at consolation. This is what happens in '*Cadenus* and *Vanessa*'.[13] Swift was bad, that is, when it came to seeing himself as the source of another's pain. Draping an elaborate mythological cloak over the naked embarrassment of Vanessa's passion, '*Cadenus* and *Vanessa*' aims to assuage pain by mixing denial with self-irony:

> *Vanessa*, not in Years a Score,
> Dreams of a Gown of forty-four;
> Imaginary Charms can find,
> In Eyes with Reading almost blind.
> (ll. 524–527)

Vanessa's infatuation can be explained only as an episode in a preposterous pastoral drama about shepherds and nymphs, about Venus and Pallas Athene and Cupid, a pastoral drama in which rationality and feeling both submit to cosmological lunacy. '*Cadenus* and *Vanessa*', to my way of thinking, is an unsatisfying poem, depending as it does on Cadenus' claim that 'Things took a Turn he never meant' (l. 731); Cadenus denies responsibility for Vanessa's pain, and in doing so denies as best he can the pain itself. Unsatisfying to the point of being cruel, the poem shows Swift trying to short-circuit feelings that accompany loss. There is no rejection here. Harold Williams' description of Swift's feelings—'embarrassed but unwilling to end the situation'—is right.[14] After Cadenus' 'last Adieu' (l. 593), everything that really matters is still to follow, including the elusive teasing and titillation of some lines that were not in the first Dublin printing ('2726'; i.e. 1726) but found their way into later editions:[15]

> But what Success *Vanessa* met,
> Is to the World a Secret yet:
> Whether the Nymph, to please her Swain,
> Talks in a high Romantick Strain;
> Or whether he at last descends
> To like with less Seraphick Ends;
> Or, to compound the Business, whether
> They temper Love and Books together;
> Must never to Mankind be told,
> Nor shall the conscious Muse unfold.
> (ll. 818–827)

Were it not for the human realities, this might be amiable prurience. In fact it is nasty. What goes wrong in '*Cadenus* and *Vanessa*' is its odd amalgam of private and public, of consolation and satire, of human feeling and cosmic farce. The poem make a useful stepping stone, on that account, from Swift's private experience to the public satires in which he turned his confrontation with pain and loss to advantage.

### *3*

What is it that pleases us as we read satire? The 'Freudian' answer would be: the display of controlled aggression. Biological theories of aggression yield a similar answer. 'In short,' says Alvin Kernan, 'aggression lies at the heart of satire.' In the face of the Eskimo flyting that he cites, it would be hard to disagree:

> I beat you
> I kill you
> I cut off your head
> I cut off your arm
> [Etc.]

Nor does Kernan's description of more sophisticated kinds of satire seem wrong. Release of aggression in satire resembles the release of energy in a game with 'rules, boundaries, referees, time limit', all of which 'prevent any disastrous killing outcome'.[16] Yet perhaps this does not tell the whole story. Games not only substitute for killing, they also enable us to come to terms with loss. That is the secret meaning of the platitude that 'it isn't whether you win or lose, it's how you play the game'. Spoken by moralists of the locker room (if any of the breed is left), this means that sporting behavior is what counts. We can reconstrue the platitude, however, as meaning that, in the game of life and death, gaining and losing, technique is what counts; for technique helps us come to terms. It is a means of pain avoidance. Antonia Wenkart describes psychiatric patients who, being unable to express their true feelings, complain of physical symptoms, fatigue or headache or the like: 'Until such time as the patient can wrench free his pain, he resorts to using devious language.'[17] The language of satire or of sport is devious in the same way. The deviousness is that of good technique. And, whether it is or isn't fair to do such violence to the old platitude about winning and losing, Swift could have understood the platitude in its reconstructed form.

Granted, the link between hostility and pain is intimate.[18] And, granted, Swift was not short on hostility:

> Keeper, shew me where to fix
> On the Puppy Pair of *Dicks*;
> By their lanthorn Jaws and Leathern,
> You might swear they both are Brethren:
> *Dick Fitz-Baker, Dick* the Player,
> Old Acquaintance, are you there?
> Dear Companions hug and kiss,
> Toast *old Glorious* in your Piss.
> Tye them Keeper in a Tether,
> Let them stare and stink together;
> Both are apt to be unruly,
> Lash them daily, lash them duly,
> Though 'tis hopeless to reclaim them,
> Scorpion Rods perhaps may tame them.[19]

Still, these lines from 'The Legion Club' not only come late in Swift's literary career (1736), they are also uncharacteristic:

satire of almost pure malediction is not like him at the height of his powers. Nor is the difference merely that, when he was at the height of his powers, he concealed his hostility better. Feeling the connection between pain and hostility, he made the tactical corrections necessary to deny not only the hostility but the pain.

According to Thomas Szasz, pain is a signal by which we perceive something wrong with the organism, something that threatens its integrity; and, on the level of communication, a cry for help.[20] One of Szasz's case histories illustrates the internalization of loss as physical pain and is instructive for the light it sheds, by comparison and contrast, on Swift's experience: the mother of a young woman in her 'late teens' dies suddenly; the daughter gets little emotional support from her older sisters, finds herself having to manage the household and comfort her father, cannot ' "let go" and mourn the loss of her mother', and finally her father commits suicide by driving his car into a bridge abutment. Soon after, she develops severe pains, apparently in the abdomen, pelvis, and lower back, and suffers episodes of anorexia and vomiting. Szasz describes her, at the start of treatment, as appearing to be 'an intelligent and introspective girl who suffered much but bore it stoically. She was neither depressed nor anxious but, on the contrary, appeared well composed.' The psychogenic origins of her pain, in Szasz's view, are these: 'It was as if the patient, having lost both parents, had no really significant object left to lose other than her body. Then, as if to make sure that she would not be taken by surprise again as she was by the death of the mother, she experienced the warning signal in a chronic manner.'[21] My point is not to hazard a *post mortem* guess about the illness that plagued Swift much of his life, commonly diagnosed as Ménière's syndrome (although it does not seem hard to invent psychic corollaries for his persistent vertigo). But can we not suppose that Swift, having lost so much, shared with Szasz's young woman the desire not to be taken by surprise again; and is it not above all in his satire, which it somehow seems right to call 'chronic', that the pain expresses itself?[22] If Swift's satire is a cry for help, however, the cry generates its own answer. In the world of his satire he discovers compensatory remedies. It is hard to resist the engaging proposition that Swift's satires are, indeed, 'well composed'.

Like other satirists, Swift gets away with murder:

> My first Prediction is but a Trifle; yet I will mention it, to shew how ignorant those sottish Pretenders to Astrology are in their own Concerns: It relates to *Partrige* the Almanack-Maker; I have consulted the Star of his Nativity by my own Rules; and find he will infallibly die upon the 29th of *March* next, about eleven at Night, of a raging Fever: Therefore I advise him to consider of it, and settle his Affairs in Time.[23]

But the nicest part of this Bickerstaffian joke on Partridge is that Swift cannot help but have anticipated Partridge's survival. How would he have felt had Partridge actually died on 29 March, at eleven o'clock at night, of a raging fever? Or, for that matter, if he had died on 28 March or 30 March? The joke, which reached its second stage in a pamphlet recounting the affecting scene of Partridge's dying hours, depends for its success on his survival; luckily for Swift, Partridge did survive and protest his existence.

Partridge's unsuspecting protest enables Bickerstaff to spring the trap with a flick of the wrist that almost has to have been planned in advance: 'Above a Thousand Gentlemen having bought his Almanacks for this Year, meerly to find what he said against me; at every Line they read, they would lift up their Eyes, and cry out, betwixt Rage and Laughter, *They were sure no Man alive ever writ such damned Stuff as this*.'[24] Either, therefore, Partridge has to disown his almanac or allow that he is no man alive. But in fact the choice is illusory. His almanac is the semblance of his life, and there is no renouncing it. *QED*. The thing to notice is not only how Swift gets away with murder (by making Partridge commit suicide) but how a living, breathing, protesting Partridge is essential to the winning of Bickerstaff's game. The whole *jeu d'esprit* has a magical cast; it has the joyfulness and surprise of magic that gives no pain:

> I am employed, like the General who was forced to kill his Enemies twice over, whom a *Necromancer* had raised to Life. If Mr. *Partrige* hath practised the same Experiment upon himself, and be again alive; long may he continue so; but that doth not in the least contradict my Veracity . . .[25]

The only necromancer is Bickerstaff-Swift, who slays Partridge but finally permits him life and, at last, wishes him a long one. The rhetorical extravaganza underlines Swift's satirical skill at breeding gain out of loss, life out of annihilation, something out of nothingness, tulips out of dung, a new creation from a confusion of waste and loss.

To go from the Bickerstaff hoax to *A Modest Proposal* seems to require a deep breath of preparation, but as another act of satiric slaughter on Swift's part—in this case a slaughter of the innocents—his scheme for cannibalizing Ireland's children profitably follows almost naturally. Is it possible to say of *A Modest Proposal* that it, too, seizes compensatory gratifications out of the abyss? In one sense, of course, it does nothing else, so many are the advantages attached to this modest proposal. The structure of Swift's thought is the same, we might think, but the content so different as to sink the analogy. But is that true? When Swift desires the politicians to ask the poor people of Ireland whether they 'would not, at this Day, think it a great Happiness to have been sold for Food at a Year old',[26] the word that does the work is 'Happiness', embedded as it is in some of Swift's trickiest syntax. Past and present come together, 'at this Day'. Only grown-ups, who at this day have lived through what they would not have lived through on the modest proposer's scheme, could understand the case in quite this way. The scheme fulfills the wish for happiness as loss is superimposed on loss, deprivation on deprivation, double negatives making an affirmative. What the people of Ireland feel is not what Job felt: they do not wish never to have been born. Nor is it quite the case that they would rather have been eaten as infants; it is that they would consider it 'a great Happiness'. They do not despair. On the contrary: the *Modest Proposal* yields a perverse but genuine comfort, even elation.

Granted, it is hard to accept the comfort in the *Modest Proposal*, but it is there. It is equally hard to accept Swift's joke, in the *Journal to Stella*, about the child that his friend Mrs. Walls is expecting and whose godfather she has asked him to be; but it *is* a joke: 'No truly, I will not be godfather to goody Walls this bout, and I hope she'll have no more. There will be no quiet nor cards for this child. I hope it will die the day after the christening.' Swift kept coming back to the joke. A month later, he announced that 'Mrs. Walls is brought to-bed of a girl, who died two days after it was christened', when in fact the child had not been born yet. Ten days later, he is at it again: 'and Walls, has she a boy or a girl? A girl, hmm, and died in a week, hmmm . . .' And, another month later: 'What, is not Mrs. Walls' business over yet? I had hopes she was up and well, and the child dead before this time.'[27] And so on, until Mrs. Walls was eventually delivered of a boy.[28] Whatever Swift's precise feelings, which are not easy to guess, the joke springs from the same habits of mind that permitted him to kill off Partridge, anticipating all the while that he would survive, and to kill off the children of Ireland to the great happiness of the poor. It is therapeutic mock-cruelty and, surely, a jousting with sensations of guilt. Even more than with Partridge, one has to wonder how Swift would have felt had the child died.

'Therapeutic mock-cruelty' brings us close to a Hobbesian—or 'banana peel'—theory of comedy. But Swift assimilates within a larger context the comedy that involves a sudden glory at someone else's discomfiture. His art rises to the understanding of comedy as recovery and gain. Consider the 'banana peel' paradigm. Someone slips on a banana peel and executes a spectacular fall. The fact that we laugh is less significant than the fact that, if the victim is injured, we stop laughing and try to help. Our laughter contains, as it were, a prediction about the outcome: the prediction is that the victim will get up and carry on. We have at once annihilated him—made him into nothing—and brought him back to life. The sudden glory is not at another's embarrassment but at our own power to recreate life. Watching someone slip on a banana peel, we behave like Swift annihilating Partridge and, in doing so, assume the same risks. The victim may be injured; Partridge might have died. In this aspect, comedy becomes a fantasy of benevolent power:

> Most Things by me do rise and fall,
> And as I please they're great and small.

Swift's riddle of the mirror opens up some of the mental processes at work in the comedy of *Gulliver's Travels*:

> Nay, bring me here the tallest Man,
> I'll squeeze him to a little Span,
> Or bring a tender Child and pliant,
> You'll see me stretch him to a Giant.

We do not usually think of Lilliputians and Brobdingnagians as compressed or stretched-out versions of ourselves and certainly not as victims of some necromantic but painless torture. Yet the riddle suggests how the little people and the big people came into being. And, once alert to such motivations, it is not hard to sense the feelings of power that go into the making of Lilliput and Brobdingnag. Whoever can bring the people of these countries to life can do *anything*. It is a pleasant commentary on the creative psychology of the *Travels* that, for all the careful measurements that went into Books I and II, the big people are a physical impossibility in the natural world.

But if the creation of Lilliputians and Brobdingnagians can be regarded as an act of benevolent despotism, the violence that Gulliver so often has to endure appears gratuitous, an act of pure imaginative aggression. So, in a sense, it is. It helps establish the norm against which Utopian fantasy will be poised. The *Travels* record a journey that begins with Gulliver suffering acute pain, moves on to banana peel situations, of which Gulliver is the most frequent victim, in Book II, then to a land full of fanciful anxieties in Book III, before finally reaching a land where—nature working all things to perfection—the inhabitants do not know pain and Gulliver's intermittent hurts serve as a sad reminder of his fallen state. Swift defines the perfection of nature as the absence of pain.[29]

Gulliver wakes up, bound and tied, in Lilliput, to an intensely painful episode:

> in an Instant I felt above an Hundred Arrows discharged on my left Hand, which pricked me like so many Needles; and besides, they shot another Flight into the Air, as we do Bombs in *Europe*; whereof many, I suppose, fell on my Body, (though I felt them not) and some on my Face, which I immediately covered with my left Hand. When this Shower of Arrows was over, I fell a groaning with Grief and Pain.[30]

The fact that this is not in the least funny—that it is an instance of pure, unqualified pain—makes it possible to plot a curve of feeling in the *Travels*. Beginning in real suffering they move on, in Book II, to Hobbesian farce—Gulliver, for example, being force-fed by a monkey—and Grand Guignol humor. A criminal's head is sliced off with a forty-foot sword: 'The Veins and Arteries spouted up such a prodigious Quantity of Blood, and so high in the Air, that the great *Jet d'Eau* at *Versailles* was not equal for the Time it lasted; and the Head when it fell on the Scaffold Floor, gave such a Bounce, as made me start, although I were at least an *English* Mile distant' (p. 120). The level of pain goes down when severed heads bounce about like India rubber. In Book III, the flappers who mediate between the Laputian sages and the real world help ward off physical disasters: they function like guardian spirits. The flapper goes with his master on walks to keep him from 'falling down every Precipice, and bouncing his Head against every Post; and in the Streets, of jostling others, or being jostled himself into the Kennel' (p. 160); if physical pain is absent, mental distress abounds. 'These People are under continual Disquietudes, never enjoying a Minute's Peace of Mind' (p. 164)—the result of their endless fretting about celestial disasters. Finally, as if in a natural progression, Gulliver comes to the land of the Houyhnhnms, where the ruling class, at least, is free from pain as well as from grief and loss. Not only do the Houyhnhnms ('if they can avoid Casualties') die peacefully of old age, 'their Friends and Relations expressing neither Joy nor Grief at their Departure' (p. 274), but Gulliver's master cannot understand what doctors are for: 'I was going on to tell him of another Sort of People, who get their Livelihood by attending the Sick; having upon some Occasions informed his Honour that many of my Crew had died of Diseases. But here it was with the utmost Difficulty, that I brought him to apprehend what I meant.' Behind this incredulity lies an inability to conceive a fallen world: 'He could easily conceive that a *Houyhnhnm* grew weak and heavy a few Days before his Death; or by some Accident might hurt a Limb. But the Nature, who worketh all things to Perfection, should suffer any Pains to breed in our Bodies, he thought impossible; and desired to know the Reason of so unaccountable an Evil' (p. 253). Even 'accidents' and hurt limbs are embarrassments in Utopia and, therefore, lightly touched on. But pains that 'breed', like living things, in our bodies are quite unaccountable.

True, Gulliver gives reasons for the pains that breed in our bodies: dissipation, gluttony, prostitution. But they are not to the point: he has substituted efficient for final causes, offering 'reasons' rather than 'the Reason of so unaccountable an Evil'. Behind the Houyhnhnm's naiveté lies the old puzzle: why does God permit evil? Why, to bring the question home, should Swift be afflicted, almost for a lifetime, with vertigo? Or with an attack of the shingles (in 1712), so violent that he spoke of it afterwards as 'miserable Torture'?[31] Or with an attack of hemorrhoids (in 1724) that 'kept me in Torture for a Week' and required 'more of the Stoick than I am Master of, to support'.[32] Or, near the end of his life, with gout:

> But I am and have been these two days in so miserable a way, and so cruelly tortured, that can hardly be conceived. The whole last night I was equally struck as if I had been in Phalaris's brazen bull, and roared as loud for eight or nine hours. I am at this instant unable to move without excessive pain, although not the thousandth part of what I suffered all last night and this morning. This you will now style the gout.[33]

'Torture' implies a torturer and Swift could not (I believe) think of pain except as inflicted by some malignant agency. This description of what 'you will now'—dispassionately—'style the gout' reaches after ways to express inexpressible pain. What can 'excessive' pain be like when multiplied a thousand times? Is it not infinite? In Houyhnhnmland Swift exercised powers as a creator that God had not just withheld but, perhaps, never thought of exercising in the first place. The devil does not figure large in Swift's theology. Perhaps the devil is God's *alter ego*.[34]

Unlike other of Swift's satires, *Gulliver's Travels* does not finally cancel pain and loss; Gulliver has to go home. There is no 'great Happiness' in the outcome, no 'new Creation'—unless we were to think of Gulliver's grudging efforts at reconciliation with Yahoo-kind as a new creation. That would be too pious. One of the last memorable images in the *Travels* recalls, at a higher level of feeling, the physical beating that Gulliver has taken in Lilliput and Brobdingnag: Yahoo pride 'breaks all the Measures of my Patience' (p. 296). The idiom (from the French: *rompre mesures*) means to foil or frustrate, but here it takes on a literal resonance. Boundaries are being shattered; the image resonates with pain. In the *Travels*, the need to cancel loss finds expression in a brief fantasy of painless life in Utopia. But the game is in a sense lost. Utopia is where there is no pain; nowhere is there no pain. *Gulliver's Travels* displays not only Swift's familiar agility in dealing with hurt but also the intensity of the hurt. In fact he knew that there was not a world elsewhere.

*4*

The magic that Swift practised, without pain, on others, he practised as dextrously on himself. In his moments of self-directed magic, he comes closest to uncovering the inner springs of his art. He engages himself in his satire more deeply than any other satirist, not only making fun or making little of himself but in fact making nothing of himself, only to rise again in glory. The 'Verses on the Death of Dr. *Swift*'[35] finish their author off but, like many another testament, aim at reconstruction: 'He gave the little Wealth he had, / To build a House for Fools and Mad' (ll. 479–480). The house that Swift built for fools and mad was, after all, not only the hospital for incurables that he endowed in his will but the monumental house of his satire. The self-reference is life-giving.

Of the places where Swift lurks in his satire, damaged or death-like yet triumphing over damage and death, two unusual and complementary instances, neither so well known as the 'Verses', repay attention. Like the 'Verses', both work variations on the themes of loss and art. The first is the strange little poem called '*Apollo*: or A Problem solved' (1731):

*Apollo*, God of Light and Wit,
Could Verse inspire, but seldom writ:
Refin'd all Mettals with his Looks,
As well as Chymists by their Books:
As handsome as my Lady's Page;
Sweet Five and Twenty was his Age.
His Wig was made of sunny Rays,
He crown'd his youthful Head with Bays:
Not all the Court of Heav'n could shew
So nice and so compleat a Beau.
No Heir, upon his first Appearance,
With Twenty Thousand Pounds a Year Rents,
E'er drove, before he sold his Land,
So fine a Coach along the Strand;

The Spokes, we are by *Ovid* told,
Were Silver, and the Axel Gold.
(I own, 'twas but a Coach and Four,
For *Jupiter* allows no more)

Yet, with his Beauty, Wealth, and Parts,
Enough to win ten Thousand Hearts;
No Vulgar Deity above
Was so unfortunate in Love.

Three weighty Causes were assign'd
That mov'd the Nymphs to be unkind.
Nine Muses always waiting round him,
He left them Virgins as he found 'em.
His Singing was another Fault;
For he could reach to *B.* in *alt:*
And, by the Sentiments of *Pliny,*
Such Singers are like *Nicolini.*
At last, the Point was fully clear'd;
In short; *Apollo* had no Beard.[36]

The discovery that Apollo is a castrato like Nicolini and therefore has no beard comes as a fine but satisfying shock to the sensibilities. Belonging to the same period as 'A Beautiful Young Nymph Going to Bed', '*Strephon* and *Chloe*', and '*Cassinus* and *Peter*', '*Apollo*: or A Problem solved' raises questions comparable to those posed by the scatological poems. Is it a pathological instance or harmlessly conventional? Is it a satire on Italian opera? Or what?[37]

Whatever else the poem may be, it is certainly a rueful meditation on the impotence of art. At the same time, rueful or not, it communicates a decisive and liberating sense of finished business: 'At last, the Point was fully clear'd.' In this connection we should recall, by way of speculation, Swift's extravagant hopes when he began his career as a poet and his quite abrupt disillusion. And, given the fact that '*Apollo* had no Beard', it is of more than passing interest that 'successful self-mutilation leads to a feeling of work well done'.[38] At the end of '*Apollo*: or, A Problem solved', a problem *has* been solved, a point has been fully cleared and the work has by all means been well done. It all brings to mind the quintessential satiric stroke that Dryden describes as leaving the severed head in place. There is no slovenly butchering here and, therefore, no pain—which is Szasz's point about self-mutilation: 'Since the body part was already lost from the point of view of the experiencing ego, its removal is *unaccompanied by pain*.' And, if Swift in fact is remembering desires, long since set aside, to be a poet of the high-aspiring and virile kind, the memory is one he would understandably have wanted to keep down: 'Implicit in such a memory is the remembrance of a previous state different from the present one and a (conscious) confrontation of these two experiences. The wish to obliterate the past (i.e. to forget) is the usual defense on the part of the ego against such memories. Evidence which reminds one of the memory is unwanted. The physical persistence of a part of the body which has been psychically amputated constitutes such an unwanted reminder of the past and this reminder is the primary motive for its removal.'[39] All of which may be translated into the terms of Swift's conversion from a Pindaric poet to a witty trifler, as he consciously thought, in octosyllabics—albeit, in the eye of history, a poet who had gained far more in the transaction than he had lost.

On this view of the poem we are in the presence of a rare occasion in Swift's life when he simply let go and with a minimum of anxiety accepted the loss of an important part of himself, probably recognizing at a deeper level of consciousness that the loss was actually a gain. The last of his early poems, 'Occasioned by Sir W—— T——'s Late Illness and Recovery' (1693),[40] comes to an extraordinarily abrupt halt as he renounces the 'malignant goddess', his Muse:

> There thy enchantment broke, and from this hour
> I here renounce thy visionary pow'r;
> And since thy essence on my breath depends,
> Thus with a puff the whole delusion ends.
>
> (ll. 151–154)

Swift the muse-ridden poet breathes his last, gratefully. If '*Apollo*: or, A Problem solved', written forty years later, incorporates an image of his career as a poet, he has no need for elaborate strategies of self-cancellation and self-renewal. All he has to do is painlessly to snip the link between present and past.

If '*Apollo*: or, A Problem solved' seems to look backward,

'Death and Daphne' (1730)[41]—from the same period of Swift's life and quite as enigmatic—seems to look ahead: in the same way as the 'Verses on the Death of Dr. *Swift*', it discounts death. Like the 'Apollo' poem, it is a poem of unconsummated love; and, as a spoof on the legend of Apollo and Daphne, shares with it a common term. Pluto, disappointed with the weekly harvest of the dead, declares that Death must marry and spawn a breed of 'Young *Deathlings*' (l. 15). Tricked out like a beau, Death heads for the upper world and, hearing of Daphne's fame, comes to visit as she plays at cards. For Daphne, described in the dedication as 'an agreeable young Lady, but extremely lean', it is love at first sight: 'For, such a Shape of Skin and Bone / Was never seen, except her own' (ll. 61–62). She revels in thoughts of the life to come below ground:

> She fancy'd, those *Elysian* Shades
> The sweetest Place for Masquerades:
> How pleasant on the Banks of Styx,
> To troll it in a Coach and Six!
> (ll. 85–88)

But disappointment waits:

> What Pride a Female Heart enflames!
> How endless are Ambition's Aims!
> Cease haughty Nymph; the Fates decree
> *Death* must not be a Spouse for thee:
> For, when by chance the meagre Shade
> Upon thy Hand his Finger laid;
> Thy Hand as dry and cold as Lead,
> His matrimonial Spirit fled;
> He felt about his Heart a Damp,
> That quite extinguish't *Cupid*'s Lamp:
> Away the frighted Spectre scuds,
> And leaves my Lady in the Suds.
> (ll. 89–100)

'Death and Daphne' is an oddity; but especially if the poem is addressed to Lady Acheson, as seems likely, perhaps not an impenetrable oddity. Swift's relationship with Lady Acheson was of the same kind as with other women in his life—pedagogical, bullying, emotionally involved.[42] In other of the poems that he wrote at the

Achesons' country estate he plays the overbearing tutor and hopelessly demanding house guest. The high-minded and romantic pedagogue of '*Cadenus* and *Vanessa*' turns into a grotesque. And in 'Death and Daphne' the protean Dean—who has played Bickerstaff, Cadenus, the Drapier, Gulliver, the modest proposer, and all the rest; and who, in another of the Market Hill poems, is said to 'merit new Employments daily: / Our Thatcher, Ditcher, Gard'ner, Baily'[43]—tries on the mask of Death, a parodic imitation of the mask of Apollo.[44] Daphne's fond belief that Elysium is the sweetest place for masquerades has a basis in the identity of opposites.

And if Swift is masquerading as Death, what gratifications does he find? Mainly that of unconsummated love. In death, that is to say, there is no death. Impotence ('He felt about his Heart a Damp, / That quite extinguish't Cupid's Lamp') has the force of suspended potency and carries an implication of possibility and power. The end of the poem leaves an open future—but without the uneasiness of the disturbing lines in '*Cadenus* and *Vanessa*' where Swift leaves to guesswork the future of tutor and pupil. The 'frighted Spectre' of Death, who scuttles off at the end of 'Death and Daphne', will no doubt go seeking a plumper bride now that he has left Daphne unceremoniously 'in the Suds'. There is still the chance of a wedding, of new Deathlings, of ironic new creations.

But what about Daphne? In fact Death has made her immortal:

> Cease haughty Nymph; the Fates decree
> *Death* must not be a Spouse for thee.

The mythological Daphne became immortal by being turned into a tree; this Daphne becomes immortal by frightening off Death the lover. The mythological Daphne, transfigured, became sacred to Apollo; this Daphne will become sacred to Death—to the poet, that is, who has given her an undying name. The trope of the poet who deals out immortality in his verse could not be more ingeniously rendered. As Death, Swift overcomes Death. In its odd way 'Death and Daphne' is an epitome of the strategies he deployed against mutability and pain.

## NOTES

1 *The Poems of Jonathan Swift*, ed. Harold Williams, 2nd ed. (Oxford, 1958), III, 934. On the authorship, dates, and publication of the riddles, see *Poems*, III, 914, 926–927.

2 Swift to Bolingbroke and Pope, 5 April 1729. *The Correspondence of Jonathan Swift*, ed. Harold Williams (Oxford, 1963–65), III, 329.

3 *Swift and Carroll: A Psychoanalytic Study of Two Lives* (New York, 1955), p. 25. Screen memories 'usually serve as a cover for other repressed memories' (Benjamin B. Wolman, ed., *Dictionary of Behavioral Science* [New York, 1973], p. 232). An example of a 'screen' or 'cover' memory is: a 'memory of a very happy holiday which helps to repress recognition that the childhood was in general miserable' (Horace B. English and Ava Champney English, *A Comprehensive Dictionary of Psychological and Psychoanalytical Terms: A Guide to Usage* [New York, 1958], p. 128). Not being a psychoanalyst, I am at a loss to know what such a memory as that of Swift's might be covering.

4 On Swift and Jane Waring, see Irvin Ehrenpreis, *Swift: the Man, his Works, and the Age* (Cambridge, Mass., 1962– ), II, 19–22.

5 *Poems*, III, 921–924. I have called this riddle one of Swift's for the same reasons as I have attributed the mirror riddle to him; they both *ought* to be by him, even if by some chance they are not.

6 *Ibid.*, III, 930.

7 In 'The Lady's Dressing Room' (*ibid.*, II, 524–530), Strephon discovers the disturbing truth that '*Celia* shits!' (l. 118). The poet proclaims that if Strephon 'would but stop his Nose' (l. 136), he would learn to love cosmetic ornament:

> He soon would learn to think like me,
> And bless his ravisht Sight to see
> Such Order from Confusion sprung,
> Such gaudy Tulips rais'd from Dung.
> (ll. 141–144)

8 A venerable *topos*, as Clive Probyn reminds me, but intensely and strangely rendered in Swift. See Norman O. Brown on Swift and 'sublimation', *Life Against Death: the Psychoanalytical Meaning of History* (Middletown, Conn., 1959), pp. 179–201.

9 Swift to Chetwode, October 1724. *Correspondence*, III, 35, 36.

10 'The Meaning of Suffering in Therapy: A Round Table Discussion', *American Journal of Psycho-Analysis*, XXI (1961), 22, 23.

11 *Correspondence*, III, 35–36.

12 Swift to Mrs. Moore, 7 December 1727. *Ibid.*, III, 254, 255.

13 *Poems*, II, 683–714.

14 *Ibid.*, II, 684.

15 For the textual history, see *ibid.*, II, 683.

16 'Aggression and Satire: Art Considered as a Form of Biological Adaptation', in *Literary Theory and Structure: Essays in Honor of William K. Wimsatt*, ed. Frank Brady, John Palmer, and Martin Price (New Haven and London, 1973), pp. 117, 124.

17 'The Meaning of Suffering in Therapy', p. 24.

18 For a helpful summary of theories of pain, see H. Merskey and F. G. Spear, *Pain: Psychological and Psychiatric Aspects* (London, 1967), pp. 169–179. I am grateful to Herant Katchadourian, who read this paper at an early stage and whose insights into the psychological issues were most helpful.

19 'A Character, Panegyric, and Description of the Legion Club', *Poems*, III, 827–839, ll. 145–158.

20 Thomas S. Szasz, *Pain and Pleasure: A Study of Bodily Feelings* (New York, 1957). See especially Part II, 'The Psychology of Pain'.

21 *Ibid.*, pp. 93, 94, 95, 98.

22 Szasz says that the question 'Where is the pain?' leads down a blind alley. But, as he says, 'there is a compulsion in all of us . . . to localize pain, and this is due, in part, to semantic habit' (*ibid.*, p. 148). By saying that Swift's pain expresses itself in his satire, I have wanted to avoid the consequences of semantic habit. One could say, in other usage, that the pain is localized in his art.

23 *Predictions for the Year 1708* in *The Prose Works of Jonathan Swift*, ed. Herbert Davis (Oxford, 1939–68), II, 145.

24 *A Vindication of Isaac Bickerstaff, Esq.* in *Prose Works*, II, 162.

25 *Ibid.*, II, 164.

26 *Prose Works*, XII, 117.

27 *Journal to Stella*, ed. Harold Williams (Oxford, 1948), pp. 129, 156, 166, 186. The dates of these entries are 16 December 1710, 5 January 1710[–11], 16 January 1710[–11], 9 February 1710[–11].

28 At least Swift's *Journal* entry for 7 March 1710[–11] (p. 208) seems to indicate the child was a boy. It is difficult, however, to separate jest from earnest in his talk about Mrs. Walls and her child.

29 For a thorough treatment of the uses of cruelty and violence in Swift, see Chapter II ('Order and Cruelty: Swift, Pope and Johnson') in C. J. Rawson, *Gulliver and the Gentle Reader: Studies in Swift and our Time* (London, 1973); originally published as 'Order and Cruelty: A Reading of Swift (with some comments on Pope and Johnson)', *Essays in Criticism*, XX (1970), 24–56. See also Paul Fussell, Jr., 'The Frailty of Lemuel Gulliver', in *Essays in Literary History, presented to J. Milton French*, ed. Rudolf Kirk and C. F. Main (New Brunswick, N.J., 1960), pp. 113–125.

30 *Prose Works*, XI, 22. Subsequent page references to *Gulliver's Travels* are given in the text, and refer to the revised edition (1959).

31 *Journal to Stella*, II, 528. The entry covers the days of 31 March–8 April: 'All these days I have been extreamly ill.'

32 Swift to Charles Ford, 2 April 1724. *Correspondence*, III, 9.

33 Swift to Mrs. Whiteway, 29 April 1740. *Ibid.*, V, 183. April seems to have been a cruel month for Swift.

34 Swift's most famous expression of the theme is in *A Tale of a Tub*: 'And, whereas the mind of Man, when he gives the Spur and Bridle to his Thoughts, doth never stop, but naturally sallies out into both extreams of High and Low, of Good and Evil . . .' (*Prose Works*, I, 99).

35 *Poems*, II, 551–572.

36 *Ibid.*, II, 597–598.

37 David Donaldson, who helped me with the research for this essay, has unearthed some reasons to think that '*Apollo*: or, A Problem solved' may have a topical cast; I have urged that he write up his findings for publication.

38 Szasz, *Pain and Pleasure*, p. 138.

39 *Ibid.*, pp. 138–139.

40 *Poems*, I, 51–55.

41 *Ibid.*, III, 902–905.

42 On Swift, Lady Acheson, and 'Death and Daphne', see Nora Crow Jaffe, 'Swift and the Agreeable Young Lady, but Extremely Lean', *PLL*, forthcoming.

43 'A Panegyrick on the D——n', *Poems*, III, 886–897, ll. 155–156.

44 Cf. Nora Crow Jaffe, 'Swift and the Agreeable Young Lady, but Extremely Lean': 'The theory that answers most questions about the poem for me is that Death is a stand-in for Swift himself.'

# 2

# 'Hack at Tom Poley's': Swift's Use of Puns

by DAVID NOKES

## *1*

In November 1716 a new plague hit London. After the pestilence of 1665 which swept away 'if Sir William Petty may be believed, Five Millions of Christian Souls, besides Women and Jews'; after the Fire which had consumed 'according to the Computation of Sir Samuel Morland, 100,000 Houses, not to mention Churches and Stables'; after the inundation of obscenity that followed 'the Abomination of Playhouses' in the land, provoking 'Even Infants [to] disfigure the Walls of holy Temples with exhorbitant Representations of the Members of Generation'; worse than all these visitations came a contagion 'more Epidemical, and, in consequence, more Fatal . . . the woful Practice of PUNNING'.[1]

Thus far the author of *God's Revenge against Punning*, whom Ault argues persuasively was none other than Alexander Pope. The epidemic had been predicted by Addison five years earlier:

> I do very much apprehend, by some of the last Winter's Productions, which had their Sets of Admirers, that our Posterity will in a few Years degenerate into a Race of Punnsters: At least, a Man may be very excusable for any Apprehension of this kind, that has seen *Acrosticks* handed about the Town with great Secresie and Applause . . .[2]

Addison had guessed right. Shortly after *God's Revenge* came the reply, *An Heroi-Comical Epistle from a certain Doctor To a certain Gentlewoman, In Defence of the Most Ancient Art of Punning.* Ault argues that this 'certain doctor' is 'not improbably Arbuthnot', and that the two pamphlets on punning are part of an extended Scriblerian joke that also takes in the eponymous Crambe's virtuoso display of the art in chapter VII of *The Memoirs of Martinus Scriblerus*. All the Scriblerians caught the punning bug, but Swift was the only chronic sufferer. He may indeed have been the carrier who brought it over from Ireland, where it is known to be endemic, for his *Journal to Stella* is full of the puns he shared with Dilly Ashe, Andrew Fountaine, and others:

> I'll tell you [a] Pun. If there was a Hackney Coach at Mr Pooley's door, what Town in Aegypt would it be; why it would be *Hecatompolis, Hack at Tom Poley's*—Silly says ppt.[3]

On his return to Ireland Swift engaged in protracted Pun-ick wars with Tom Sheridan, another remorseless punster. Between them they produced *Ars Punica, Sive Flos Linguarum, The Art of Punning*, or *the Flower of Languages . . . In Thirty-Four Rules, by Tom Pun-sibi*, hunting down homophones long after any real ingenuity or spontaneity was gone. Addison regarded all such word play with condescension. A pun, he said, in *Spectator* No. 61, was a 'jingle of words':

> I shall here define it to be a Conceit arising from the use of two Words that agree in the Sound, but differ in the Sense. The only way therefore to try a Piece of Wit, is to translate it into a different Language, if it bears the Test, you may pronounce it true; but if it vanishes in the Experiment, you may conclude it to have been a Punn.

According to this definition, pun depends solely upon a similarity of sounds. Hence Addison's strictures bear the same magisterial smack as his censure of Italian opera—another entertainment where sound conspired to drive out sense. But technically, what he has defined is a *homophone*, which is only one form of pun. Tom Pun-sibi offers a similar definition, but much less censoriously:

> Punning is an Art of harmonious Jinggling upon *Words*, which passing in at the *Ears*, and falling upon the *Diaphragma*, excites a titillary Motion in those Parts, and this being convey'd by the *Animal Spirits* into the *Muscles* of the *Face*, raises the *Cockles* of the *Heart*.

Actually Pun-sibi is not over-nice in his terminology. In section VI of the general Instructions for teaching this art, he counsels that candidates

Must every Day of their Lives repeat *six* synonimous Words, or Words like in Sound, before they be allowed to sit down to Dinner. Such as:

| | | | |
|---|---|---|---|
| Assent | Ascent | Alter | Altar |
| A lass | Alas | A peer | Appear |
| Bark | Barque | Barbery | Barberrie |

Clearly he doesn't mean *synonymous* words at all, since all the examples he gives are of simple homophones with no pretensions to any similitude of sense. What is curious is that both definitions restrict puns to their least interesting form. The concept that both neglect is the *homonym*, the single word with two or more separate meanings. These are those myriad words of all work, fast or cast, die or tie, see or saw. These are puns too, but puns that depend upon consubstantiated meanings, not simply chiming sounds:

> So to one neutrall thing both sexes fit,
> We dye and rise the same, and prove
> Mysterious by this love.

The serious literary punster, as opposed to the after-dinner would-be wit, uses homophones like 'sun' and 'son' only where rhyme stimulates a reconsideration of reason:

> There should I see a Sunne by rising set,
> And by that setting endless day beget.[4]

Swift, though he enjoyed his games of crambo and his 'punick wars', knew the ironic force of such punning as this, as Denis Donoghue has shown: 'Swift throws a rope around several cognate terms, and pulls them down with a low synonym.' The implication, Donoghue argues, is that 'the genius of Language itself is on Swift's side'.[5] Similarly Donald Davie has praised Pope's 'gravity' pun in the *Dunciad* for being so much more than a homophone:

> This is a much better pun than the one in Shakespeare about how, when someone is dead, he'll be a 'grave' man. For Shakespeare's pun is a matter of merely accidental likeness of sound, whereas Pope's feels back along the lines of etymological development, to a genuine likeness of meaning.[6]

Both Augustans share the Joycean trick of making revelations out of *double entendres*. Epiphanies, Joyce calls them, acts of verbal magic that give old words a rub and make them new, offering not a jingle of words, but a jangle of ideas. To adapt Joyce's metaphor, Swift's puns are not so much epiphanies as incarnations, a constant process of words becoming flesh. With the apparatus of his 'physicological system' Swift transubstantiates words into 'things' to prove there's no trick in his argument. He is like a conjuror with an incredulous audience. Here, touch it, feel it, he says—quite solid, right?—when we know that at any moment he will turn all that solidity back into airy nothingness.

Swift shows his greatest virtuosity with puns in *A Tale of a Tub*. There is the tailor-worshippers' use of 'invest':

> They held the Universe to be a large *Suit of Cloaths*, which *invests* every Thing: That the Earth is *invested* by the Air; The Air is *invested* by the Stars; and the Stars are *invested* by the *Primum Mobile*.

With his surrealistic imagery of beech trees wearing 'sparkish periwigs' and the sea being a 'waist-coat of water-tabby', Swift gives a wholly novel cast to a traditional homiletic theme. By reviving a dead metaphor he actually requires us to focus on the quality and width of the brothers' coats, drawing us all the while to his triumphant conclusion:

> it will follow in due Course of Reasoning, that those Beings which the World calls improperly *Suits of Cloaths*, are in Reality the most refined Species of Animals, or to proceed higher, that they are Rational Creatures, or Men.
>
> (p. 78)

The *reductio ad absurdum* is the result of interweaving the two separate meanings of *invest*: to clothe, or to confer authority. Papal *bulls* is a more obvious pun, developed with cruder vigour:

> they would *Roar*, and *Spit*, and *Belch*, and *Piss*, and *Fart*, and *Snivel* out *Fire*, and keep a perpetual *Coyl*, till you flung them a Bit of *Gold*.
>
> (p. 112)

The pun on 'the wise man's Rule of *Regarding the End*' plays with all possible meanings of that phrase, from a meditation upon mortality to arse-wiping. The word 'critic' too becomes a homonym with three distinct meanings:

> By the Word, *Critick*, at this Day so frequent in all Conversations, there have sometimes been distinguished three very different Species of Mortal Men . . .
>
> (pp. 92–3)

The 'abstract' meaning of the word is a person of taste and discrimination, with 'a true Relish of the *Sublime* and the *Admirable*'; a secondary meaning is 'Restorers of Antient Learning from the Worms'; but Swift concentrates upon his third, physical interpretation. These critics, like walkers in the filthy streets of Edinburgh, 'observe the Colour and Complexion of the Ordure . . . take its Dimensions . . . paddling in, or tasting it . . .'

Ian Watt's comments upon the 'ironigenic' tendencies of language at this time—particularly of abstract discourse—are relevant here. Swift's puns demonstrate the potentially fissile nature of all sorts of apparently simple words. They are revealed as consubstantiated units which, under persistent ironic pressure, may be split off into their separate component elements, which then resettle in layers, according to their respective specific gravities. Pun performs the Scriblerian trick of revealing the interdependence of the bathos and the sublime.

'Zeal' has just such a range of meanings, at least according to Swift:

> *Zeal*; which is, perhaps, the most significant Word that hath been ever yet produced in any Language: As, I think, I have fully proved in my excellent and *Analytical Discourse* upon that Subject; wherein I have deduced a *Histori-theo-physilogical* account of *Zeal*, shewing how it first proceeded from a *Notion* into a Word, and from thence in a hot Summer, ripened into a *tangible Substance.*
>
> (p. 137)

This process of linguistic ripening describes Swift's technique of 'incarnation' exactly. Puns are at the heart of this ironic trick, though developed and augmented by a full supporting range of rhetorical devices. Working outwards from specific puns, the process of incarnation can be seen turning several other abstract notions into really rather surprisingly tangible substances.

## 2

There is a tendency within eighteenth-century society to provide its satirists with a vocabulary newly enriched with ambiguities as the ironic spin-off from those very processes of change which the satirists most acutely deplored. Donald Davie has shown how the 'new science' provided just such a sub-stratum of ambiguities, readily exploitable in puns.[6] Much the same tendency can be found in the areas of finance, and of language itself, both linked by the central concept of *currency*. Any number of metaphorical bridges can be thrown across this current; one coins a new phrase; slang debases the currency of language, and so on. But the links between the institutions of language and finance go deeper than the coincidence of these scarcely living metaphors. Both depend upon the assumption of some normative and negotiable value. A guinea must mean the same to two men who wish to trade in guineas; liberty must mean the same to two philosophers who wish to discuss human societies. Yet negotiability imposes its own strains. Away from the mint, in mouths and pockets everywhere, the value of a word or coin is subject to the arbitrary operations of fashion, opportunity and market forces. They are worth what they will fetch. The Tory opponents of paper money, who clung to a gold standard of known intrinsic value, had clear affinities with the philosophers who wished to fix language for ever. Critics of linguistic corruption expressed themselves in terms of coin-clipping, and vice-versa. Chesterfield described how his 'fair countrywomen'

> take a word, and change it, like a guinea into shillings for pocket-money, to be employed on the several occasional purposes of the day.[8]

Many Augustans shared the desire for some kind of linguistic Bretton-Woods to put a stop to this devaluation. But Locke at the beginning of the century, and Johnson fifty years later, were equally contemptuous of such vain idealism. 'To enchain syllables', Johnson wrote emphatically in his Preface to the *Dictionary*, 'and to lash the wind are equally the undertakings of pride, unwilling to measure its desires by its strength . . .' The market must determine what a word was worth; there was no ultimate court of appeal with authority to overset usage. Yet to Swift the idea of sanctioning usage implied enfranchising the ignorant to pervert language in a hand-to-mouth process of devaluation. His *Proposal for Correcting, Improving and Ascertaining the English Tongue* (*1712*) aimed at restricting the anarchic power of one man, one voice by 'fixing our language for ever'. The irony of this attempt —an irony noted by others—is that Swift thereby aligns himself with materialists, like Bishop Wilkins, whom his satires constantly ridicule. It is an irony we find repeated throughout his life. As a Christian humanist, Swift wished to leave men free to find their own path to salvation through this world of challenging moral ambiguities where things are often not what they seem. As a satirist he strews his writings with specious analogies, logical culs-de-sac, rhetorical booby-traps to expose the unwary. Yet all this disruptive energy goes underground when he poses as a public figure of church and state. His sermons reveal an orthodox, unsmiling Anglican, articulating a stern and simple policy of obedience to authority. His *Examiner* writings, less dour than the sermons, express another stern and simple party-line. Socially, Swift felt the need for stability was paramount, and he was prepared to suppress eccentricities and support conformity to maintain it. The contradiction between his instinctive allegiance to Man's intellectual freedom and his equally instinctive recognition of the social benefits of conformism is visible in *Gulliver's Travels*, in one notorious scheme of the Academicians of Lagado:

> many of the most Learned and Wise adhere to the new Scheme of expressing themselves by *Things*, which hath only this Inconvenience attending it: that if a Man's Business be very great, and of various Kinds, he must be obliged in Proportion to carry a greater Bundle of *Things* upon his Back, unless he can afford one or two strong Servants to attend him. I have often beheld two of those Sages almost sinking under the Weight of their Packs, like Pedlars among us; who when they met in the Streets would lay down their Loads, open their Sacks, and hold Conversation for an Hour together; then put up their Implements, help each other to resume their Burthens, and take their Leave.[9]

Swift has no answer to the problem of 'ascertaining' words. So he covers his confusion in ambiguities. His process of incarnation here exploits materialism without endorsing it. In his relentless catechism of fixed terms he does not turn words into things to give them a known value, but to bombard us with innumerable synonyms as in *A Tale of a Tub*:

> . . . Air being a heavy Body, and therefore . . . continually descending, must needs be more so when loaden and press'd down by Words; which are also Bodies of much Weight and Gravity, as it is manifest from those deep *Impressions* they make and leave upon us.
>
> (p. 60)

There is a parallel with Swift's sages struggling with their weighty packs in Pope's *Epistle to Bathurst.* Here the currency is money, and Pope is arguing for the stability of barter:

> Had Colepepper's whole wealth been Hops and Hogs,
> Could he himself have sent it to the Dogs?

Pope's imagery reduces bank-bills back to their collateral objects, and introduces a vein of surrealistic fantasy:

> Astride his Cheese Sir Morgan might we meet,
> And Worldly crying coals from street to street.

But what is Pope's case? Tories were certainly suspicious of the mushroom growth of banks and joint-stock companies, not least because Whigs held a virtual monopoly of them. The débâcle of the South Sea Bubble—a Tory counter-measure—was an object lesson in the airy nothingness of share certificates. Yet nobody argued *seriously* for the abolition of money, except Pope, apparently:

> What Riches give us let us then enquire:
> Meat, Fire, and Cloaths. What more? Meat, Cloaths, and Fire.
> Is this too little? Would you more than live?[10]

Pope's strong suit is fantasy. When one examines the philosophical axioms of the poem, and their logical implications, one encounters yawning chasms across which the couplets hang like frail rope-walks. Essentially the *Epistle to Bathurst* depends upon an asserted analogy between the natural cycle of the seasons, and a putative ethical cycle in human behaviour:

> Ask we what makes one keep and one bestow?
> That POW'R who bids the Ocean ebb and flow.

We may indeed ask which power this is, dividing the world so firmly between getters and spenders, since such a regulating force of Providence must entail a serious infringement of free will, and hence of individual redemption. Pope's neat gardening impulse to separate wheat from tares approaches the Calvinist division of the world between fallen and chosen in a pre-existing moral order that transcends individuals. Mandeville's *Fable of the Bees* illustrates the naïveté of such thinking. The sub-title of Mandeville's work, 'Private Vices, Public Benefits', works in exactly the same way as Pope's notorious apothegm in the *Essay on Man*, 'All Partial Evil, Universal Good'. Yet Mandeville was consciously embracing a utilitarian morality of the greatest happiness of the greatest number. He argued that corruption was a *good* thing, since capitalism depended upon incentives and exploitation to develop a dynamic and sophisticated society with benefits for all. This amoral celebration of the power of the market to create its own values scandalized contemporaries. Yet Pope's formulation depends upon just such a balance of benefits. It is an interesting indication of contemporary preoccupations that while the idea of a moral loss-leader was abhorrent in the social world, it was accepted, at least until Voltaire's *Candide*, as a defining characteristic of divine Providence. Like Johnson on language, Mandeville cut through the make-believe, and declared the independence of money from traditional and authoritarian forms of control. He showed, to the horror of humanists, that money could pre-empt a new morality based upon community development rather than personal integrity, and initiated a new phase in the philosophical tussle over means and ends.

The central point about the currencies of language and finance is that they are *enabling* forces; they are the fluids that animate a society and make it dynamic. By the same token, they can make or break the values of that society, belonging to no master, and at the service of the highest bidder, philosopher or politician, Allen Bathurst or Jonathan Wild. Defoe saluted this enabling power:

> . . . O Money, Money! What an Influence hast thou on all the Affairs of the quarreling, huffing Part of this World, as well as upon the most plodding Part of it! Without Thee Parliaments may meet, and Councils sit, and Kings contrive, but it will all be to no

> Purpose, their Councils and Conclusions can never be put into Execution! Thou raisest Armies, fightest Battles, fittest out Fleets, takest Towns, Kingdoms, and carriest on the great Affairs of the War; All Power, all Policy is supported by Thee, even Vice and Vertue act by thy Assistance, by Thee all the great Things in the World are done. Thou makest Heroes, and crown'st the Actions of the mighty; *By Thee*, in one Sence Kings reign, Armies conquer, Princes grow Great, and Nations flourish.[11]

The pictures drawn by Swift and Pope celebrate a *disabling* force in society; conversation fatally impeded by these pedlar's packs of things; trade obstructed by hundreds of oxen, and tons of coal. Acting like extended puns, these images perform the same act of incarnation, and present a thoroughly static society, not subject to the elusive democracy of the market-place where bank-bills, and words of mouth pass current. But the metaphors are fantastic and surreal; their very comic effect inhibits us from taking the disabling intention seriously.

Swift and Pope deliberately overpitch their effects, as in the reason Swift gives for the Academicians of Lagado desiring to abandon language:

> . . . it is plain, that every Word we speak is in some Degree a Diminution of our Lungs by Corrosion; and consequently contributes to the shortening of our Lives.
>
> (p. 169)

This is an absurd physico-logical parody of the true concern which Swift shared, that misuse of language would lead to the corrosion of the culture which depended upon language for expression. The problem is as before; theoretically Swift and Pope share a belief in free will; in practice they prefer a form of benevolent despotism that eliminates the worst excesses of freedom. Money, language and science all hold out the prospect of unlimited freedom. They work strange alchemy upon their possessors, converting them from rational beings into visionaries determined to recreate the world according to their desires. Paper credit is like an Aeolist fantasy—insubstantial, yet of potentially limitless powers. The form is ludicrously out of proportion to the content, and it is this discrepancy which so often provides the satirists with their best effects. The mock-heroic genre itself is the literary codification of just such discrepancies. A bank-bill is adaptable to all men's wishes and ruling passions; yet it is out of touch with reality, with *things*. It is a promise written upon air, and will stand as readily a cipher for a million as for a hundred pounds. It is an image of anarchy to be so frail, and yet so powerful—the discrepancy violates the natural laws of fitness and harmony, so dear to the classical mind:

> Pregnant with thousands flits the Scrap unseen,
> And silent sells a King, or buys a Queen.
> (*Epistle to Bathurst*, ll. 77–8)

Pun exploits these discrepancies, while acquitting the satirist of specific responsibilities for the resulting ambiguities. Puns dam up the easy flow of the currencies of finance and language by insisting that they bear the full freight of objects for which they circulate as ciphers. There is a simple, almost child-like delight in such obstructionist tactics, seeing dead metaphors brought back to life at the most inconvenient moments, and plausible abstractions transubstantiated into the most intractable actualities. Thus the 'inspiration' of the Dissenters if literalized into a taking in of wind, 'with every Man a Pair of Bellows applied to his Neighbour's Breech, by which they blew up each other'.

Swift and Pope did not wish to abolish money, or language, or science, or faith—the fantastic exaggeration of their imagery makes that clear. But they did wish to offer some restraints to their easy circulation. The two currencies of money and language were too powerful to be independent of all controls save those of the market-place. One's attitude to them naturally depended upon which elements in society one felt were likely to exert the greatest influence on a 'free' currency. It is significant that all the uses of paper credit noted by Pope are corrupt; gambling, bribery, seduction. He makes no mention of ordinary mercantile activities.

By contrast, in the *Drapier's Letters*, Swift was confronting a real, not a metaphorical threat of a debased currency. Wood's halfpence were of such inferior metal that they must inevitably drive out all the gold and silver from Ireland:

> Mr WOOD made his HALF-PENCE of such *Base Metal*, and so much smaller than the *English* ones, that the *Brazier* would hardly give you above a *Penny* of good Money for a *Shilling* of his.

Using a familiar technique of mock-serious computation to establish his case, Swift presents another vignette of a disabled society:

> The common Weight of these HALF-PENCE is between four and five to an *Ounce*; suppose five, then three Shillings and four Pence will weigh a Pound, and consequently *Twenty Shillings* will weigh *Six Pounds Butter Weight.* Now there are many hundred *Farmers* who pay Two hundred Pounds a Year Rent: Therefore when one of these *Farmers* comes with his Half-Year's Rent, which is One hundred Pound, it will be at least Six hundred Pound weight, which is Three Horses Load.[12]

The point is that Swift is here addressing himself to 'the Shop-Keepers, Tradesmen, Farmers and Common People of Ireland' to resist the imposition of Wood's coins. He is therefore using the free circulation of currency as a *positive* value in a prosperous and civilized society. It is Wood, the enemy, who is seen to be obstructing the free flow of trade, and all the comedy of that clogged-up currency is directed against him. So, while the imagery is identical with that used by Pope in the *Epistle to Bathurst*, the conclusion is entirely different. Was Swift more optimistic then, about Man's capacity for organizing a free *and* moral society, than Pope? Or is Empson right to suspect that the force of all Swift's physico-logical puns derives from a subconscious fear that, after all, Hobbes may be right, and that the 'spirit' may be no more than a chemical compound? The punster clouds his meanings in perpetual ambiguities, trusting to neither the word nor the flesh, and always the more ambiguous when his intentions seem most clear. There is something disturbingly crude about the literal-mindedness with which Swift dismisses holy water as a 'universal pickle', and derides the Catholic doctrine of transubstantiation. The energy released against one branch of Christian theology seems sufficient to destroy several more. This is a kind of materialism which, once generated, develops a logic of its own. Swift plays his own transubstantiation trick endlessly; confronting modest proposers who think only in statistics with hecatombs of baby-flesh; or, in reverse, by turning 'things' back into words, confuting the objectivity of scientists with displays of syllogistic pyrotechnics. The only consistent element is the vitality of the trick itself, a vitality born of rhetorical pressures which make each word as much an area of moral struggle as a man's soul. In each one the conflicting claims of free will and determinism are played against each other, only to have the conflict left, as it must be, unresolved. The vitality of these verbal games also reminds us of the philosophy of 'vive la bagatelle' that pervaded meetings of the Scriblerus club. John Dennis's testy remark that 'he that would pun, would pick a pocket' is adduced by Pope as evidence of the critic's ill-nature. And Tom Pun-sibi concludes his study of the subject with the observation that 'punning is a virtue that most effectually promotes the end of good fellowship, which is laughing'.

In the *Drapier's Letters* Swift presents Wood as an alchemist in reverse, taking in gold, and giving back only dross:

> the *Fellow* will not so much as give us good *Brass* or Copper for our *Gold* and *Silver*, nor even a Twelfth Part of their Worth.

His activities are thus directly analogous to those of Pope's dunces who imitate Virgil's praise of Augustus as the bringer of the new Golden Age:

> This, this is he, foretold by ancient rhymes
> Th'Augustus born to bring Saturnian times . . .[13]

The pun here is explained by Pope in a note: 'The ancient golden age is by poets stiled Saturnian', he writes, 'but in the chymical language, Saturn is lead.' The Saturnian age of the Hanoverians was not one of golden culture but of leaden dullness. The discrepancy between these two meanings is a fine example of the devaluation which Swift and Pope both feared in the transition from a classical model for society, to a scientific one. Yet the pun which highlights this discrepancy also demonstrates the ingenuity that can reconcile the two extremes.

## NOTES

1 *The Prose Works of Alexander Pope 1711–1720*, ed. Norman Ault (Oxford, 1936), Introduction, pp. cx–cxii.

2 *The Spectator*, ed. Donald F. Bond, 5 vols. (Oxford, 1965), I, 259–63; No. 61, 10 May, 1711.

3 *Journal to Stella*, ed. Harold Williams, 2 vols. (Oxford, 1948), II, 641; 19 March 1712/13.

4 John Donne, 'The Canonization', ll. 25–7; 'Good Friday, 1613. Riding Westward', ll. 11–12.

5 Denis Donoghue, *Jonathan Swift: A Critical Introduction* (Cambridge, 1969), p. 49.

6 Donald Davie, *The Language of Science and the Language of Literature, 1700–1740* (London, 1963), p. 49.

7 *A Tale of a Tub*, etc., ed. A. C. Guthkelch and D. Nichol Smith, second edition (Oxford, 1958), pp. 77–8. Subsequent references are to this edition and are given in the text.

8 *The World*, No. 101, 5 December, 1754.

9 *Prose Works*, ed. Davis, XI, 169–70. Subsequent references are given in the text.

10 *Epistle to Bathurst*, ll. 53–4, 44–50, 81–3.

11 *A Review*, vol. IV, No. 106; 16 October, 1707.

12 *The Drapier's Letters*, *Prose Works*, ed. Davis, X, 6–7.

13 *The Dunciad*, ll. 319–21.

# 3

# Swift and the Human Predicament

by CLIVE T. PROBYN

*1*

Erasmus complained that his childhood had been tortured by it; Bacon said that though it was the 'art of arts' it had shrunk to the level of 'childish sophistry and ridiculous affectation'; Marlowe's Faustus rejected it in favour of the 'metaphysic of magicians'; Milton consigned it to 'some waste corner' at the foot of Parnassus, and in 1673 wrote a masque populated by some of its terminology (*At a Vacation Exercise*), a flight of fancy induced by compulsory study of it; the titular hero of Butler's *Hudibras* is an expert in it, 'An art t'incumber *Gifts* and wit, / And render both for nothing fit'. Pope's Dunces are adept in its obscurantist use; Swift hated it, but his memory retained and his satirical technique utilized its methods and procedures in great detail. The villainy of Thornhill in Goldsmith's *The Vicar of Wakefield* (1766) is first signalled by a parade of its jargon; Smollett's Matthew Bramble in *Humphry Clinker* (1771) deplores its necessity; Johnson thought a lecture on it was overvalued at twopence; Boswell buttonholed James Harris in a London street in order to belabour a joke at the former's expertise in it; Mrs.Thrale thought people should know about it in order to defend themselves against its practitioners; Fielding invoked an intuitive form of it to describe Dr. Harrison's love for Amelia; Gibbon attributed his conversion from Catholicism to reading Crousaz's book about it.

The subject was logic. In Europe between the Restoration in 1660 and the end of the eighteenth century a book about logic appeared, on average, once every three weeks.[1] The simplest, everyday language today betrays concepts derived from Aristotelian logic: *genus, species, difference*. To be in a *predicament* now suggests being trapped in a difficult or dangerous situation. But once it meant something more specific: being in one of Aristotle's categories of classification, definable, labelled, pigeonholed. In the eighteenth century logic was still the art of arts, the introduction to all other forms of educated discourse, and was studied alongside the other six liberal arts of grammar, rhetoric, music, arithmetic, geometry and astronomy. It was a compulsory part of all higher and some lower education, a central part of the normal experience of educated men. In Abraham Cowley's poem *The Tree of Knowledge* (1656) one of its oldest diagrammatic symbols, the series of dichotomies known as Porphyry's tree, merges into the symbol of forbidden knowledge:

> The sacred Tree midst the fair Orchard grew,
> The Phoenix Truth did on it rest,
> And built his perfumed Nest.
> That right Porphyrian Tree which did true Logick shew,
> Each Leaf did learned Notions give,
> And th'Apples were Demonstrative.
> So clear their colour, and divine,
> The very shade they cast did other Lights out-shine.

Cowley refers here to the Aristotelian logic which had dominated mens' minds for more than fifteen hundred years. He charts its decline into mere 'Probabilities', 'Rhetorick' and 'Fallacies', into 'slight and with'ring Leaves!' Milton wrote a logic-book, so did Hobbes, Isaac Watts, John Wesley, and John Stuart Mill; but by the early eighteenth century the reputation of logic had been sullied by specialization, a reactionary and fossilized school and university curriculum, and by its associations with scholasticism. In Prior's *Alma:or the Progress of the Mind* (1718) it has become the art of confusing an opponent by a bullying and futile syllogistic, an endless civil war of words:

> I could, Thou see'st, in quaint Dispute,
> By dint of *Logic* strike Thee mute;
> With learned Skill, now push, now parry,
> From Darii to Bocardo vary,

And never yield, or what is worst,
Never conclude the Point discours'd.
(Canto III, 380–5)

Pope's *Essay on Man* (1733–4) deplores the 'subtle schoolmen' whose philosophy is 'More studious to divide than to unite' (II, 81–2); the *Essay on Criticism* (1711) reflects with public satisfaction the decline of 'Scotists and Thomists', and all the other disputant scholastics, and their degradation 'Amidst their kindred Cobwebs in Duck-Lane' (1. 445), a place for learned lumber and second-hand books. In *The Dunciad* the very title of the poem evokes Duns Scotus, perhaps the first scholastic philosopher, and the dunces themselves, like their progenitor, are experts in syllogistic reasoning. Since Locke has been expelled (IV, 196), the dunces establish their mindlessness by 'Demonstration thin, and Theses thick, / And Major, Minor, and Conclusion quick' (II, 241–2), turning the three parts of the syllogism into a kind of verbal gymnastics. Swift's image of the Aeolists in section VIII of *A Tale of a Tub* is a burlesque of scholastic philosophy and also includes a syllogistic 'proof' of their flatulent philosophy: '*Words are but Wind*; *and Learning is nothing but Words*; Ergo, *Learning is nothing but Wind*'. In the *Tale* Peter is described as 'the Scholastick Brother' and he it is who bends his father's will in order to make it mean whatever suits his purposes, 'searching farther Evasions, and solving everlasting Contradictions'.

Logic provided a perfect target and vehicle for the satiric lexical brilliance of the Scriblerus group. The climax of their satire is reached in the *Memoirs of Martinus Scriblerus*, composed between the years 1714 and 1727, the joint effort of Arbuthnot, Parnell, Gay, Oxford and Swift. Chapter VII extracts a rich satirical life from the corpse of scholasticism by relating the efforts of Martin's father to beat the elements of ancient logic and metaphysics into his son's skull through the agency of a tutor, Conradus Crambe (described as cousin to Mr. Swan, 'Gamester and Punster in the City of London'). Tutor and tutee inhabit opposite and conflicting mental worlds. Martin's is bounded by sensible objects, Crambe's by a literal response to words alone: the ensuing attempts to understand concepts and general ideas are thus comically bedevilled by opposing attitudes towards words as signs of objects and the objects themselves. In sheer desperation Cornelius offers the baffled Martin a 'sensible image': the coachman is sent for and describes a fight he has witnessed between 'a fair man, a Sergeant in the Guards; the other black, a Butcher; the Sergeant hath red Breeches, the Butcher blue; they fought upon a Stage about four o'clock, and the Sergeant wounded the Butcher in the leg.' Cornelius translates this incident into its Aristotelian logical constituents in order to show the baffled Martin 'how the fellow runs through the praedicaments' (i.e. the ten predicaments or categories of Aristotle's logic: substance, quantity, quality, relation, action, passion, where, when, site and habit—being the labels of every thing that can be said of a thing in relation to every other thing in nature):

> Men, *substantia*; two, *quantitas*; fair and black, *qualitas*; Sergeant and Butcher, *relatio*; wounded the other, *actio & passio*: fighting, *situs*; Stage, *ubi*; four a Clock, *quando*; blue and red Breeches, *habitus*.[2]

Martin mishandles the other fundamental tool of Aristotle's logic, i.e. the five predicables of genus, species, difference, property and accident, by confusing a definition with a description. He complains that an advertisement for a lost or stolen dog should be defined as '*An irrational animal of the Genus caninum*, &c.' Cornelius makes Martin happy by inventing a description *and* a logical definition: 'An Italian Greyhound, of a mouse-colour, a white speck in the neck, lame of one leg, belongs to such a Lady. Greyhound, *genus*; mouse-coloured, etc. *differentia*; lame of one leg, *accidens*; belongs to such a lady, *proprium*.' Crambe's theory of the syllogism is a sexual one, manipulating the ambiguous potential of terms such as *copulative* (in the proposition 'man is a rational animal' the word *is* functions as the copulative), the terms *male* for the major premise, and *female* for the minor. The personifying of logical terms is amusing, and seems endless in a predictable sort of way. In the *Memoirs* satire and sense are mixed up, and what appears on the face of it to be mere *bagatelle* turns out to be far more significant in relation to other more serious effects. The cultural world of Swift had clearly digested the terms and methods of traditional Aristotelian logic and had assimilated its elements into their mental world picture.

In the Scriblerian *Memoirs* the logical fantasy does not go beyond a satire on scholasticism, but in *A Tale of a Tub* (begun, according to Sheridan, when Swift was still a student at Trinity College, Dublin, where he rebelled against scholastic logic and refused to study it), the central allegory of the tailor-worshippers and the professors who define man as a 'Micro-Coat' produces a logical fantasy and intellectual comedy of a high order. The proposition that man is 'a compleat Suit of Cloths with all its Trimmings . . . Religion a *Cloak*, Honesty a *Pair of Shoes* . . . Self-love a *Surtout*, Vanity a *Shirt*, and Conscience a *Pair of Breeches*' is immediately recognizable as a logical travesty, an inversion of inner and outer, a fantasy on the predicament of *habitus* in a literal sense, and the source for Swift's radical conviction that the abstractions of reason are dangerously and tragically related to the humiliating limitations of a rational intelligence grounded, like the abstract language upon which it relies, in the physical world.

Though the technicalities of scholastic logic were ripe for satirical exposure, and remained firmly associated with pedantry throughout the eighteenth century in general, the classifications and even the illustrative terms first used by Aristotle continued to enjoy a vigorous life. The reasons for this are not hard to find. The university curriculum was virtually unchanged from medieval times until the last quarter of the eighteenth century in respect of classical philosophy, and thus generated a continuing need for texts which were traditional in their logical concepts. Locke's revisionary attitude towards scholasticism had not convinced everyone. In certain branches of science Aristotelian categories flourished with a new life. In linguistics the traditional logical frameworks proved essential to analysis; and the very fact of the long dominance of scholastic logic, together with an increasing post-Lockean interest in the psychology of thought (often referred to as simply the art of thinking) led to important efforts to rehabilitate logic as a necessary accomplishment of the well-educated man. The terms and procedures of Aristotle's logic were truly commonplace in the eighteenth century, a fundamental educational discipline, a shared habit of mental procedure, an agreed way of labelling the external world. R. S. Crane's definition of the term *commonplace* describes the notion exactly:

> *disjecta membra* of philosophic or scientific systems that have survived, independently, as parts of a common stock of usable notions and patterns of reasoning upon which all educated men can draw . . . wherever they occur, they represent not so much what the writers in whose treatises, essays, poems, or novels we find them are thinking *about* as what they are thinking with.[3]

Though the particlar subject of this essay is Swift, there are examples of this commonplace assimilation of logic everywhere in the period. An obvious example is found in Johnson's remark to that champion of all things Aristotelian, James Harris, that 'To be distinct, we must talk *analytically*. If we analyse language, we must speak of it grammatically; if we analyse argument, we must speak of it logically.' Boswell admired the work of Harris, but received the following rebuff from Johnson:

> BOSWELL: 'He says plain things in a formal and abstract way, to be sure: but his method is good: for to have clear notions upon any subject, we must have recourse to analytick arrangement.' JOHNSON: 'Sir, it is what every body does, whether they will or no. But sometimes things may be made darker by definition. I see a *cow*, I define her, *Animal quadrupes ruminans cornutum*. But a goat ruminates, and a cow may have no horns. *Cow* is plainer.'[4]

Johnson's retort reveals an informed dislike. His words and his mental set are shaped by the logical context of Harris's work: his reply is in strictly logical terms, defining an object by its genus and specific difference (*animal* and *quadrupes ruminans cornutum*), but he clearly objects to the conversion of plain truths into the specialisms of an intellectual system. Boswell feels no need to explain the mode of Johnson's retort: even though it seems to be a scholarly dialect, it is nevertheless one which is familiar to his contemporary readers. Fielding defined his art with the aid of an empirical and a philosophical inflection: 'I describe not men, but manners; not an individual, but a species' (*Joseph Andrews*, Bk. III, i), but his *Essay on the Knowledge of the Characters of Men* opens in the style and with the terminology of logical distinctions: 'Those who predicate of Man in general, that he is an Animal of this or that Disposition, seem to me not sufficiently to have studied Human Nature . . . Nor is it perhaps a less proper Predicament of the Genius of a Tree, that it will flourish so many Years, loves such a Soil, bears such a Fruit, &c. than of Man in general, that he is good, bad, fierce, tame, honest, or cunning.'

## *2*

Thomas Sheridan's *Life of Swift* (1784) relates Swift's many efforts to come to terms with the logic of his day as a student at Trinity College, Dublin, in particular the 'old treatises on logic writ by Smiglecius, Keckermannus, Burgersdicius, &c.', which formed a compulsory requirement of his first degree. He eventually rejected them all on the grounds that they taught 'the art of wrangling' instead of the art of reasoning. With the confidence of maturity Swift looked back to his painful experience with logic and, in Sheridan's words, told his tutor (possibly St. George Ashe, whose own pronouncements on logic suggest a sympathetic audience for Swift's objections), 'he was contented with that portion of reason which God hath given him, and he would leave it to time and experience to strengthen and direct it properly; nor would he run the risk of having it warped or falsely biassed, by any system of rules laid down by such stupid writers, of the bad effects of which he had but too many examples before his eyes, in those reckoned the most acute logicians.' As a result Swift was 'stopped of his degree the first time of sitting for it, on account of his not answering in that branch.' Everyone knows the result of Swift's stubbornness. Concessions were made to his logical insufficiency and he was allowed to graduate only by special grace.

But what is usually overlooked is the tenacity of Swift's memory of the experience:

> In going through the usual forms of disputation for his degree, he told me he was utterly unacquainted with the logical terms, and answered the arguments of his opponents in his own manner, which the Proctor put into the proper form. There was one circumstance in the account which he gave of this, that surprised me with regard to his memory; for he told me the several questions on which he disputed, and repeated all the arguments used by his opponents in syllogistick form, together with his answers.
> (pp. 5–6)

The statutes in Trinity College in force at this time required logic to be studied in the first of the four-year B.A. degree, the chief texts being Porphyry and his commentators. In the second year Aristotle's *Organon* was studied (i.e. any collection of the logical writings), with the rubric that 'what relates to logic shall be handled logically, that is, syllogistically, not with flourishes of rhetoric.' These conditions of logical study remained in force, substantially, until 1760. With Swift's logical problems it is almost certain that he would have turned to the logic-book of a Trinity College tutor, Narcissus Marsh's *Institutiones Logicae* (1679), specially designed for the College. Here recent scholarship has uncovered the tracks of the logical basis of Swift's fourth part of *Gulliver's Travels*, and of the more general relationship between Swift's concept of man, not as a rational animal, as countless logics defined him, but as an animal *capable* of reason yet characteristically driven by a subversive irrationality. The logical implications of Swift's emendation to the traditional definition *animal rationale* are worth detailed attention.[5]

In 1725 Swift wrote a letter to Pope explaining the way he reacted to groups and individual persons. He added a few lines about his artistic intention in a treatise which he was completing about the rational capabilities of man. In critical discussions of *Gulliver's Travels* there is no more frequently quoted piece of evidence:

> I have ever hated all Nations, Professions, and Communities; and all my love is towards Individuals: for Instance, I hate the Tribe of Lawyers, but I love counsellor such a one, and Judge such a one: 'Tis so with Physicians (I will not speak of my own Trade) Soldiers, English, Scotch, French, and the rest. But principally I hate and detest that animal called Man, although I hartily love John, Peter, Thomas, and so forth. This is the system upon which I have governed myself many years (but do not tell) and so I shall go on till I have done with them. I have got Materials towards a Treatise, proving the falsity of that definition *Animal ration*ale, and to shew it should be only *rationis capax*. Upon this great foundation of Misanthropy (tho' not in Timon's manner) the whole Building of my Travels is erected; and I never will have peace of mind, till all honest men are of my opinion: By consequence you are to embrace it immediately, and

> procure that all who deserve my esteem may do so too. The matter is so clear, that it will admit of no dispute; nay, I will hold a hundred pounds that you and I agree in the point.[6]

These few lines have proved as vexing as anything in the *Travels*. One might readily agree with Swift that it is humanly impossible to relate emotionally to abstract masses of individuals. But need we *hate* them? We might readily agree that emotional relationships can only exist between individuals, but need we necessarily '*hartily love*' them? We might justifiably love or hate the same object without agreeing to Swift's antithesis of individual versus group. As an argument Swift's paragraph is an ambivalent combination of an intellectual *system* and a personal testament. The second half reads like banter, particularly so if we remember Swift's implacable hatred for *all* systems of abstract speculation, and his unremitting satire in *A Digression on Madness* on those who insist on bending everybody and everything to their own versions of reality. The paragraph is crucial to our understanding of the philosophical basis of *Gulliver's Travels* and is vital as a statement of intent, but its emotional extremism and arbitrary classification of humanity are absurd. It is also illogical. If Swift loved individual members of professional and national groups, then it is not the groups of individuals he objects to *per se* but the mental habit of generic classification according to specific skills and properties, and the effect of such specialisation on the human personality.[7]

Swift is thus ostensibly basing a love-hate antithesis on a prior classification of humanity into *individuals* whom he can know and other *individuals* whom he cannot know. This division is justified by the assertion that the common definition of man as *animal rationale* is not a definition at all: it is not even a description, but merely a capability more or less deployed in behaviour. Bolingbroke put the point shrewdly in a postcript to a letter:

> P.S. Pope and you are very great Wits, and I think very indifferent Philosophers. If you despised the world as much as you pretend, and perhaps believe, you would not be so angry with it . . .
> . . . Your definition of *Animal Rationis capax*, instead of the common one *Animal Rationale*, will not bear examination: define but Reason, and you will see why your distinction is no better

than that of the Pontiff Cotta; between *male ratio*, and *bona ratio*. But enough of this.[8]

The interpretative problems caused by adding a fictional vehicle to a philosophically dubious proposition could never have been foreseen, even by Swift. But, if we examine the sources of Swift's philosophical ideas, particularly for the fourth voyage of *Gulliver's Travels*, we may be able to see that Swift's satirical imagination had transferred into literature not only the terms but also some fundamental problems of contemporary epistemology.

The logic-books of Swift's time were much concerned with the necessary distinctions to be drawn between genus, species, and individual. The citation of *animal rationale* is utterly commonplace; so is the example of the horse as an *irrational* animal. For example, Thomas Good's *A Brief Tract of Logick* (1677: based on Brerewood's *Elementary Logick* of 1614) is almost entirely devoted to variations of this one syllogism: *Homo non est Equus*, or *nullus Homo est Equus*; *Ergo, Nullus Equus est Homo*. Good gives the following illustration of the five types of proposition (genus, species, differentia, proprium, accident):

> *Petrus est Animal*; *Animal* is the *Genus*, or the Common Kind of *Peter*: for if you ask what kind of creature *Peter* is, I answer he is an *Animal* or sensitive Creature. *Petrus est Homo*; homo is the Species or the special Kind of *Peter*: *Peter est rationalis*; *rationalis* is the Difference by which Peter is distinguished from a Beast which is unreasonable: *Petrus est risibilis*; *risibilis* is the Propriety of *Peter*, for it is only Proper to Man to laugh.
>
> (p. 26)

Swift's definitions of man in the letter to Pope are part of an assumed cultural context, but with certain changes made to the usual logical assumptions in the fourth voyage of Gulliver. Gulliver is the individual man, the rational animal; but by this definition so are the Houyhnhnms. The common example of the horse as an irrational animal is reversed and the view of human reason which Gulliver both narrates and exemplifies emerges as a poor parody. The remaining term of the argument in the fourth voyage is the *Yahoo*, the ape-like brute without speech or reason which according to Porphyry's scheme of classifications is the antithesis of man as a *rational animal*. Gulliver's human demoralisation is complete, and his rational confidence crumbles when he is nearly raped by an eleven year old female Yahoo: 'For now I could no longer deny, that I was a real *Yahoo*, in every Limb and Feature, since the Females had a natural Propensity to me as one of their own Species', as he delicately puts it. The prospect and physical possibility of cross-breeding between species is an appalling challenge to received philosophical classifications as well as to man's physical dignity at the summit of creation. Gulliver's repulsion is not particularly remarkable, but Swift's imaginative ability to dramatise an intellectual paradox (rational horses, irrational anthropoids) in emotional and sexual terms is a unique fusion of a logical system and of anthropological implication.

The chief topic of Gulliver's conversation with the Master Horse is 'the Nature of Manhood' (p. 224), seen predominantly and eventually almost exclusively from the Houyhnhnm point of view. Gulliver's clothes are put at the same level as his reason: accidental attributes, not essential parts either of his being or of his definition. His feet are too soft to walk on without protective devices (shoes); the location of his eyes prevent sideways vision; his hands cannot support the weight of his body, and so on. Groups such as those of the legal and medical professions, and particularly politicians, are seen as consequences of human corruption, products of human inadequacy and not organizations to satisfy human needs. Thus Gulliver describes the nobility in particular as a consummation of vice, 'The Imperfections of his Mind run parallel with those of his Body, being a Composition of Spleen, Dulness, Ignorance, Caprice, Sensuality and Pride' (p. 241). The apparent virtue of the Houyhnhnms crushes Gulliver's residual pride in belonging to the human race and he capitulates to the Master Horse's estimate (p. 243):

> he looked upon us as a Sort of Animals to whose Share, by what Accident he could not conjecture, some small Pittance of Reason had fallen, whereof we made no other Use than by its Assistance to aggravate our *natural* Corruptions, and to acquire new ones which Nature had not given us.
>
> . . . our Institutions of *Government* and *Law* were plainly owing to our gross Defects in *Reason*, and by consequence, in *Virtue*; because *Reason* alone is sufficient to govern a *Rational* Creature; which has therefore a Character we had no Pretence to challenge.

The Master Horse, like Swift, prefers to define man by his performance and not by his philosophical theories. Indeed, human 'Systems of *Natural* Philosophy' are treated with sarcastic contempt. The Master Horse shows Gulliver that 'Controversies, Wranglings, Disputes, and Positiveness in false or dubious Propositions, are evils unknown among the Houyhnhnms.' Gulliver attends the Houyhnhnm Grand Assembly with all the zeal of a new convert. The subject of the debate is always the same, the extermination of the Yahoos. If the Houyhnhnm world has the surgical sterility of a genetic laboratory its positive advantage, it seems, is that there are in it none of the messy complexities, failures and tensions of its human counterpart. No reasoning is necessary here because all truths are self-evident and therefore meet with universal assent. Only the Yahoos spoil the picture; they are the unregenerate, primal animality which has always provided the obstacle to a perfect world based on rational principles. The Houyhnhnms consider the propositions that the Yahoos are aboriginals, or perhaps more recent intruders into their world. Gulliver puts forward the thesis of racial degeneration from an original parent species which could exist elsewhere in a less degenerate state, and of which he himself could be a member. He accordingly suggests that the Houyhnhnms try racial engineering and deal with the Yahoos in the way his own countrymen deal with their horses: i.e. selected breeding by castration, but with the aim of complete extermination of the species. This ultimate horror of racial genocide is the last step in Gulliver's total alienation from his own kind. He admits that

> when I thought of my Family, my Friends, my Countrymen, or human Race in general, I considered them as they really were, *Yahoos* in Shape and Disposition, perhaps a little more civilised, and qualified with the Gift of Speech; but making no other Use of Reason, than to improve and multiply those Vices, whereof their Brethren in this Country had only the Share that Nature allotted to them. When I happened to behold the Reflection of my own Form in a Lake or Fountain, I turned away my Face in Horror and detestation of my self; and could better endure the Sight of a common *Yahoo*, than of my own Person.
>
> (p. 262)

There is no more intense vision of self-loathing than this. Gulliver's glimpse of a rationalist Utopia makes his own life a hell on earth. The Houyhnhnms, naturally, regard him as having no place in their society, for he is neither Yahoo nor Houyhnhnm but a hybrid, a cross-bred species, and hence a freak of nature which must be expelled as a threat to Houyhnhnm mastery. Though Gulliver returns to his own kind he can never regard himself as a part of it. Intellectually he will always be looking over his shoulder in aspiration to the cool rationality of the Houyhnhnms, driven to do so by the disgust which he will always feel for his animal proximity.

When Swift's substitution of *animal rationis capax* for *animal rationale* is put in its philosophical context his misanthropy (though not his savage indignation) can be properly understood as a point of view rather than a recommended rule of conduct. The first point that needs to be made is that the definition Swift preferred is by no means unique to Swift. Philosophers and logicians got there first. Watts remarked on the insufficiency of the definition in 1725:

> The common definition of Man, viz, *a rational animal* is very faulty, 1. Because the *Animal* is not rational; the Rationality of Man arises from the Mind to which the Animal is united. 2. Because if a Spirit should be united to a *Horse*, and make it a rational Being, surely this would not be a *Man*: 'Tis evident therefore that the *peculiar Shape* must enter into the Definition of a *Man* to render it just and perfect, and for want of a full Definition thereof all our Definitions are defective.[10]

The anonymous author of *A Philosophical Dissertation upon the Inlets to Human Knowledge* (Dublin, 1740) demotes rationality from an essential differentia of man to a property, an occasional but not a continuous activity in human behaviour:

> I cannot but look on the common definition of man as *animal rationale*, to be somewhat *defective*. I think it might be altered for the better, though that would not be compleat, to define him *animal rationabile*, if *rationabile* may be allowed to signify the capacity of receiving and not the actual exercise of reason . . . This definition is proper, whereas Aristotle's is not which makes him *animal rationale*, as if he were actually and not only poten-

> tially so, by his specific nature, without any foreign help of culture.[11]

One piece of evidence suggests that Swift's logical point in *Gulliver's Travels* had been well and truly taken by his contemporary audience. In *The Logicians Refuted: In Imitation of Dean Swift* (possibly by Goldsmith) there are the following lines:

> Logicians have but ill defin'd
> As rational, the human kind;
> Reason, they say, belongs to man,
> But let them prove it if they can.
> Wise Aristotle and Smiglecius,
> By ratiocinations specious,
> Have strove to prove with great precision,
> With definition and division,
> *Homo est ratione praeditum*;
> But for my soul I cannot credit 'em.

The author of this piece proceeds to show the moral superiority of the beasts (including 'honest quadrupeds', and even of the ape, whose ruling passion is 'malice') over man's viciousness, much in the way of Rochester's *Satyr against Mankind*, which includes the comment that 'Man differs more from Man, than Man from Beast', a sentiment also found in Plutarch, Montaigne, Sedley, and Locke's *Essay* (IV, xx, 5): 'there is a difference of degrees in men's understandings, apprehensions, and reasonings, to so great a latitude, that one may, without doing injury to mankind, affirm, that there is a greater distance between some men and others in this respect, than between some men and some beasts.' The burden of all such revisions to the standard philosophical definitions of man was that human diversity and human perversity could not be comprehended by traditional means. The undeniable fact of biological similarities between monkey and man (discussed at length in Tyson's *Orang-Outang, Sive Homo Sylvestris*, 1699, and in Monboddo's *Origin and Progress of Language*, 1773), worked over the same area explored by Swift's satiric imagination. But scientific caution ruled out the moral implications which were Swift's exclusive concern: Monboddo adds, 'Though I hold the Orang Outang to be of our species, it must not be supposed that I think the monkey or ape, with or without a tail, participates of our nature; on the contrary, I maintain that, however much his form may resemble ours, yet he is, as Linnaeus says of the Troglodytes, *nec nostri, nec sanguinis*.'[12]

The overwhelming question in Gulliver's fourth voyage is the validity of the Houyhnhnms as rational symbols. Gulliver's linguistic inquisitiveness is rewarded with the information that Houyhnhnm means horse, but signifies in its etymology '*The Perfection of Nature*' (IV, iii). The word is a phonetic rendering as close as Gulliver can make to '*English Orthography*.' As we have noted, some of Swift's contemporaries were aware that the fourth voyage involved logical terms and definitions, and at least Bolingbroke seems to have noticed that the fourth voyage also involved a logical *problem*. The challenge to received epistemology lay virtually dormant, however, until the middle of the nineteenth century. John Stuart Mill noticed that the fourth voyage illustrated a problem at the very root of inductive logic. In chapter two of his *System of Logic Ratiocinative and Inductive* (1843–72) Mill argues that if Swift's Houyhnhnms were to be discovered in the real (as opposed to the imaginary) world, then their definition would provide a logically insoluble problem. Any definition of man as a *rational animal*, Mill continues, is insufficient and provisional because 'Such a definition . . . is always liable to be overset by the discovery of new objects in nature' (i.e. a species of rational animal without the external form of *man*):

> All concrete general names are connotative. The word *man*, for example, denotes Peter, Jane, John, and an indefinable number of other individuals, of whom, taken as a class, it is the name. But it is applied to them, because they possess, and to signify that they possess, certain attributes. These seem to be corporeity, animal life, rationality, and a certain external form, which for distinction we call the human. Every existing thing, which possessed all these attributes, would be called a man; and anything which possessed none of them, or only one, or two, or even three of them without the fourth, would not be so called. For example, if in the interior of Africa there were to be discovered a race of animals possessing reason equal to that of human beings, but with the form of an elephant, they would not be called men. Swift's Houyhnhms [*sic*] would not be so called. Or if such newly-discovered beings possessed the form of man without any vestige of reason, it is probable that some other name would be found for them.[13]

In the newly-discovered world of the Houyhnhnms that 'other name' is *Yahoo*. Similarly, the most vexing philosophical aspect of this voyage lies in the dichotomy between the individual and the class or group. Swift, as we know, claimed to love individuals—'John, Peter, Thomas, and so forth'—but hated 'that animal called man'. The problem of discriminating between the two is such that even Mill has no solution to offer. Book III, chapter iii, of *A System of Logic* ends with a question and a plea:

> Why is a single instance, in some cases, sufficient for a complete induction, while in others, myriads of concurring instances, without a single exception known or presumed, go such a very little way towards establishing an universal proposition? Whoever can answer this question knows more of the philosophy of logic than the wisest of the ancients, and has solved the problem of induction.

The complete induction works both ways: the Houyhnhnms conclude from Gulliver's example that humanity in general is largely irrational and corrupt, and Gulliver concludes from their argument about his physical proximity to the Yahoos that they must be right. Misanthropy is the only *logical* conclusion for him.

But the reader knows better. It is significant that Mill's observations on *Gulliver's Travels* are made in a chapter *Of Names*. Gulliver's name connotes *gull, gullible*, hence credulity and unreliability, an interpretation explicitly invited by the legend attached to his 'portrait' in the 1735 edition (*splendide mendax*, or magnificent liar). As narrator he is dogged from the outset by Swift's satirical uncertainties: his own validity is in question. Is it possible, then, that Swift's most complex emblem of rationality, the Houyhnhnms, completely lack such thematically undercutting associations? If Swift intended to treat the Houyhnhnms *critically* we might expect some hint of their insufficiency in their names. If so, such a device should arise naturally from the context and should also refer specifically to their status as rational symbols. Satirically reductive, homophonic puns are a commonplace in Swift. In the *Discourse to Prove the Antiquity of the English Tongue*, *Achilles* becomes *A kill-ease*; *Diomede/die a Maid*; *Ajax/a Jakes*; *Peloponnesus/Pail up and ease us*; and so on. The homophonic puns are functional, travestying classical and heroic dignity by a sexual or scatological reduction. Other examples (from *A Modest Defence of Punning*, 1716) travesty polysyllabic or technical terms by a kind of physical enactment of their meaning: thus *coruscat* becomes *Chorus of Cats*; *Scholar* becomes *sculler*. Latin and Greek derivations such as *asafoetida* becomes *Asaph et Ida*; sudorific becomes *sued her I feck*; and *licanthropy* becomes *lick on through Pye*.

In the *Memoirs of Martinus Scriblerus*, in a logical context, terms are *animated*: *copulative* is given a sexual function, so are the male and female forms of the syllogism. In the *Battle of the Books* the books of the Ancients and Moderns grow limbs, wear headgear and armour, and do battle with other animated books. The very terms of the fourth voyage are animated terms of the Aristotelian syllogistic. Aristotle warns against the logical error of confusing resemblance with essence:

> We must also see whether the resemblance tends towards the ridiculous, for example, that of a monkey to a man, whereas the horse bears no resemblance: for the monkey is not more handsome than the horse, although he is more like a man.[14]

Significant names are an organic part of the fantasy-voyage tradition, to which *Gulliver's Travels* belongs. More's *Utopia* coined significant names from Greek, as did Rabelais. Joseph Hall's *Mundus Alter et Idem* uses many synthetic words coined from Latin, Greek, French, Italian, Spanish and German. Defoe's account of a lunar voyage, in *The Consolidator* (1705), uses anagrammatic names and words with Latin and Greek roots. As Kelling points out,[15] Gulliver gratuitously mentions his broad linguistic knowledge of 'High and Low Dutch, Latin, French, Spanish, Italian, and Lingua Franca.' In classical logic and rhetoric there had always been a technique or topic of argument which inferred a meaning from proper names. In his *Rhetoric* Aristotle gave several examples of this sort of onomastic argument: Draco the legislator ('his laws were not those of a man, but of a dragon, so severe were they'); Polus ('Thou art ever Polus [colt] by name and colt by nature'); and Hecuba's comment on Aphro-dite in Euripedes' *Troades* ('And rightly does the name of the goddess begin like the word aphro-syne (folly) ). Quintilian discussed the device; Cicero used it to make a contemptuous pun on the surname of Verres ('boar-pig'). It is a commonplace in Greek drama not only as a pun but as an indicator of character or destiny. The closest lexicographical link to *Houyhnhnm* is *homonym*, which not only sounds like Swift's invented word but also provides meanings pertinent to the logical substructure for Swift's symbolic creatures and expressed intentions in the fourth voyage.

The common meanings of the term *homonym* is the use of two words identical in sound and sometimes in spelling, but with different meanings (e.g. heart/hart; mole/mole). The term thus describes a state of phonetic identity and semantic ambivalence. Its more specialized scientific usage describes a name given to a species or genus that has been used at an earlier date for a different species or genus and is therefore rejected. In this latter sense the rational horse has usurped the label and definition *animal rationale* (previously the exclusive definition of *man*), and Gulliver consequently rejects its former validity. The earliest usage in this sense (recorded by the *OED*) is long after Swift's time, but the fact is that the word originates not in scientific classifications but in logic, and usually in contexts dealing with classification and proper methods of analysis. It is the first word ('ομώνυμα) of Aristotle's *Categories*:

> Things are equivocally named, when they have the name only in common, the definition (or statement of essence) corresponding with the name being different. For instance, while a man and a portrait can properly both be called 'animals' these are equivocally named. For they have the name only in common, the definitions (or statements of essence) corresponding with the name being different. For if you are asked to define what the being an animal means in the case of the man and the portrait, you give in either case a definition appropriate to that case alone.[16]

Quintilian's manual of rhetoric, the *Institutio Oratoria*, elaborates on the term *homonym* (looking forward to Locke's distinction between a nominal and a real essence) by ascribing to it the sense of ambiguity and obscurity: 'For example, the word *taurus* may be unintelligible unless we make it clear whether we are speaking of a bull, or a mountain, or a constellation, or the name of a man, or the root of a tree.' Various logic-books published before, during and after Swift's lifetime maintain the logical currency of *homo-*

*nym*: it may be found in Burgersdicius (1626: seven English editions between 1637 and 1680); in Milton's pupil Edward Philips's logic-book (1648)—'Homonymous, things of several kinds, having the same denomination, a Term in Logick'; in Isaac Watts' *Logick* (1725)—which gives the synonym *ambiguous*; in James Harris's *Hermes* (1751), 'One word may be not homonymously but truly and essentially common to many particulars past, present and future.' A particularly important inflection is added to this debate in the acrimonious dialogue between John Locke and Bishop Stillingfleet in the 1690s. Locke tried hard to impress upon the Bishop that the names *Peter*, *James* and *John* could equally well denote horses as men, and could even apply to baboons. Driven to sarcasm the Bishop replied that 'My man *Peter* and I can sit and chop Logick together, about our Country Affairs, and he can Write and Read, and he is a very sharp Fellow at a Bargain; but my *Horse Peter* can do none of these things, and I never could find any thing like *Reason* in him, and do you think I do not know the Difference between *a Man* and *a Beast*?'[17] The sheer size of the problem of the same words used in different senses (e.g. man, motion, humanity, animality) led Locke to propose a synthetic language, free from associated meanings, and to recommend the compilation of a pictorial dictionary, wherein 'words standing for things which are known and distinguished by their outward shapes should be expressed by little draughts and prints made of them.' Such a dictionary would be especially useful in teaching the language of 'remote countries or ages.' The notion appears in Swift's Academy of Lagado, except that the *Things* themselves are entirely to replace the denotative symbols (*Words*).

In summary, therefore, several things emerge from this complex and inter-related logical and philosophical background. First, the term *homonym* is associated with a logical context of ambiguity and ambivalance; secondly, Swift's rational horses (and his Yahoo-monkeys) are to be found also in logical contexts, most recently in the 1690s; thirdly, the Houyhnhnms as symbols represent a problem of definition and are conceived as a logical paradox (an *animal rationale* which is not, however, *man*). Swift's imagination, I would suggest, dramatised a logical debate in *Gulliver's Travels* and made the very definition *animal rationale* a homonym itself. Preposterously for us, but actually for Gulliver, horse and man can at least initially both be designated by the definition *animal rationale*, for they each share the same nature. The lexical and semantic link between them is not only the logical context stemming from Aristotle through Locke, but also a simple homophonic pun.[18] *Homonym* has two morphemes (*same/name*), and in addition to its lexicographical sense also suggests *man-name*. *Houyhnhnm* cannot be thus easily broken up into morphemes, but if we substitute the phonologically linked *homonym* by its logical alternative (i.e. *equivocal*) we produce a term which suggests both a literal pun on the horse's characteristics (*horse speaking*) and a critical judgement on their status in Swift's discussion of the nature of man. As symbols the Houyhnhnms are ambivalent, and their names indicate their natures, just as Gulliver's name indicates his nature. Swift thus underscores their ambivalence as rational symbols by associating them with a term from logic which describes an apparently similar (rational) faculty shared with man, but which actually conceals physical and moral dissimilarities. This is precisely Gulliver's dilemma. In IV, vii, Gulliver reports the opinion of the Master Horse:

> as I agreed in every Feature of my Body with other *Yahoos*, except where it was to my real Disadvantage in point of Strength, Speed and Activity, the Shortness of my Claws, and some other Particulars where Nature had no Part; so, from the Representation I had given him of our Lives, our Manners, and our Actions, he found as near a Resemblance in the Disposition of our Minds.

In all essentials Gulliver has already admitted, with horror, that he recognizes his kinship if not identity with the Yahoo: 'I observed, in this abominable Animal, a perfect human Figure' (IV, ii). Whereas it is easy for Gulliver to reject the Yahoo because of spontaneous physical disgust, the Houyhnhnms are irresistible as rational companions, even though in outward form they are not men and neither are they subject to a whole range of human emotions from joy to grief. In their own minds (like Gulliver's expressions of veracity are to himself) they are sincere and honest, and everything is clear and distinctly definable. The clarity of their vision is of the kind which permits urbane discussion of genocide for the Yahoos and eugenics for themselves. They are totally unconscious of their own being. In human terms they are preposterous. Mendacity does not exist in their society, therefore they have no word for lying (IV, iii), a piece of intellectual self-deceit which is self-evidently absurd. My suggestion of a homophonic link between *homonym* and *Houyhnhnm* may, even in spite of its contextual probabilities, seem nothing more than etymological accident, or an unconscious memory of the logic-books of Swift's youth. But it should be remembered that Swift was an expert in such things. The third voyage (written after the fourth) contains in Lagado an extensive array of linguistic ingenuity—cyphers, universal language schemes, acrostics, anagrams and secret codes, and the Lagadian cryptologists are, like Walpole's political agents, 'very dextrous in finding out the mysterious Meanings of Words, Syllables and Letters.' Minor phonetic adjustments are essential to any pun and in Swift's case would be rudimentary tricks from an expert antagonist of dark meanings. And, as we have seen, he was particularly interested in homophonic puns. The phonetic and semantic relationship (in the satirical context) between *Houyhnhnm* and *homonym* suggests that Swift too was manipulating a traditional onomastic element of fantasy voyages, thereby hinting at the spurious logical validity of the Houyhnhnms' rational ideal behind their and Gulliver's backs.[19] With the equivocal horses this splendid liar has found his perfect home in a convoluted paradox, among a non-human and inhumane species supremely ignorant of their own ambivalence.

Locke showed that the infinite shades of gradation between one species and another in the natural world could not be comprehended by simple definitions. Swift showed in *Gulliver's Travels* that man's animal nature was not merely part of a traditional logical definition but an undeniable imperative in his conduct, and that to underestimate its part in determining human actions and institutions was to risk Gulliver's fate, i.e. the absurd and ultimately tragic delusion that we can always and entirely be motivated by the rational part of our dichotomous natures. Swift's contemporary readers, having been vexed by a vivid re-enactment of this ancient paradox of man's nature, are left to ponder the moral significance for themselves. For Locke it was a matter for complaint that educated readers of his generation, 'bred up in the Peripatetick philosophy', too readily believed that 'the Ten Predicaments [were] exactly conformable to the nature of things.'

In his own way Swift was illustrating the same dichotomy between the logical labels which the mind attaches to the world and the world's awkward habit of sliding away beneath them. The homonymous term *animal rationale* is as applicable to horses in Houyhnhnmland as it is to Swift's vision of human behaviour in Augustan England. The rational self-esteem of both is at best ambivalent, at worst a solipsistic delusion. But it is also characteristic of Swift's method that such an implication, though tragic in its significance, is comic in its mode of expression. The pun is the lowest form of wit because it reduces meaning to the level of a phonemic accident. It confuses normally separated categories of meaning. In Swift's hands that confusion elicits a brief but dazzling moment of disorientation whereby the denotative certainties of language are shattered by linguistic contingency. Its function is to tell us something about the Lockean treacheries of language and classification, in all their provisional, imprecise nominalism. Thus Swift's linguistic comedy, in which logic plays an important part, breaks epistemological taboos by making 'meaning' itself *elude* language. To Swift and his age the Houyhnhnm represented a potent myth of supreme rationality: for modern critics the Houyhnhnm *is* a perfect example of what Barthes calls an 'ideographic system . . . where the forms are still motivated by the concept which they represent while not yet, by a long way, covering the sum of its possibilities for representation'.[20]

## NOTES

1 Almost 2,400 books wholly or partly on logic appeared between 1660 and 1800, including anonymous works, translations and reprints, with peaks in 1675, 1694, 1737, 1748. See Wilhelm Risse, *Bibliographica Logica*, 2 vols. (Hildesheim, 1973). The eighteenth century lacks studies which relate elementary and university education to its larger cultural and literary context, unlike the seventeenth century. Cf. M. Joseph, *Rhetoric in Shakespeare's Time* (1947); T. W. Baldwin, *William Shakespeare's Small Latin and Less Greek* (1944); Hardin Craig, *The Enchanted Chain* (1936); W. J. Ong, *Ramus Method and Decay of Dialogue* (1958). For the eighteenth century, see W. S. Howell's surveys, *Eighteenth Century British Logic and Rhetoric* (Princeton, 1971), and *Logic and Rhetoric in England, 1500–1700* (Princeton, 1956). W. T. Costello, *The Scholastic Curriculum at Early Seventeenth Century*

*Cambridge* (Cambridge, Mass., 1958), and W. A. L. Vincent, *The Grammar Schools: Their Continuing Tradition, 1660–1714*, 1969), are useful introductions. For a general survey, see R. Blakey, *Historical Sketch of Logic* (1851) and W. and M. Kneale, *The Development of Logic* (Oxford, 1962).

I have restricted footnote references in this essay (part of work-in-progress) to a bare minimum. Place of publication is London, except where stated.

2 *The Memoirs of Martinus Scriblerus* (New Haven, 1950), ed. Charles Kerby-Miller, pp. 119–20. For a commentary on the logical background, see pp. 243–261.

3 R. S. Crane, 'Philosophy, Literature, and the History of Ideas', *The Idea of the Humanities*, 2 vols. (1967), I. 176. First published in 1954.

4 *Boswell's Life of Johnson*, ed. G. B. Hill, rev. L. F. Powell, 6 vols. (Oxford, 1934–50), III, p. 245. See also my forthcoming essay in *Modern Language Review*, 'Johnson, James Harris, and the Logic of Happiness', which discusses this passage in some detail.

5 My starting point is R. S. Crane's article, 'The Houyhnhnms, the Yahoos, and the History of Ideas', *Reason and Imagination: Studies in the History of Ideas 1600–1800*, ed. J. A. Mazzeo (1962), pp. 231–53. I also summarise some evidence discussed in my article 'Swift and Linguistics', *Neophilologus*, LVIII, 4 (1974), 425–39. For information on logical studies at TCD, see K. Theodore Hoppen, *The Common Scientist in the Seventeenth Century* (1970), and Constantia Maxwell, *History of Trinity College Dublin, 1591–1892* (Dublin, 1946).

6 *Correspondence of Jonathan Swift*, ed. Harold Williams, 5 vols. (Oxford, 1965), III, 103. Cf. also III, 118.

7 Ian Watt discusses Gulliver's function as *persona* in relation to the individual-general dichotomy in 'The Ironic Tradition in Augustan Prose', *Stuart and Georgian Moments: Clark Library Seminar Papers on Seventeenth and Eighteenth Century English Literature*, ed. Earl Miner (1972), pp. 161–88.

8 To Swift, 10 December, 1725: *Works of Pope*, ed. W. Warburton, 10 vols. (1754), X, p. 58. Bolingbroke probably refers to the last paragraph of Cicero's *De Natura Deorum* (II, lxvii, 168).

9 *Prose Works of Jonathan Swift*, ed. Herbert Davis and others, 14 vols. (Oxford, 1939–62), XI, 251. All subsequent references are to this edition and are given in the text.

10 Isaac Watts, *Logick; or, the Right use of Reason . . . in the Affairs of Religion and Human Life, as well as in the Sciences* (1725), pp. 170–1. Watts's later, more popularly styled work, *The Importance of the Mind* (1742), a supplement to the art of logic, was cited more than 150 times in the first volume of Johnson's *Dictionary*. Few books gave him greater pleasure: see the *Preface* to Dodsley's *The Preceptor* (1748) for Johnson's essay on logic.

11 Quoted in A. O. Lovejoy, 'Monboddo and Rousseau', *Essays in the History of Ideas* (Baltimore, 1958), p. 55.

12 *Origin and Progress of Language* (1773), 5 vols., I, 311.

13 *Collected Works of John Stuart Mill* (Toronto and London: in progress), Vol. VII, ed. J. M. Robson (1973), pp. 31–2. Mill varies his choice of names for individuals in several drafts of this paragraph. Elsewhere (p. 975) he selected the unusual apostolic combination John, Peter, Thomas, used by Swift in his letter to Pope, and which Crane tracked down to Marsh's *Institutio Logicae*, the TCD logic-book. Nearly all references made by Mill to Swift are specifically to the fourth voyage. Mill's copy of *Gulliver's Travels* is in Somerville College Library, Oxford, and though not demonstrably by Mill alone there are marginal annotations against every passage dealing with the definition of man. Against the third paragraph of chapter five the annotation reads: 'foolish disputes with simple terms.' For further remarks on denotation, predication and the Houyhnhnms, see *A System of Logic*, p. 1042. Mill incorrectly spells Houyhnhnms in all cases up to the fourth edition (1856).

14 *Topica*, translated by E. S. Forster (1960), p. 395.

15 H. D. Kelling, 'Some Significant Names in *Gulliver's Travels*', *Studies in Philology*, XLVIII (1951), 769.

16 *The Categories*, translated by H. P. Cooke (1960), p. 13. The *OED* is deficient in tracing logical terminology. Some of the gaps have been filled by Roland Hall's series of articles in *Notes and Queries*, CCVII–CCXVII (1963–72).

17 *The Bishop of Worcester's Answer to Mr. Locke's Second Letter* (1698), p. 162. See also Rosalie L. Colie, 'Gulliver, the Locke-Stillingfleet Controversy and the Nature of Man', *History of Ideas News Letter*, II (1956), 59–60.

18 Logicians, of course, recognize the pun as a device of argument. Watts (p. 95) mapped out the path from logic to wit: 'Among the Words which are equivocal in *Sound Only*, and not in *Writing*, there is a large Field for Persons who delight in *Jests* and *Puns*, in *Riddles* and *Quibbles*.'

19 There have been many other attempts to decipher the word Houyhnhnm. Most suggest a phonetic rendering of 'whinny'; some suggest 'Who inhuman' as its significance. The justification for my own suggestion is that it arises from the known intellectual substructure and differs in no way from Swift's use of reductive homophonic puns elsewhere. Moreover, Swift's symbol and meaning arise from a common root: the Greek term ἄλογον means 'irrational' and, in modern Greek, 'horse'. For other suggestions, see Marjorie W. Buckley, 'Key to the Language of the Houyhnhnms in *Gulliver's Travels*', *Fair Liberty was all his Cry*, ed. A. N. Jeffares (1967), p. 278.

20 Roland Barthes, *Mythologies*, translated by Annete Lavers (1972), p. 127.

# II

# IRISH AND ENGLISH POLITICS

# 4

# The Hibernian Patriot's Apprenticeship

by ANGUS ROSS

When Swift mounted his horse at Letcombe Regis under the Berkshire Downs, on Monday 16 August 1714 and riding north made for Holyhead and Dublin, it has seemed he closed one half of his writing career and opened the other. Since the beginning of his literary education under Sir William Temple's cosmopolitan tutelage at Moor Park in Surrey, he had for twenty years sought the approbation of the 'Men of Wit and Tast' to whom he appeals in *An Apology for the Tale of a Tub*.[1] These were largely the leaders of wit and style in London, 'the Town' without qualification. They were the intellectual heirs of Temple, men like Addison, Arbuthnot, Bolingbroke, Congreve, Prior and the rest, all who were the opposite of 'the Sour, the Envious, the Stupid, and the Tastless, which he mentions with disdain'.[2] Against the impulse in his writing towards wit, fantasy and burlesque, from which he created for that audience *A Tale of A Tub* and its related pieces, the *Bickerstaff* papers and similar *jeux d'esprit*, a contrary pressure exerted itself towards the didactic, the serious and grave. This gave shape to the fragment of *The History of England* written between 1697 and 1700, *A Project for the Advancement of Religion, and the Reformation of Manners. By a Person of Quality*, twice printed in 1709, and *The History of the Four Last Years of the Queen*, substantially written during 1712 and 1713. He combined both divergent currents in a spate of political pieces such as *A Discourse of the Contests and Dissensions between the Nobles and Commons in Athens and Rome, with the Consequences they had upon both those States*, printed in 1701, and his polemical writing for the

Harley ministry, with which he extorted recognition, trust, dependence and some reward from certain English grandees. All this, in total might be called his English career.

After 1714,

> Pursu'd by base envenom'd Pens,
> Far to the Land of Slaves and Fens . . .[3]

another scene opens for him. Despite his hope expressed to Charles Ford in August 1714 just after he arrived in Dublin, that he might 'keep my Resolution of never medling with Irish Politicks',[4] all his prose writing with the one great exception of *Gulliver's Travels* was written for Irish occasions. It is true that before the appearance of his first Irish pamphlet of this period, *A Proposal for the Universal Use of Irish Manufacture in Cloaths and Furniture of Houses &c. Utterly Rejecting and Renouncing Everything wearable that comes from England*, which appeared on the streets of Dublin in 1720, he spent some time framing two elegiac pieces touching on his extrusion from England and his withdrawal from English political affairs. These are *Memoirs, Relating to that Change which happened in the Queen's Ministry in the Year 1710*, written in 1714, published in 1765, and *An Enquiry into the Behaviour of the Queen's Last Ministry, with Relation to their Quarrels among themselves and the Design charged upon them of altering the Succession of the Crown*, written between 1715 and 1721, also published in 1765. This pause and backward look may indicate the difficulty Swift had in disengaging himself from his years at the Court in England, as well as the danger he was in if he shewed any political initiative under the new dispensation. Nevertheless, to posterity he is best known as the 'Hibernian Patriot', the 'Drapier' who electrified the people of Dublin in 1724 and 1725, the 'projector' of *A Modest Proposal* for the alleviation of Ireland's misery in 1729, and finally as the writer of *Gulliver's Travels*, published in 1726, which has much of Ireland in it revealed by the circumstances of those several remote nations. Yet, it is worth asking if the prose pieces Swift wrote before 1714, before he returned to live in Dublin, are not also in some measure Irish writing, and a discussion of this point, as well as underlining some aspects of his genius, may also make some contribution to the tangled discussion of Swift as an Irish writer.

It may seem rash for an outsider to enter these troubled waters, beset with reefs and powerful cross-currents, where even Irish writers and critics commend themselves to the waves with good-luck spells. 'Is there such a thing as an Irish literature,' asks Frank O'Connor at the start of his entertaining and ingenious essay, *The Backward Look*, fending off ill-fortune by adding, 'or is it merely two unconnected subjects linked together?'[5] Andrew Carpenter in a recent essay makes a similar sign by mentioning '. . . the personality of Irish writing (if such a thing can really be said to exist).'[6] I have in mind, however, a far more modest enquiry than the nature of Irish writing, namely some speculations on the possible influence on a few prose texts written by Swift before 1714, of his Irish birth, upbringing and connections.

At the risk of dull repetition, a short statement of Swift's fraught heritage should be set out. Born in Dublin on 30 November 1667 of poor English parents, he was consigned to a lowly place in the tiny English group owing allegiance to the Church of Ireland by law established which dominated a large, alien Catholic population. A recent writer has, using hearth tax data for 1732–33, estimated the Catholic population in that year at about 1,407,000, and the Protestant population at about 527,000.[7] Of the latter, however, the majority would be Ulster presbyterians, disenfranchised, disabled from sitting in parliament or holding office, without direct political responsibility. It has also been credibly suggested that in 1703, as a result of the confiscation following the Treaty of Limerick by which on 3 October 1691, William III ended James II's attempt to lead an armed Irish Catholic resurgence, the Catholics retained only about 14 per cent of all the land in Ireland, no doubt generally the poorest in quality, compared with more than half in 1641 when they rose in rebellion against Protestant domination.[8] Thereafter the policy of Swift's Anglo–Irish land-owning co-religionists was to keep their political domination, and by the exercise of power continually retain the Catholic population in a state of landless dependency, and the Ulster Presbyterians disenfranchised. This could only be done by relying on the metropolitan power of royal and parliamentary rule from London to supply military force, which in turn meant a tacit agreement on the part of the Anglo–Irish politicians, gentry and nobility to accept English supremacy over a 'depending' kingdom. The historical process which had brought to pass this state of affairs might be succinctly, if crudely, characterized as a stalemate in a struggle against the powerful, centralising English power, which unified England under the medieval monarchy; conquered Wales; absorbed the Scottish kingdom; and destroyed the decentralized Celtic gaelic-speaking kingdoms of Ireland. In Ireland, distance, the problem of remote administration, the size and populousness of the peripheral territory complicated by cultural factors, including the language difference and sixteenth-century religious struggles within the Christian church, all united to continue the impasse which the Anglo–Norman invaders had run into at a very early period. Frank O'Connor identifies this as 'the real disaster of Irish history, for the Normans could not rule the country themselves, but they were strong enough to prevent anyone else's ruling it'.[9] The successive waves of English (and Scottish) colonists and placemen that were invited into the country by successive English governments, Tudor, Stuart and Cromwellians, produced another disturbing factor in what a contemporary of Swift's called 'the discredit which is grown upon the constitutions or settlement of this kingdom'.[10] This was the feature of colonial society that particularly irked Swift in his own situation, the self-perpetuating rule of 'dog eat dog', in which each generation of exploiters considers its predecessors fair game, even though they are of the colonizing group. In such desperate circumstances it is not surprising that Swift at times rejected his 'Irishness' with revulsion, claiming like many another before, and after, him that he was English of the English, as in an often quoted letter he wrote from Dublin as late as 14 June 1737, to the second earl of Oxford, the son of the Lord Treasurer:

> I loved My Lord your father better than any other Man in the World, although I had no obligation to him on the Score of Preferment, having been driven to this wretched Kingdom (to which I was almost a Stranger) by his want of power to keep me in what I ought to call my own Country; though I happened to be dropped here, and was a Year old before I left it, and to my Sorrow did not dye before I came back to it again.[11]

Nevertheless, the fact of his Irish birth was something Swift could not get round, and it in effect governed his career. On the practical level, it gave him his education at Kilkenny School and Trinity College, Dublin, and eventually pressed him as a priest into the Church of Ireland. His years in the English household of Sir William Temple, diplomat, writer and courtier, had yet an Irish connection too, for the urbane baronet was of an important Anglo–Irish family. His father, Sir John Temple, was Master of the Rolls in Ireland, and he himself inherited the office, though he drew his salary as an absentee and carried out his duties by deputy. Acting as Temple's secretary, Swift must have been introduced to the extensive Irish lobby in London (and England in general), which would be well worth close investigation as a political and social connection of English importance. Sir William Temple refers to this in his *Essay Upon the Advancement of Trade in Ireland*:

> This subordinacy in the government [of Ireland], and emulation of parties, with the want sometimes of authority in the governor (by weakness of his credit and support at court) occasions the perpetual agencies or journies into England of all persons that have any considerable pretences in Ireland, and money to pursue them; which end many times in long abodes, and frequent habituating of families there, though they have no money to support them, but what is drawn out of Ireland. Besides, the young gentlemen go, of course, for their breeding there; some seek their health, and others their entertainment in a better climate or scene: by these means the country loses the expence of many of the richest persons or families at home, and mighty sums of money must needs go over from hence into England, which the great stock of rich native commodities here can make the only amends for.[12]

Many of Swift's deepest and longest-held views and judgements took their rise from his education with Temple, and the *Essay* is of further value in offering an important parallel with Swift's close grasp of the significance of economic analysis in history and politics, particularly the history and politics of Ireland.

The most obvious places to find threads linking Swift's early writing with his later Irish pieces would be in early works discussing unequivocally Irish events or questions. Of his prose works written before 1714, four out of some fifty-six have wholly Irish subject matter, though others have sporadic Irish references. The four are:

*The Story of the Injured Lady. Written by Herself. In a Letter to her Friend. With his Answer* [written, 1707]
[*Prose Works*, IX, 1–12]

*A Letter from a Member of the House of Commons in Ireland to a Member of the House of Commons in England, concerning the Sacramental Test.* 1708 [*Prose Works*, II, 109–25]

*A Letter to a Member of Parliament in Ireland upon Chusing a new Speaker there* [1710] [*Prose Works*, II, 129–35]

*A short Character of His Ex*[*cellency*] *T*[*homas*] *E*[*arl*] *of W*[*harton*] *L*[*ord*] *L*[*ieutenant*] *of I*[*reland*]*. With an Account of Some Smaller Facts.* 1710
[*Prose Works*, III, 175–85; 231–40]

Looked at together, they offer evidence that Swift had a continuous, passionate interest in the national well-being of Ireland linking his early writing with those of the Drapier, though what constituted his 'Ireland' in the ambiguous politics of this time is not a straightforward question.

*The Story of the Injured Lady* was written in the spring of 1707,[13] but never printed by Swift, probably because the allegory of the piece dies in risible banality, which in another mood the author of *A Tale of A Tub* might have vivified in quite a different manner. The tenor and vehicle become entangled, just as Milton's poem 'The Passion' goes aground on the image

And I (for grief is easily beguild)
  Might think th'infection of my sorrow loud
Had got a race of mourners on som pregnant cloud.

This forces him to add 'This subject the Author finding to be above the years he had, when he wrote it, and nothing satisfi'd with what was begun left it unfinished.' Swift finished his piece, but the interference in the allegorical development was probably the same in both cases, unwanted sexual overtones. Swift's failure may suggest that for him too, imaginatively the topic was not matched as yet, by humbling experience and introspective feeling. He had indeed two years earlier contrived a successful sexual image in a savage attack on Lord Cutts, appointed one of the Lords Justices to carry on the government of Ireland in the absence of the Lord Lieutenant, where the predatory male (Cutts/England) damages the surrendering female (Ireland); but in *The Description of a Salamander*,[14] the aggressor is a poxy old Beau and the receptive Nymphs are two notorious whores. The 'injured lady' whines, however, that she is 'undone by the common Arts practised upon easy credulous Virgins.' A triangular situation is set up, improbably enough, setting the wooer (England) between two unequally dowered mistresses, one attractive and complaisant (Ireland), the other 'tall and lean, and very ill-shaped . . . she hath a stinking Breath . . . Scolding and Cursing are her common Conversation' (Scotland). The rhetoric of genteel romance inhibits the knock-about possibilities of the 'family' allegory common at the time, in which Ireland is the sister of England, just as Peg (Scotland) is the raw but likeably individualized sister in Arbuthnot's *John Bull* pamphlets.[15] The Scottish comparison throws us on to a more interesting aspect of *The Story*. Swift's piece was clearly prompted by the close attention he and others in Dublin, where he was then staying towards the end of a period of Irish residence, paid during 1706–7 to the violent arguments inside and outside the Edinburgh parliament house over the 'Articles' for a proposed union of Scotland and England. By the Act of Security of 1703, the Scottish Estates of Parliament, long docile under the manipulation of the London government, had blundered into some independence, and declared that the successor to the crown of Scotland on the demise of Queen Anne was a matter for them. They intimated that unless Scotland obtained equal privileges in trade and navigation with England, they would not offer the succession to the family of Hanover as provided by the English Act of Settlement. Engaged in the War of the Spanish Succession, the administration of Godolphin and Marlborough could take no chances of a pro-French, Jacobite intervention north of the border, and pushed for an incorporating union with the Scots. In Swift's eyes, this beggarly nation were successfully screwing undeserved privileges from the metropolitan power, privileges foolishly denied to the *English* colonists of Ireland.

In personal terms, the episode probably strengthened Swift's hostility to the Scots, exacerbated as it was by the powerful and coherent Ulster presbyterian interest, which the London government sought to conciliate, but which Swift held to be the greatest threat to his church. *The Story*, in terms of Swift's political thought, shows him advancing the doctrine developed in William Molyneux's argument *The Case of Ireland's Being Bound by Acts of Parliament in England Stated* (Dublin, 1698). This book, which was much admired by Swift, is a fundamental statement of the Anglo–Irish rejection of the complete subordination of Ireland to the English government and an assertion of the theory that Ireland was a sister kingdom with an independent parliament. The theory was based on a clear-cut, intellectualized interpretation of past events, and the actual behaviour of the Irish parliament contradicted it almost at every point. In it, however, the stage is set for a peculiarly Swiftian confrontation of thought and action, ideal and actuality, awaiting only the vivifying of a really powerful satirical imagination to bring to life the political argument of, for example, *Gulliver's Travels*.

In general terms, the English government in forcing the Union of Scotland and England and the reduction of Ireland to a closely controlled dependancy, was following not only its own strong, centralist tendencies, but a trend throughout Europe in the seventeenth and eighteenth centuries. Louis XIV was active in terminating the independence and privileged status of feudal appanages of the French crown, and perhaps the best instance of the movement lies in the fate of the Catalans. The unsuccessful rebellion, on cultural and historical grounds, of the latter, against absorption into Spain, was exploited by the maritime powers in their struggle against France in the War of the Spanish Succession. Swift summarily dismissed them to oblivion, when in 1714 it suited him in *The Publick Spirit of the Whigs* to belabour Steele for an inept political rhetoric of sensibility:

> Having mentioned the *Catalonians*, he puts the Question, *Who can name the* Catalonians *without a Tear*? That can I; for he hath told so many melancholy Stories without one Syllable of Truth that he hath blunted the Edge of my Fears . . .[16]

That was ungenerous. Swift's predicament in Ireland was one which could be generalized in Europe, and the aftermath of the oppression of the Irish, both colonized and colonizers, like that of the experience of the Catalans, is with us yet.

*A Letter from a Member of the House of Commons in Ireland to a Member of the House of Commons in England, concerning the*

*Sacramental Test* is the very first of Swift's Irish writings to be published as part of a political controversy, albeit in this case an English one. In 1708, Swift was in London as an emissary of the Irish Church, to obtain the remission of the first fruits, a small tax on stipends exigible by the crown. The Whig Junto, Sunderland, Wharton, Somers, Halifax and Cowper, then reaching their greatest power, were expected to press in the parliament of 1709 for the repeal of the Test Act. The connection between Swift's mission and the threatened political move was a galling one, and Swift's reaction to it shows how his Irish background and office put immense strain on his political thinking. The English Test Act was passed by Parliament in 1673, and assented to by Charles II as a condition for the voting of supply for the Dutch War. It required all office-holders in the country, civil or military, to take the communion sacrament according to the form of the Church of England; make a Declaration against transubstantiation; and take the oaths of allegiance and supremacy. This package was intended to disable Catholics and non-conformists from holding offices or places, and to frustrate any exercise of the royal prerogative in their favour in return for their support. In 1704 the Test was extended to Ireland by the High Tories then in the ministry, as part of an anti-popery act. The anti-Catholic provisions were part of the series of 'penal laws' designed to cripple and terrorize the Catholics, but the Test was aimed at the continued exclusion of the presbyterians from parliament and office. Swift all his life supported the Test Act as a bulwark of the Church of Ireland against disorder, anarchy and revolution, and reiterated his support of it in a 'Publisher's Advertisement' that accompanied the 1735 reprint of this piece. Yet, like many churchmen, he was uneasy over the claims made by the legislature and the executive to direct the affairs of the church. This is one of the threads in his unfinished piece 'Remarks upon a Book, Intitled *The Rights of the Christian Church asserted*', written the year before, in 1707.[17] A yet harder yoke bore on Swift as an Irish churchman, because just at this time, although he had been led to believe that the remission of the first fruits had been granted, this turned out not to be the case, and he was receiving hints from his Junto patrons that the agreement of the Church of Ireland to the repeal of the Irish Test might be the price for the financial benefits.[18] The Junto's reasons for repealing the Test Act were partly that they represented a current of latitudinarian, if not sceptical, toleration of religious belief and practice, but also that they sought to conciliate the dissenters as voters and as a political interest. In English political terms, the ministry were contemplating the repeal of the Test in Ireland to prepare the way for its repeal in England, and in Swift's eyes this was 'the Parliament here [in London] interfering in things purely of *Ireland*, that have no relation to any interest of theirs.'[19] This sentiment Swift put into two of the best paragraphs, of his *Letter . . . Concerning the Sacramental Test*, an early formulation of his Irish views:

> I do not frequently quote Poets, especially *English*, but I remember there is in some of Mr. *Cowley's* Love Verses, a Strain that I thought extraordinary at Fifteen, and have often since imagined to be spoken by *Ireland*.
>
> *Forbid it Heaven my Life should be*
> *Weigh'd with her least Conveniency.*
>
> In short, whatever Advantage you propose to your selves by repealing the *Sacramental Test*, speak it out plainly, it is the best Argument you can use, for we value your Interest much more than our own. If your little Finger be sore, and you think a Poultice made of our *Vitals* will give it any Ease, speak the Word, and it shall be done; the Interest of our whole Kingdom is, at any Time, ready to strike to that of your poorest *Fishing Town*; it is hard you will not accept our Services, unless we believe, at the same Time, that you are only consulting our Profit, and giving us Marks of your Love. If there be a Fire at some Distance, and I immediately blow up my House before there be Occasion, because you are a Man of Quality, and apprehend some Danger to a *Corner of your Stable*; yet why should you require me to attend next Morning at your Levee, with my humble Thanks for the Favour you have done me?[20]

In one of the most significant parts of the essay, Swift says

> I must desire you to take Notice, that the Terms of *Whig* and *Tory*, do not properly express the different Interests in our Parliament.[21]

Swift goes on to claim that the Irish House of Commons is made up 'on the one side of *moderate Whigs*, and, on the other, of [a small number of] *Presbyterians* and their *Abettors*.' Without going into the intricacies of this, it is enough to suggest that Swift's experience of the Irish situation, in which a small English group of landowners characterized by the shibboleth of adherence to the Church of Ireland, by metropolitan support, kept its power over a larger, relatively prosperous group of politically disabled presbyterians and a vast population of culturally differentiated Catholics, could not but influence his theory of the state, his picture of the church, and his analysis of the English political scene.

After a year in England, soliciting the men in power for the crown's remission to the Church of Ireland of the first fruits and diverting the town with the Bickerstaff papers, Swift spent a year from July 1709 to August 1710 in Ireland. *A Letter from a Member of Parliament in Ireland upon Chusing a new Speaker there* was written during this Irish sojourn, and clearly intended for the press in Dublin as a contribution to the political skirmishing that took place there before the Irish parliament re-assembled on 19 May 1710. When the parliament had been prorogued at the end of the previous year, Alan Broderick, speaker of the Irish House of Commons, had been promoted to the office of Lord Chief Justice of the Queen's Bench in Ireland and to the peerage as Lord Middleton. A new speaker had to be elected at the opening of the new session. Broderick had in 1708 taken a leading part in pressing for the repeal of the Test Act. His conduct at that time caused Swift in his nervousness at this possibility to write in unmeasured terms to Archbishop King:

> If it became me to give ill Names to all Things and Persons, I should be at a Loss to find bad enough for Villany and Baseness of a certain Lawyr of Ireld . . .[22]

At some later date, Swift incorrectly endorsed the eight-page holograph manuscript of *A Letter*, now in the Forster Collection, 'Writt in Ireland upon chusing a new Speaker there 1708 (as I rememb.).' In subject, this piece which Swift never printed goes with *A Letter . . . concerning the Sacramental Test*, and the confusion of dates on his part is understandable. It underlines the importance of the Test Act for Swift as an Anglo-Irishman, and as a priest in the Church of Ireland. The anti-Presbyterian purpose of the Test, which was not primarily aimed at the Catholics who were politically disabled in other ways, is clearly shown when Swift writes:

> You know very well, the great Business of the High-flying Whigs, at this Juncture, is to endeavor a Repeal of the Test Clause. You know likewise that the Moderate Men, both of High and Low Church, profess to be wholly averse from this Design, as thinking it beneath the Policy of common Gardners to cutt down the only Hedge that shelters from the North.[23]

As the new parliament was about to meet, the Dublin government, under instruction from the English ministers, were following up their project of repealing the Test Act by arranging for John Forster, the Recorder of Dublin and a supporter of the repeal, to be elected Speaker. Swift, in opposing this, argues that support for the Test unites all 'Moderate Men'. And so it might in the Irish situation, where the English party labels did not fit. All 'moderate' Anglo–Irish landowners sought to preserve their dominant status, a consideration absent from English controversy. Swift therefore seeks in addressing his Irish audience to make opposition to the Test the mark of the wild men, to whom in addition he applies the term 'high-flying', normally associated in England with the extreme Tories and Jacobites. Either the piece missed its time, or Swift thought it below his standard, and it did not see print until 1765, but it preserves the brooding passion of his concern with Irish politics.

The last of the four Irish pieces Swift wrote before 1714 is also the most substantial. It ranks with his greatest political satires and is therefore more complex than the other wholly Irish essays. It is interesting to note, however, that the specifically Irish elements which give it form and tone have tended to be neglected by his editors in favour of more general and English considerations. The 1711 title page is not straightforward. *A Short Character of His E[xcellency] T[homas] E[arl] of W[harton] L[ord] L[ieutenant of I[reland]* is to be accompanied with *An Account of some smaller Facts, during His Government, which will not be put into the Articles of Impeachment.* The broader short-title commonly used, *A Short Character of the Earl of Wharton*, may be justified by Swift's abhorrence of Wharton's character and public activities in general, as shown in other passages of his writing, but it loses the heavy Irish resonance, and the threat of an impeachment for Irish conduct. Thomas Wharton, fifth baron and first Earl of Wharton and one of the Whig Junto, was made Lord Lieutenant of Ireland in Spring 1708. Six years later Swift acidly gave an explanation for this appointment:

> In which publick Service [managing elections and converting young men of quality to Whig doctrines] he contracted such large Debts, that his Brethren were forced out of mere justice to leave *Ireland* at his Mercy; where he had only time to set himself right.[24]

There were several reasons, personal and public, for Swift's aversion to the Earl's character and conduct. As Lord Lieutenant, Wharton supported the repeal of the Test Act and actively leant on the Church of Ireland for their agreement to the repeal in return for the remission of the first fruits; Swift claimed that he was received by the Earl as a suppliant for the remission 'with sufficient coldness' and at a second meeting arranged by Lord Somers 'as drily as before';[25] Wharton may also have refused to appoint Swift his chaplain. In the latter case, if it be true, he missed a remarkable double, since Addison was his secretary. Other considerations outside the scope of this essay clearly entered into Swift's publicly expressed dislike and contempt for the statesman, millionaire, politician and shameless rake, but the piece obviously starts from a complex of personal and Irish matters. *A Short Character* is dated '*London*, Aug. 30, 1710', but is clearly framed from material dating from before and after that date, the day Wharton resigned his lieutenancy to return to England. Swift in fact landed in England in Wharton's suite in September 1710, to realize his career as an English political controversialist. The pamphlet first appeared anonymously, without imprint, some time in December 1710, when Swift had already begun his series of *Examiner* papers for Harley's ministry, and it thus bridges his Irish activities and his London achievements. It was perhaps conceived as a possible weapon in future impeachment proceedings, when it became clear that with the fall of the Junto, one by one, Wharton's political days were numbered. Indeed, Swift first centred a paragraph on Wharton in his second *Examiner* essay of 9 November, on political lying, then devoted part of his fourth of 30 November to an attack on Wharton as a corrupt provincial governor. This took the form of a witty imitation of Cicero's attacks on the pro-praetor Gaius Verres who

> had been the *Roman* Governor of *Sicily* for three Years; and on return from his Government, the *Sicilians* entreated *Cicero* to impeach him in the Senate; which, he accordingly did, in several Orations . . .[26]

On 8 December, Swift wrote to his ladies in Dublin:

> Here's a damned libellous pamphlet come out against lord Wharton, giving the character first, and then telling some of his actions: the character is very well, but the facts indifferent.[27]

By 1 January 1711, Swift's authorship was suspected in Dublin, as he notes to the same correspondents:

> The Bishop of Clogher shewed you a pamphlet. Well, but you must not give your mind to believe those things; people will say any thing. The character is here reckoned admirable, but most of the facts are trifles. It was first printed privately here; and then some bold cur ventured to do it publickly, and sold two thousand in two days: who the author is must remain uncertain. Do you pretend to know, impudence? How durst you think so?[28]

William King, Archbishop of Dublin and a stubborn leader of the Anglo–Irish interest against untrammelled pro-English manipulation on the part of the Castle, perhaps maliciously claiming ignorance of the authorship, wrote an old-fashioned remonstrance at the attack on Wharton to its satirical author:

> We have published here a Character of the Earl of *Wharton*, late Lord Lieutenant of *Ireland*. I have so much christianity and justice as to condemn all such proceedings. If a governor behave himself ill, let him be complained of and punished; but to wound any man thus in the dark, to appeal to the mob, that can neither inquire nor judge, is a proceeding that I think the common sense of mankind should condemn. Perhaps he may deserve this usage, but a good man may fall under the same.[29]

Clearly, Swift was not as yet to be a prophet in his own country. He forgot, if he had ever seriously supported, the plan of impeaching Wharton, as his new friends in power decided that punishing their predecessors would set too dangerous a precedent. In another letter to Swift, almost a year later, the Archbishop had a different, and sadder, Anglo–Irish reason for leaving Wharton alone.

> If we could impeach, as you can in *Great Britain*, and bring the malefactors to account, I should be for it with all my endeavour; but to show our ill-will when we can do no more, seems to be no good policy in a dependent people . . . I reckon, that every chief governor who is sent here comes with a design to serve first those who sent him . . . The only difference between governors, as to us, is to have a good-natured man, that has some interest in our prosperity, and will not oppress us unnecessarily . . .[30]

The tone of Swift's pamphlet is quite different from such, almost oriental, resignation. His piece opens with two splendidly defiant paragraphs, which since they foreshadow much of Swift's later Irish writing, bear quotation:

> The Kingdom of *Ireland*, being governed by Deputation from hence, its Annnals, since the *English* Establishment, are usually digested under the Heads of the several Governors: But, the Affairs and Events in that Island, for some Years past, have been either so insignificant, or so annexed to those of *England*, that they have not furnished Matter of any great Importance to History. The Share of Honour, which Gentlemen from thence have had by their Conduct and Employments in the Army, turneth all to the Article of this Kingdom; the rest which relateth to Politics, or the Art of Government, is inconsiderable to the last Degree, however it may be represented at Court by those who preside there, and would value themselves upon every Step they make, towards finishing the Slavery of that People, as if it were gaining a mighty Point to the Advantage of *England*.
>
> Generally speaking, the Times which afford most plentiful Matter for Story, are those in which a Man would least chuse to live; such as under the various Events and Revolutions of War, the Intrigues of a ruined Faction, or the Violence of a prevailing one, and lastly the arbitrary, unlawful Acts of oppressing Governors. In the War, *Ireland* hath no Share but in Subordination to us; the same may be said of their Factions, which, at present, are but imperfect Transcripts of ours: But the third Subject for History, which is arbitrary Power, and Oppression; as it is that by which the People of *Ireland* have for some Time, been distinguished from all her Majesty's Subjects, so being now at its greatest Height under his Excellency *Thomas* Earl of *Wharton*, a short

> Account of his Government, may be of some Use or Entertainment to the present Age, although, I hope, it will be incredible to the next . . .[31]

Swift's version of the Chinese curse, 'May you live in interesting times!' which opens the second paragraph is worthy of the depth of feeling in *Gulliver's Travels* and gives some sign of how the contemplation of Irish affairs affects him personally. After the generalization of the miniature preface, four short introductory paragraphs follow, establishing the *persona* of the speaker, a London man of wealth and fashion who receives Wharton's visits. This leads in to the 'character' proper. The 'character', in turn, is succeeded by an account of Wharton's 'Actions, only during the Time he was Governor of *Ireland*, which were transmitted to me by an eminent Person in Business there [i.e. an Irish government place-holder]'. Thereafter, there comes a farrago of allegations which, in the hands of a Maria Edgeworth or a Charles Lever, would furnish out a set of fictional sketches of the 'Humours of Ireland'. This last section, clearly the 'Facts during His Government which will not be put into the Articles of Impeachment' of the 1711 title-page, is relegated by Herbert Davis in his edition to an Appendix, no doubt on account of Swift's own dismissive phrases quoted earlier from the *Journal*. The opening sentences of these 'trifles' unroll divertingly enough, however, as in for example, 'The Earl of Rochester's Regiment of Dragoons was embarked for Her Majesty's Service abroad . . .'; 'Mrs. *Lloyd*, at first coming over, expected the Benefit of the Box-money . . .'; 'He met Lieutenant General Langston in the Court of Requests . . .'; 'As for the Business of the Arsenal . . .'; 'His Excellency being desirous, for a private Reason, to provide for the worthless Son of a worthless father . . .' There seems no reason to think that these 'Hints', as he calls them, 'to any Person, who may hereafter have a Mind to write Memoirs of his Excellency's Life' are not written by Swift. They frame, as it were, the more sombre assonances of the attack in the 'character', the literary overtones of 'the Nature of a Serpent, a Wolf, a Crocodile or a Fox . . .' They suggest that in Ireland it is impossible to be even a Villain on a grand scale; everything is tinged with the flat, the everyday and the ridiculous.

After this discussion of four undeniably Irish pieces from Swift's *œuvre* before 1714, we may move into more speculative areas. Is it, we may ask, possible to discern any specific marks of his Irish experience in his *English* political pieces? It may be, and perhaps these marks could be said to add some of the most powerful and effective touches to his English political journalism. One of Swift's strengths as a writer, found even in his earliest pieces, is his ability to combine clear, crisp, weighty generalizations with effective, local controversy. The two paragraphs quoted above from *A Short Character of the Earl of Wharton* give one fine example of this, and another useful one may be found in the three opening paragraphs of his first, brilliant public success, *A Discourse of the Contests and Dissensions between the Nobles in Athens and Rome*, written and published in 1701, which begins:

> It is agreed, that in all Government there is an absolute unlimited Power, which naturally and originally seems to be placed in the whole Body, wherever the executive Part of it lies. This holds in the Body natural: For wherever we place the Beginning of Motion, whether from the Head, or the Heart, or the animal Spirits in general, the Body moves, and acts by a Consent of all its Parts. This unlimited Power placed fundamentally in the Body of a People, is what the best Legislators of all Ages have endeavoured, in their several Schemes, or Institutions of Government, to deposite in such Hands as would preserve the People from Rapine, and Oppression within, as well as Violence from without. Most of them seem to agree in this; that it was a Trust too great to be committed to any one Man, or Assembly; and therefore they left the Right still in the whole Body; but the Administration, or executive Part, in the Hands of *One*, the *Few*, or the *Many*: Into which three Powers, all independent Bodies of Men seem naturally to divide . . .[32]

Such passages, evidence of historical and comparative political thinking he had done while working with Sir William Temple, give even his most polemical pamphlets a tone of substance, lacking in the efforts of most of his opponents. The juxtaposition of political generalization and specific attack, rash, witty, often unfair, generates an enjoyable tension in his best work, which keeps the reader on his toes. This particular tension seems to be a form of a peculiarly Swiftian turn of mind. He seeks clear-cut, black and white, perfect pattern, and at the same time responds to and engages with anarchic diversity, imperfection, the kaleidoscope of human behaviour. At the level of writing prose, he is the master of terse finality, and bewildering wit, fantasy and burlesque. His political generalizations are of a particular kind; specifically, his doctrine most often seems to be nostalgic, conservative, the analysis of an Englishman looking from outside at an idealized England and English constitution. His political activity, on the other hand, often seems to be opportunistic, personal, aggressive, without doubt the politics of an Englishman in the Irish situation, or of an Anglo–Irishman from the periphery assaulting the preserves of the centre. Take, for example, a paragraph in *The Sentiments of a Church of England-Man with respect to Religion and Government*, written in 1704 but not printed until the publication of his *Miscellanies in Prose and Verse* of 1711:

> It is a *Church-of*-England *Man's* Opinion, that the Freedom of a Nation consists in an absolute *unlimited legislative* Power, wherein the whole Body of the People are *fairly* represented; and in an *executive* duly *limited*: Because on this Side likewise, there may be dangerous Degrees, and a very ill Extream. For when two Parties in a State are pretty equal in *Power, Pretensions, Merit* and *Virtue*, (for these two last are, with relation to Parties and a Court, quite different Things,) it hath been the Opinion of the best Writers upon Government, that a Prince ought not in any sort to be under the Guidance, or Influence of either; because he declines, by this Means, from his Office of presiding over the *Whole*, to be the head of a *Party*; which, besides the Indignity renders him answerable for all publick Mismanagements, and the Consequences of them: And in whatever State this happens, there must either be a Weakness in the Prince or Ministry, or else the former is too much restrained by the Nobles, or those who represent the People.[33]

This passage is from a piece which, as is shown by the circumstances of its printing, represents Swift's considered thoughts. It also incidentally shows clearly the problems, religious and philosophical, that were raised by his Anglo–Irish heritage. The paragraph is not written in terms of a dynamic of political struggle, nor does it really represent the political system in England as it actually existed in Queen Anne's reign. Swift's mention of 'dangerous Degrees and a very ill Extream' directs our attention to the apocalyptic nature of his political doctrine. He constantly suggests that all institutions are trembling on the brink of disaster if some quite fragile balance is disturbed. Such is his attitude, as we have seen, to the repeal of the Test Act. Of course, this is a response to some degree forced on him by the Irish situation, where in terms of political theory the Anglo–Irish domination *was* on the edge of the abyss. Swift's occasional apocalyptic tone is put to excellent use in handling English political matters in his *Examiner* papers, and a good instance is to be found in no. 24 of Thursday, 18 January 1710 on [The Ruined Party's Hopes and the Madness of the People]:

> It is *Machiavel's* Observation, that the People, when left to their own Judgement, do seldom mistake their true Interests; and indeed they naturally love the Constitution they are born under; never desiring to change but under great Oppressions. However, they are to be deceived by several Means. It hath often happened in *Greece*, and sometimes in *Rome*, that those very Men who have contributed to shake off a former Tyranny, have, instead of restoring the old Constitution, deluded the People into a worse and more ignominious Slavery. Besides, all great Changes have the same Effect upon Commonwealths that Thunder hath upon Liquors; making the *Dregs* fly up to the Top: The lowest *Plebeians* rise to the Head of Affairs, and there preserve themselves by representing the Nobles and other Friends to the old Government, as Enemies to the Publick. The encouraging of new Mysteries and new Deities, with the Pretences of further Purity in Religion, hath likewise been a frequent Topick to mislead the People. And, not to mention more, the promoting false Reports of Dangers from Abroad, hath often served to prevent them from fencing against real Dangers at Home. By these and the like Arts, in Conjunction with a great Depravity of Manners, and a weak or corrupt Administration, the Madness of the People hath risen to such a Height, as to break in Pieces the whole Frame of the best instituted Governments. But however, such great Frenzies being artificially raised, are a perfect Force and Constraint upon human Nature; and under a wise steddy Prince, will certainly decline of themselves; settling like the Sea after a Storm; and then the true Bent and Genius of the People will appear. Ancient and Modern Story are full of Instances to illustrate what I say. In our own Island we had a great Example of a long Madness in the People, kept up by a thousand Artifices like intoxicating Medicines, until the Constitution was destroyed; yet the Malignity being spent,

> and the Humour exhausted that served to foment it; before the Usurpers could fix upon a new Scheme, the People suddenly recovered, and peacably restored the old Constitution.[34]

As a priest in the Church of Ireland, Swift was an officer in an important Irish *political* institution. The particular religio-political status of the Church of Ireland was, of course, only a specific instance of a dilemma that has always characterized the institutionalized religion of Christendom. The specific political demands on him as a Churchman did cause Swift acute embarrassment. He had a well-developed historical view of the Christian church and Christian tradition, a view which could at times transcend his own age, and which despite its partisan nature, gives the fable of *A Tale of a Tub* a particular authority. Rubbing against this wider view at every turn, however, was the bleak reality of the Church of Ireland, a small, beleaguered outpost in the inadequate pay of a small band of exploitive invaders. In *The Sentiments of a Church of England-Man*, he declares, 'I believe, I am no *Bigot* in Religion; and I am sure, I am none in Government.'[35] Such an easy, broad declaration might be just possible in England, where only small minorities dissented from the Church by law established, but transferred to Ireland, such stout support for the state Church demanded support for the penal laws enacted to terrorize the huge majority of Catholic christians in the exercise of their religious duties. Speaking as a 'Church of England-Man', Swift declares that

> He thinks it highly just, that all Rewards of Trust, Profit, or Dignity, which the State leaves at the Disposal of the Administration, should be given only to those, whose Principles direct them to preserve the Constitution in all its Parts.[36]

In excluding minorities, this might be argued in troublous times to be hard but necessary. In chapter VIII of *Gulliver's Travels*, the King of Brobdignag is made to say in comment on Gulliver's account of his own dear, native country,

> He laughed at my odd kind of Arithmetick (as he was pleased to call it) in reckoning the Numbers of our People by a Computation drawn from the several Sects among us in Religion and Politicks. He said, he knew no Reason, why those who entertain Opinions, prejudicial to the Publick, should be obliged to Change, or should not be obliged to Conceal them. And as it was Tyranny

> in any Government to require the first, so it was Weakness not to enforce the second: For a Man may be allowed to keep Poisons in his Closet, but not to vend them about for Cordials.

In Ireland, however, the penal laws did attempt by economic pressure to make men change their opinions, and along with the Test Act, excluded in law, whatever happened in fact, the preponderant mass of the population, Catholic and Presbyterian, in favour of a small section of English land-owners. The situation placed the Church itself in a vulnerable situation, totally dependant on the beneficiaries of such ferocious exclusion and on their over-seas power support. Swift's abhorrence of

> the Humour of the Age, in delighting to fling scandals upon the Clergy in general; which, besides the Disgrace to the Reformation and to Religion it self, casts an Ignominy upon the Kingdom . . .[37]

difficult enough to sustain in England, became impossible in the face of the rapacity of the Irish parliament. It is constant involvement with insoluble Irish problems like these that gives particular ferocity to Swift's satirical passages on European history in *Gulliver's Travels*, the account of the *Big-Endians* and *Little-Endians* for instance in Book I.

Swift's urge for clear statements at the same time as realizing and expressing complex truths is not to be explained only in terms of his Irish experience, but the contemplation of insoluble conflicts certainly did not lessen the tension. His Irish background allowed him to over-simplify his theoretical account of English politics, no dis-service for a clear and powerful argument. In this he somewhat resembles another Anglo–Irish writer, George Bernard Shaw, who made equally remarkable imaginative use of an outsider's view of English society, seeing both more and less, perhaps, than an Englishman of England. The cultural ambivalence of Anglo–Irishmen like Swift has been generalized as a quality of Anglo–Irish literature. J. C. Beckett, in a discussion of Swift, Burke and Goldsmith, calls it ambivalence or ambiguity of outlook, and suggests that it led to the detachment and aggressiveness of the insecure.[38] Andrew Carpenter in a suggestive essay already cited calls it the double vision of Anglo–Irish writers, claiming that it gives a particular depth to their work. He speculates that life in

Ireland since the Battle of the Boyne has been 'a more enigmatic and ambiguous affair than life in England.'[39] Whatever the quality be called, and however derived or stimulated, it is certainly present in Swift's work even before his permanent move to Ireland in 1714, and informs his English as well as his Irish pieces.

To conclude, something must be said about Swift's thoughts on language. Here, if anywhere, we may expect to find some evidence and influence of his Anglo–Irish culture. Swift wrote two important pieces before 1714, of relevance to such an enquiry. These are, a letter which Steele printed in *The Tatler*, no. 230, on Thursday, 28 September 1710,[40] and *A Proposal for Correcting, Improving and Ascertaining The English Tongue; in a Letter to . . . Robert Earl of Oxford*, dated 22 February 1711–12 and printed in May 1712.[41] The significance he attached to the latter, and similarly to his views on language, is indicated by the fact that he published it over his own name. This distinction is shared among his many works by only four others, his first appearance in print, *Ode to the Athenian Society*, and the volumes he edited of Sir William Temple's works. Swift suggests in the title of *A Proposal* that his subject is the 'English Tongue' but a remark he made on 21 February shows that it is rather the relation between *speech* and *language* which is his concern:

> I have been 6 hours to day morning writing 19 Pages of a Lettr to day to Ld Treasr, about forming a Society or Academy to correct and fix the English Language. (Is English a Speech or a Language?)[42]

Swift's *Proposal*, though short, is quite a complicated piece. Its linguistic thinking has been attacked as naïve, but that is because it is as much about prose style, as about language in any technical sense. His stress on the relationship between the best style and the best conversation, without exhausting the meaning of the essay, seems to be quite an important part of it. Following Sir William Temple and earlier writers, Swift makes 'propriety', a social judgement, the test of style. In a brief historical excursus on 'Improvements . . . Corruptions . . . Refinements' to English in the preceding hundred years, he attacks

> that Licentiousness which entered with the *Restoration*; and from infecting our Religion and Morals, fell to corrupt our Language:

> Which last, was not like to be much improved by those, who, at that time made up the Court of King *Charles* the Second . . . so that the *Court*, which used to be the Standard of Propriety, and Correctness of Speech, was then, and I think hath ever since continued the worst School in *England*, for that Accomplishment.[43]

Swift's feeling for the relationship between good conversation and good prose style is shared by Dryden, who in a famous passage in the 'Preface' to *Sylvae: or the Second Part of Poetical Miscellanies*, published in 1685, asserts that

> The properties and delicacies of the English [language] are known to few; 'tis impossible even for a good wit to understand and practise them, without the help of a liberal education, long reading, and digesting of these few good authors we have amongst us, the knowledge of men and manners, the freedom of habitudes and conversation with the best company of both sexes . . .[44]

In short, like Dryden, Swift is concerned with style as 'social gesture.' In this he is associated with his fellow Scriblerian, the Scotsman Dr. Arbuthnot, and contrasted with later writers like Johnson, Boswell, Gibbon. Here we are not concerned with anything specifically Irish, but with men from the periphery making their way by exercising a talent for writing. Swift and Arbuthnot were courtiers; they adopted the propriety of good society, of the court, as a means of becoming accepted at the centre. As we have seen, however, Swift finds as usual the institution less than perfect. Johnson and Boswell adopted a more 'public' style, dependent less on conversation and society, and more on written correctness, and learned or codified norms. It is noticeable that the prose style of Swift, Arbuthnot and Gay is plainer, more direct, more 'conversational', even less 'correct', than the more elaborated, structured style of Johnson, Boswell, Gibbon or Burke. Of course, this is only one aspect, though an important one, of Swift's prose style. He was also a master of gnomic utterance, and delighted in using where appropriate in parody, irony and joking all the improprieties of tone and the informalities of feeling he deplores in *A Proposal*. It may be that his Irish background alerted him to the variety of language registers, made him more open, less censorious or at least more adept at using them. It is clear that Swift's notion of prose style is a social one, that would commend itself to a brilliant and skilful outsider wishing to make his mark in the metropolis. The earlier *Tatler* paper also focusses on 'the great Depravity of our Taste . . . the continual Corruption of our English Tongue . . . all new affected Modes of Speech, whether borrowed from the Court, the Town or the Theatre . . .'[45] Swift offers a letter in 'this [new] Way of Writing' and it is worth noting his insistence on the aural quality of writing. Now, it may be that Swift's language could be discussed in terms of its relationship with Anglo–Irish speech, or even Gaelic, in the way that Vivien Mercier suggests is possible to support his thesis of *The Irish Comic Tradition*,[46] but it is enough here to suggest that Swift's Anglo–Irish heritage may be plausibly linked with his theory of style and his own far more adventurous artistic practice, and that here too, his writing before 1714 has its Irish interest.

## NOTES

1 *Prose Works*, I, 11.
2 *Prose Works*, I, 2.
3 *Poetical Works*, ed. Herbert Davis (Oxford, 1967), p. 509.
4 *Correspondence*, II, 127. Swift to Charles Ford, [August] 1714.
5 Frank O'Connor, *The Backward Look: a Survey of Irish Literature* (1967).
6 Andrew Carpenter, 'Double Vision in Anglo–Irish Literature' in Andrew Carpenter, ed., *Place, Personality and the Irish Writer: Irish Literary Studies*, I (Dublin, 1977), 188.
7 F. G. James, *Ireland in the Empire: 1688–1770* (Cambridge, Mass, 1973), Appendix, p. 315 ff.
8 J. G. Simms, *The Treaty of Limerick* (Dundalk, 1961), pp. 195–6.
9 *Ibid*., p. 85.
10 Sir William Temple, *An Essay Upon the Advancement of Trade in Ireland* (Dublin, 1673), reprinted in *Miscellanea* (1679; appeared 1680).
11 *Correspondence*, V, 46–7.
12 Temple, *An Essay*, para. 8.
13 Godfrey Davies, 'Swift's *The Story of the Injured Lady*', *Huntington Library Quarterly*, 6 (1943), 473–89.
14 *Poetical Works*, pp. 58–60; see also pp. 471–74, *An Excellent New Ballad: Or, The True English Dean to be hang'd for a Rape* for another variation on the same theme, especially ll. 61–64: 'If Maidens are ravish't, it is their own Choice, / Why are they so willful to struggle with men? / If they would but lye quiet, and stifle their voice, / No Devil nor Dean could Ravish 'em then'.

15 eds. A. W. Bower and R. A. Erickson, *John Arbuthnot: The History of John Bull* (Oxford, 1976), pp. 50 and lxvii–lxviii.
16 *Prose Works*, VIII, 62.
17 *Prose Works*, II, 65–107 cf. *Remarks upon a Book, Intitled, The Rights of the Christian Church asserted* 1707; *Prose Works*, II, 65–107.
18 *Correspondence*, I, 85. Swift to Archbishop King, 10 June 1708.
19 *Correspondence*, I, 76. Swift to Dean Stearne, 15 April 1708.
20 *Prose Works*, II, 114.
21 *Prose Works*, II, 118.
22 *Correspondence*, I, 81. Swift to Archbishop King, 15 April 1708.
23 *Prose Works*, II, 131.
24 *The History of the Four last years of the Queen*; *Prose Works*, VII, 10.
25 *Memoirs Relating to that Change which happened in the Queen's Ministry in the Year 1710*; *Prose Works*, VIII, 121.
26 *Prose Works*, III, 27.
27 *Journal to Stella*, ed. Harold Williams, 2 vols. (Oxford, 1948), I, 115.
28 *Journal to Stella*, I, 148.
29 *Correspondence*, I, 207.
30 28 July 1711; *Correspondence*, I, 243.
31 *Prose Works*, III, 177–8.
32 *Prose Works*, I, 195–6.
33 *Prose Works*, II, 23–4.
34 *Prose Works*, III, 64–5.
35 *Prose Works*, II, 2.
36 *Prose Works*, II, 6.
37 *Prose Works*, II, 9.
38 J. C. Beckett, *The Anglo-Irish Tradition* (1976), 143 ff.
39 *op. cit.*, p. 188.
40 *Prose Works*, II, 173–177.
41 *Prose Works*, IV, 5–21.
42 *Journal to Stella*, II, 493.
43 *Prose Works*, IV, 10.
44 ed. George Watson, *John Dryden: Of Dramatic Poetry and Other Critical Essays*, (1962), p. 20.
45 *Prose Works*, II, 173–4; 177.
46 Vivian Mercier, *The Irish Comic Tradition* (Oxford, 1962).

# 5

# *The Conduct of The Allies*: The Question of Influence

by J. A. DOWNIE

*1*

Swift arrived in London in September 1710, in the wake of the change of government engineered by Robert Harley, on a mission from the Irish Church to sue for the gift of Queen Anne's Bounty. Soon, 'weary of the caresses of the great men out of place', he was 'talking treason' against the Whigs, comforted by the thought of 'some Advances' that Harley had 'formerly made' towards him. When he gained access to the new prime minister in connection with the first-fruit negotiations, he was quickly convinced that Harley 'would do every thing' to bring him over to his side.[1] Harley gave Swift *The Examiner* to edit. Beginning on 2 November 1710, Swift published a regular series of essays in the Tory paper which was not to cease until June 1711 and the end of the parliamentary session.

*The Examiner* was an extreme 'right-wing' organ, inaugurated immediately prior to the dismissal of Lord Treasurer Godolphin in August 1710. It called for an extensive government inquiry into the management of the late ministry, and urged that corrupt public servants should be brought to account. One of its original sponsors was Henry St. John, soon to be appointed secretary of state in the ministerial reshuffles. He had given *The Examiner* a cause in his *Letter to the Examiner*, which argued that England had been forced to pay for a major share of the War of the Spanish Succession, now in its eighth year, while instead of making peace at the earliest favourable opportunity, the allies had prolonged hostilities to gain for themselves a more advantageous settlement while England footed the bill. This was a popular theme. War-weariness was rife throughout the kingdom. Taxes were high, harvests poor, and there was a general clamour for peace. One of the priorities of the new government was to make peace. Along with other High Church stalwarts such as Francis Atterbury, Dean of Christ Church, Matthew Prior, and John Freind, Henry St. John penned the early issues of *The Examiner*, and the paper quickly found an audience for the views it was putting forward.

Harley, on the other hand, was concerned that the allies should not be confirmed in their fears that the change of government would mean a precipitous move for a settlement at any price. Similarly at home he chose to propound a moderate line on the ministerial changes, at least until the new administration was secure. As Swift perceptively remarked during the October elections, 'Mr. Harley himself would not let the Tories be too numerous'.[2] Although the government was, by now, clearly a Tory one, with the mass resignation of the remaining Whig officers in September, Harley wished to administer without recourse to party considerations. Swift was recruited to moderate *The Examiner*'s extreme stance.[3] When, in an early one of his contributions, Swift resolved 'to let the remote and uninstructed Part of the Nation see, that they have been misled on both Sides, by mad, ridiculous Extreams, at a wide Distance on each Side from the Truth; while the right Path is so broad and plain, as to be easily kept, if they were once put into it',[4] he was following Harley's more moderate lead, and for a time the ultra-Tory periodical reflected a new editorial policy. Eschewing traditional party labels, Swift claimed to offer 'Country' arguments in the good old cause of the public interest. 'I would be glad to ask a Question about *two Great Men* of the late Ministry, how they came to be *Whigs*?', he demanded, 'And by what figure of Speech, half a Dozen others, lately put into great Employments, can be called *Tories*?' (III, 15). Marlborough and Godolphin, the chief ministers of the previous ministry, could hardly be called model Whigs, although they led a Whig government. As for the Tory credentials of Harley and his closest supporters, they were far from unimpeachable. Swift suggested, in this way, that the conflict between Whig and Tory was illusory.

It was typical of Harley to choose a *quondam* Whig to address the Tories, and to lead them into the path of moderation. Six years earlier he had used the same tactics in employing Daniel Defoe. Prior to 1710 Swift's political associates had been Whigs, and some of his closest friends had been turned out of office as a result of the ministerial revolution. Somers, to whom Swift had dedicated his *Tale of a Tub*, lost his place as Lord President, while Richard Steele lost the editorship of the official newspaper, *The London Gazette*. Harley did not expect Swift to become a Tory. He could advocate some policies and still retain his integrity as an Old Whig, suspicious of Court intrigue, and vigorously against continental commitments. But Swift soon began to display genuine Tory attitudes, as if converted by his new role. The man primarily responsible for his changing beliefs was Henry St. John.

Swift did not meet St. John until 11 November 1710,[5] by which time he had already published two issues of *The Examiner*. Nonetheless from his first acquaintance with the secretary his conversion to St. John's views can be documented. St. John was a party man. He had a vastly different conception of the ministerial revolution. He wanted 'to fill the employments of the kingdom, down to the meanest, with Tories'.[6] Like the Tory backbenchers, he wished to see investigations into the mismanagements of the late ministry, and the impeachment of the Whig leaders, and, above all, of Marlborough and Godolphin. Throughout January 1711 Swift was closetted in 'business' conferences with the secretary. 'I was forwarding an impeachment against a certain great person', he explained to Stella on the 31st, 'that was two of my businesses with the secretary, were they not worthy ones?'[7] In the spring of 1711, until he relinquished the editorship with the issue for 7 June, *The Examiner* mirrored this change of heart, as the ministerial paper once more took up an increasingly hard Tory line. In fact there is more than a hint that Harley finally took steps, when elevated to the peerage as Earl of Oxford in May 1711, to remove Swift from his position.[8]

Swift stayed in London. He explained that there was one more business the government wanted him for, 'and when that is done, I will take my leave of them'.[9] In the summer of 1711 Matthew Prior was dispatched to France to formulate the preliminaries upon which the actual negotiations for peace could be based. He returned to England with the French diplomat, Mesnager. The Mesnager convention between Britain and France was duly signed, without consulting the allies, to whom, bound by treaty obligations, any steps towards a settlement should have been reported. Anxious to make peace, the Oxford ministry chose to make a nice distinction between a separate treaty, which was against the terms of the Grand Alliance, and separate treaty negotiations. A propaganda campaign was launched to prepare the way for the announcing of the signing of the Mesnager convention. On 27 November 1711 Swift published, as the culmination of this campaign, *The Conduct of the Allies, and of the Late Ministry, in Beginning and Carrying on the Present War.*

*2*

In indicting the allies and the Godolphin ministry in the *Conduct of the Allies*, Swift pulls no punches. The thesis he propounds so energetically shows no trace of political moderation, instead it closely resembles the *Letter to the Examiner*. The usual explanation is that St. John influenced the subject matter of the later pamphlet. According to A. D. MacLachlan, the 'inspiration' for the *Conduct of the Allies* emanated from St. John: 'Far from Swift's being the tool of the chief minister, the chief minister was forced to trim his sails to the hurricane produced by Swift's—and St. John's—propaganda'.[10] While writing the *Examiner* during the period that Swift was falling under the secretary's spell, he referred his readers to a projected discourse 'by it self', should they wish to see considered the 'Conduct of the late Ministry, the shameful Mismanagements in *Spain*, or the wrong Steps in the Treaty of Peace' (III, 87–88). That the secretary supplied Swift with information for the *Conduct of the Allies* is beyond doubt: he even disappeared on a trip to Hampton Court with the manuscript of the pamphlet in his pocket. Entries in the *Journal to Stella* make it quite evident that Swift sought the opinion of St. John extensively. Consequently the secretary was influential in the state of the final draft. Swift wrote to Stella on 30 October:

> I was to-day in the city concerting some things with a printer, and am to be to-morrow all day busy with Mr. Secretary about the same. I won't tell you now; but the ministers reckon it will do abundance of good, and open the eyes of the nation, who are half bewitched against a Peace. Few of this generation can remember any thing but war and taxes, and they think it is as it

> should be: whereas 'tis certain we are the most undone people in Europe, as I am afraid I shall make appear beyond all contradiction.[11]

From Swift's excited tone, we can gauge the outspoken nature of the tract in question, and it is apparent that he believed in the 'conspiracy thesis' he was to put forward in connection with the allies and the late ministry.

The principal success of Swift's polemical strategy consisted in his ability to present apparently objective evidence to endorse feelings already held by the majority of his audience. He confirmed the vague belief of the country squire that he was being exploited to subsidize not only a long and futile war which had already been won, but also to line the pockets of corrupt ministers and greedy allies. By formulating his arguments on a factual basis, he provided a concrete framework for these previously abstract ideas. He demonstrated precisely *how* the allies and the Whigs had conspired to defraud the national wealth of the kingdom by 'proving' from supposedly objective source materials, that such a conspiracy really existed. And he did so in terms that led the reader to assume that he was reading facts paraded without a structured argument. The art of the *Conduct of the Allies* lies not in the use of more expected Swiftian rhetorical devices such as irony and satire, but in the manner in which Swift impresses himself on his audience as a plain speaker, frank, ingenuous, when in fact he is quite the opposite. He takes this polemical approach to the extent that he might almost be said to be assuming a persona—a mask through which he can address the landed man.

The effectiveness of the *Conduct of the Allies* is best understood in relation to the timing of the publication of the pamphlet, and in consideration of the audience for which it was intended. Richard Cook observes that 'the immediate *raison d'être* of Swift's Tory pamphlets was the molding of public opinion for particular ends, and it is in terms of these persuasive goals that the tracts can be best understood'.[12] The *Conduct of the Allies* did not attempt to preach to the unconverted. It made no attempt to win over the Whigs. It sought to provide cogent reasons for the ministerial stance on the question of peace on the announcement of the Mesnager convention: reasons that could be followed and propounded by government sympathizers in the House of Commons. In addition it was expected that the pamphlet would appeal to the mass of country gentlemen outside parliament, traditionally Tory in sentiment, who paid the taxes that maintained the war-machine, and who exerted considerable influence in the election of parliament-men. The meeting of parliament on 7 December was the date at which the *Conduct* aimed. Then the debates over peace were to take place, and explanations for the conduct of the present ministers over the peace negotiations would need to be forthcoming. Forewarned is forearmed, and Swift attempted to forearm ministerial supporters.

Things did not go according to plan. Although the *Conduct of the Allies* sold at a rate that even astonished Swift himself—a second edition of the pamphlet, called for after only two days, was sold out within five hours, and by 7 December the tract was in its fourth edition—its preparations for the debates on the question of peace were pre-empted by the tactics of the opposition. The Earl of Nottingham opened the debate in the Lords, and spoke vehemently for a motion of 'No Peace without Spain'.[13] Surprisingly the motion was carried, and the discussion of the conduct of the allies was postponed. Oxford, despite Swift's pessimism, regrouped his forces, created at a stroke twelve new court peers to ensure a majority, and headed off the opposition offensive. Then Swift's pamphlet came into its own. It was no coincidence that during the debate on the conduct of the allies in the Commons in February 1712, Swift was able to report to Stella with great satisfaction that 'those who spoke, drew all their arguments from my book, and their votes confirm all I write'. As he pointed out: 'the Court had a majority of a hundred and fifty: all agree, that it was my book that spirited them to these resolutions'. When the votes were printed, he observed that they were 'almost quotations' from the *Conduct of the Allies*, 'and would never have passed, if that book had not been written'.[14] By the end of January 1712 the *Conduct* had passed through six editions, and a total of 11,000 copies had been sold.

## *3*

The polemical approach of the *Conduct of the Allies* is essentially historical. Swift patiently explains, through the presentation of carefully chosen historical facts, the treaty obligations of Britain and her allies, and the way in which they have been wilfully ignored. In the tone of a man who knows much more than he can, or ought to, say, Swift contrives to supply the impression that he is letting the reader into some tremendous state secret. Back-bench Tories and independent country gentlemen implicitly believed in the corruption of the previous ministers. They wanted to be told that they had been right, but they needed to feel that they were making the discovery for themselves without prejudice. Swift adopts an attitude of ill-concealed exasperation that he should even be obliged to explain at all matters that were self-evident to the most imperceptive mind. From the opening remarks of the Preface, he displays this incredulity when faced with opposition to a peace that would end a prolonged war which was proving ruinous to the landed man:

> I Cannot sufficiently admire the Industry of a sort of Men, wholly out of Favour with the Prince and People, and openly professing a separate Interest from the Bulk of the Landed Men, who yet are able to raise, at this Juncture, so great a Clamour against a Peace, without offering one single Reason, but what we find in their *Ballads*. I lay it down for a Maxim, That no reasonable Person, whether *Whig* or *Tory* (since it is necessary to use those foolish Terms) can be of Opinion for continuing the War, upon the Foot it now is, unless he be a Gainer by it, or hopes it may occasion some new Turn of Affairs at home, to the Advantage of his Party; or lastly, unless he be very ignorant of the Kingdom's Condition, and by what Means we have been reduced to it.
>
> (VI, 5)

Having begged the question most forcefully, emphasizing the thesis that the war had been protracted for motives of private interest, and to the detriment of the nation at large, Swift reveals his design to let the reader see for himself the evidence to uphold the 'conspiracy theory'. In his Preface he sets the scene for the discourse itself, but more than that, he practically tells his audience on which side their sympathies ought to lie. There is no attempt to be objective about the subject in the Preface, or to allow the reader to draw his own conclusions from the evidence Swift was about to present in a supposedly objective way. The *Conduct of the Allies* was propaganda in the most accepted sense of the term, to the extent that Swift selected his sources, omitting entirely any evidence that did not support his case, and distorting any that might not, in his eyes, be sufficiently unambiguous. Step by step the pamphlet takes the most ignorant reader from point to point, hammering its message home. Its logical progression appears almost pedantic, but it is unmistakable and irresistible. There had been a conspiracy to exploit the landed man, Swift argued, telling the Tories precisely what they wanted to hear.

Swift adopted a pseudo-objective vein at the beginning of the pamphlet itself, listing calmly 'the Motives that may engage a wise Prince or State in a War'. Excluding an invasion situation, Swift argued against a monarch exerting his forces to a degree at which the danger of forfeiting the prosperity of his kingdom was a real threat. This was especially so when the war was the more immediate concern of a neighbouring country. In such a context it was reasonable, Swift felt, to consider 'which Party has the deepest share in the Quarrel':

> If a House be on fire, it behoves all in the Neighbourhood to run with Buckets to quench it; but the Owner is sure to be undone first; and it is not impossible that those at next Door may escape, by a Shower from Heaven, or the stillness of the Weather, or some other favourable Accident.
>
> (VI, 8–9)

This was a peculiarly apt image for Swift's purpose. Not overflowing with generous humanitarian impulses, it nonetheless fitted in admirably with the country gentleman's view of continental commitments. Obviously, preparations had to be made against the threat of fire spreading to Britain, but there was no need to use British resources to combat the fire in Spain, or indeed in the Spanish Netherlands, at least not on the scale that those most closely affected would be obliged to expend. It was for the United Provinces and the Emperor to fetch most of the water to douse the conflagration: there was no need for the British to send a fire-engine. Following exactly the thinking of the majority of Tories on the war, Swift posited the example of a prince 'so generous, as to contribute more than the Principal Party' to the general war-effort. Having firstly exposed the imprudence of the extent of British treaty obligations, he turned to the situation at hand. The hypothetical prince who was prepared to contribute more than he was obliged to subdue an enemy, Swift argued,

> ought at least to have his Share in what is conquered from the Enemy: Or, if his Romantick Disposition transports him so far, as to expect little or nothing of this, he might however hope, that the Principals would make it up in Dignity and Respect; and he would surely think it monstrous to find them intermedling in his Domestick Affairs, prescribing what Servants he should keep or dismiss, pressing him perpetually with the most unreasonable Demands, and at every turn threatning to break the Alliance, if he will not comply.
>
> (VI, 9)

Here, in the opening pages of the *Conduct of the Allies*, still, it must be remembered, ostensibly discussing an hypothetical case, Swift has aroused the indignation of his partisan audience in illustrating the insulting behaviour of the allies towards Britain. He is not without his tacit criticism of the war at the outset: 'if his Romantick Disposition transports him so far' is clearly meant to be ironic. But essentially Swift accepts the terms of the situation, and then invites conclusions on whether or not Britain has been treated justly by her allies. In 1710, contemporaries would recall, the Dutch had remonstrated with Queen Anne when she decided to change her government, and they had accused her of breaking the terms of the treaty of alliance in initiating negotiations with France on her own behalf. By expressing the relationship between Britain and her allies in this light, Swift sought to cut the ground from under the feet of the Whigs when the problem of Spain came to be debated.

From the abstract Swift came down to the particular. After an historical survey of the wars in which England had taken part since 1066, he analysed the obligations she had contracted at the start of the War of the Spanish Succession. 'I think', he put forward, 'it plainly appears . . . that *England* ought no more to have been a Principal in this War, than *Prussia*, or any other Power, who came afterwards into that Alliance' (VI, 13). Finally he summed up the situation in concrete terms, propounding the naked thesis for which the reader had been prepared:

> that no Nation was ever so long or so scandalously abused by the Folly, the Temerity, the Corruption, the Ambition of its domes-

> tick Enemies; or treated with so much Insolence, Injustice and Ingratitude by its foreign Friends.
>
> (VI, 15)

He proposed to prove three basic points 'by plain Matters of Fact':

> *First,* That against all manner of Prudence or common Reason, we engaged in this War as Principals, when we ought to have acted only as Auxiliaries.
>
> *Secondly,* That we spent all our Vigour in pursuing that Part of the War which could least answer the End we proposed by beginning of it; and made no Efforts at all where we could have most weakned the Common Enemy, and at the same time enriched our Selves.
>
> *Lastly,* That we suffered each of our Allies to break every Article in those Treaties and Agreements by which they were bound, and to lay the Burthen upon us.
>
> (VI, 15–16)

The emphasis has changed, as Swift goes on the offensive. The war, suddenly, is unwise if England is to act as 'principals'; the question of the Spanish peninsula is answered by suggesting that the Whigs were not prepared to expend any resources there until the war in Spain had been lost, despite the ostensible title of the conflict; finally, Swift attempts to cover up the government's unorthodox peace overtures by blaming the allies for worse indiscretions—it was absurd to complain that Britain had transgressed the terms of the Grand Alliance when they had been infringed on so many occasions by her allies. The boot was placed firmly on the other foot. Instead of having to explain away ministerial conduct, Swift called the allies and the late ministry to account for their own proceedings. As an honourable treaty the Grand Alliance had ceased to exist. Swift took the argument one stage further. He accused the allies and the late ministry of conspiracy.

To the Tory squire, party considerations mattered less than corrupt governments, high taxation, the national debt, and expensive continental commitments. Swift probed deep into the psyche of the country gentleman, exploiting his prejudices about monied men, and playing on his fears that there had been a plot to undermine the landed interest. By the end of the *Conduct of the Allies*, Swift has presented the full-blown 'conspiracy thesis', weaving a net of such a scope that it is difficult for the reader to see how so many things could have happened without rampant self-interest dominating the dealings of the late ministry. And, of course, most of Swift's readers were biassed. Swift made great use of the symbol of the 'family' as a collective noun for the Marlboroughs and their hangers-on. This, in itself, was suggestive of intrigue. By insinuating that the late ministers, under the leadership of Marlborough and Godolphin, had been involved in a scheme to accrue to themselves all political and economic power in the state, he pricked the latent anxieties of the independent country gentlemen, habitually ignorant and suspicious of courts. 'With these Measures', he pointed out, 'fell in all that Sett of People, who are called the *Monied Men*; such as had raised vast Sums by Trading with Stocks and Funds, and Lending upon great Interest and Praemiums; whose perpetual Harvest is War, and whose beneficial Way of Traffick must very much decline by a Peace' (VI, 41). These, he observed, were the real reasons for such an outcry against a peace:

> It is the Folly of too many, to mistake the Eccho of a *London* Coffee-house for the Voice of the Kingdom. The City Coffee-houses have been for some Years filled with People, whose Fortunes depend upon the *Bank, East-India*, or some other Stock: Every new Fund to these, is like a new Mortgage to an Usurer, whose Compassion for a young Heir is exactly the same with that of a Stock jobber to the Landed Gentry. At the Court-end of the Town, the like Places of Resort are frequented either by Men out of Place, and consequently Enemies to the Present Ministry, or by Officers of the Army: No wonder then, if the general Cry, in all such Meetings, be against any Peace either *with* Spain, or *without*; which, in other Words, is no more than this, That discontented Men desire another Change of Ministry; that Soldiers would be glad to keep their Commissions; and, that the Creditors have Mony still, and would have the Debtors borrow on at the old extorting Rates, while they have any Security to give.
>
> (VI, 53–54)

*4*

As I have remarked, it is usual to point to Henry St. John as the source of Swift's ideas in the *Conduct of the Allies*. Irvin Ehrenpreis observes that the secretary principally offered him 'advice and suggestions', echoing other scholars.[15] Certainly passages in the *Conduct* resemble St. John's written views as expressed in his correspondence and in print. In the *Letter to the Examiner* he noted that Britain embarked on the War of the Spanish Succession 'To restore the *Spanish* Monarchy to the House of *Austria* . . . and to regain a Barrier for *Holland* which lay naked and open to the Insults of *France*; [these] were the Wise and Generous Motives, which engag'd *Britain* in the present War'. He went on: 'We engag'd as *Confederates*, but we have been made to proceed as *Principals: Principals* in expence of Blood and of Treasure, whilst hardly a *Second* Place in Respect and Dignity is allow'd to us' (III, 222–23). In the summer of 1711 St. John wrote to the British envoy in Prussia when the new king was making a mockery of British diplomacy:

> In short we have by several false measures brought ourselves to that pass, that a king, who is hardly a freeholder, treats us *de haut en bas*. We must get out, my good friend, as well as we can, and not only the present generations of Britons, but future ages, will I dare say, learn by our example not to plunge themselves too deep in a war on the continent.[16]

There can be no doubt of St. John's wholehearted concurrence in Swift's argument in the *Conduct*. His stance over the clash between the landed and the monied interests has often been quoted: the latter was 'a new interest . . . a sort of property . . . not known twenty years ago, [which] is now increased to be almost equal to the terra firma of our island'.[17]

What has passed virtually unnoticed, despite its bearing on the writing of the *Conduct of the Allies*, is Oxford's attitude to the 'conspiracy thesis'. It is often assumed to be fundamentally different to that of Swift and St. John in the autumn of 1711. Discussing the *Conduct*, one writer claims that: 'These polemics may have taken their cue from Harley's presumed policies, but they went far beyond any pressure or persuasion he may have wished to put on [the Dutch leaders], and they contradicted his attempts to retain moderate support'.[18] Yet Swift was careful to stress that the *ministers* believed good would come of the pamphlet. He was at pains to point out to Stella that 'three or four great people' were consulted in his attempts to verify all the allegations made in the tract. It would have been strange had the Lord Treasurer not been one of them. The manuscript was circulated freely and alterations were made by consecutive ministers. Copies were sent 'to the great men' on 26 November prior to publication. Oxford 'had it by him on the table' when Swift called to see him the following day, and it is inconceivable that the prime minister could not have prevented it being made public, if, as has been claimed, the *Conduct* changed government policy against the government's wishes, forcing the peace issue to a settlement regardless of the demands of the allies.[19] The idea that the moderate Oxford was required to bow to the potency of the propaganda disseminated by the pen of Jonathan Swift is untenable. It is more far-fetched than the contention that Marlborough was dismissed as a direct result of the *Conduct of the Allies*. Oxford had all the powers of a chief minister. He concurred in the publication of Swift's pamphlet. Further, it can be demonstrated that he chose to accentuate the attack on the allies and the late ministry.

As soon as the pamphlet began 'to make a noise', Swift began revising it for a second edition. He noted that the 'lord treasurer made one or two small additions'.[20] Oxford also incorporated more of his ideas into the authorial fourth edition. These can, of course, be indentified simply by comparing the first four editions of the *Conduct of the Allies*. Although we cannot be sure which of the inserted passages were Oxford's work, all of them extended the original theme of the pamphlet, driving home the assault on the allies. Other than numerous typographical emendations, there were no other changes. No passages were deleted. One might have expected Oxford, if he were indeed distressed at the immoderate tone adopted by Swift, to have tried to play down the severity of the language. Clearly he did not. All the additions were factual, and none sought to qualify the pamphlet's thesis. The most important was a further instance of the ill-mannered way in which Queen Anne had been treated by the Emperor, Charles of Austria, on whose behalf England had put an army into the field in the Iberian peninsula to support his claim to the Spanish monarchy:

> Her Majesty borrowed Two hundred thousand Pounds from the *Genoese*, and sent it to *Barcelona*, for the Payment of the *Spanish* Army: This Mony was to be re-coined into the current Species of *Catalonia*, which by the Allay is lower in Value 25*l. per Cent.*

> The Queen expected, as she had Reason, to have the Benefit of this Re-coinage, offering to apply it All to the Use of the War; but King *Charles*, instead of consenting to this, made a Grant of the Coinage to one of his Courtiers; which put a stop to the Work: And when it was represented, that the Army would Starve by this Delay, his Majesty only replied, *Let them Starve!* and would not recal his Grant.
>
> (VI, 32–33)

This anecdote, which almost certainly originated with Oxford, is related in the same emotive manner in which Swift had presented similar instances of allied misconduct. There would have been little point in Oxford suggesting minor emendations to the *Conduct of the Allies* had he been in fundamental disagreement with its thesis.

That Oxford did not take issue with Swift over the theme of his pamphlet is hardly surprising, despite the assumption that the prime minister did not share St. John's enthusiasm for a separate peace with France without the agreement of the allies. In 1708 Oxford had penned an attack on the management of the Godolphin ministry which surpassed even the most direct criticisms of Swift's tract. 'Plaine English to all who are Honest, or would be so if they knew how', although never published in Oxford's lifetime, lived up to its title. It was a most savage indictment of the Marlborough family:

> In short necessary services are starved to enrich an overgrown family. Spaine is sacrific'd to their ambition & avarice, our fleet made so unwieldy & expensive in order to make an army necessary, & a ship cannot be built without some of the family having a footing in it & in one word you have nowhere abroad the army you pay for, neither are any accounts made up at home which relate to the Warr. Every year we are amused with chimerical designs in order to cover the cheats & misapplications of money and whilst one family share amongst them the wealth of the nation, who have more yearly coming in from the Public, besides all their secret byways of gain, than Queen Elizabeth had to succour France, relieve Holland, secure Ireland & fight with Spain & yet of this immense sum which they annually hoard up, not one of them has thought fit to lay out *one shilling upon land*; They will not give so small a Heritage as that to the Country of their fidelity, neither will they pay one farthing to the Public Rates

> while the Poor freeholder stoops down under the heavy weight of multiplied and continued taxes.[21]

Here, in miniature, we have the second half of the thesis propounded by Swift in the *Conduct of the Allies*: 'that no Nation was ever so long or so scandalously abused by the Folly, the Temerity, the Corruption, the Ambition of its domestick Enemies'. We should not overlook the fact that the pamphlet dealt not only with the allies, but also with the Godolphin ministry, which the Tory backbenchers accused of mismanagement. The structure of the work entailed the consideration of both as part of the conspiracy thesis. Harley was the first to write on the subject of the extravagancies of the Marlboroughs. He was the first to coin the term, 'the Family'. 'It is plain', he wrote, 'that everything they do is calculated to support either the power or profit of one family' (p. 101). This was in 1708. Three years later Swift's attack on the family was a crucial feature of his censure of the conduct of the late ministry. 'Whether this War were prudently begun or not', he postulated, 'it is plain, that the true Spring or Motive of it, was the aggrandizing a particular Family, and in short, a War of the *General* and the *Ministry*, and not of the *Prince* or *People*; since those very Persons were against it when they knew the Power, and consequently the Profit, would be in other Hands' (VI, 41).

Similarities between certain passages in 'Plaine English' and in the *Conduct of the Allies* can be noted, especially with regard to the recurrence of a number of phrases about the family that served to endorse the conspiracy thesis. Where Harley talked about Spain being 'sacrific'd' to the 'ambition' and 'avarice' of the family, Swift observed that 'our Armies, both in *Spain* and *Portugal*, were made a Sacrifice to Avarice, Ill-conduct, or Treachery' (VI, 21). This was most evident when Spain was under discussion. The final section of Swift's pamphlet, the most polemical, concerns the question of 'No Peace without Spain', and its relevance to the peace negotiations (VI, 45–64). Swift actually reprinted the eighth article of the Grand Alliance to demonstrate that 'there is not in any of these, the least mention of demanding *Spain* for the House of *Austria*, or of refusing any Peace without that Condition' (VI, 46). It is in the next few pages that he ties in the ends of the conspiracy thesis he has woven, with an attack on the stock-jobbers who lived off the war, to the ruin of the landed man, and with accusations that the war had been prolonged for the advantage of the family. 'What Arts have been used to possess the People with a *strong Delusion*, that *Britain* must infallibly be ruined, without the Recovery of *Spain* to the House of *Austria*?' (VI, 58), Swift demanded, 'If we must now Surrender *Spain*, what have we been Fighting for all this while?':

> The Answer is ready; We have been Fighting for the Ruin of the Publick Interest, and the Advancement of a Private. We have been fighting to raise the Wealth and Grandeur of a particular Family; to enrich Usurers and Stock-jobbers; and to cultivate the pernicious Designs of a Faction, by destroying the Landed-Interest. The Nation begins now to think these *Blessings* are not worth Fighting for any longer, and therefore desires a Peace.
> (VI, 59)

Harley had advanced similar reasons:

> As long as these rule victorys obtained are employd for their private advantage & profit & not to the end designd for obtaining a safe & honourable peace, but to aggrandise themselves & to prolong that war by which they get such vast wealth & secure to themselves so much power; for you must not expect peace abroad until they have subdued all their enemies at home.
> (p. 101)

The most striking similiarity between the two tracts involved the use of Matthew 23, v. 4: 'For they bind heavy burdens and grievous to be borne, and lay *them* on men's shoulders; but they *themselves* will not move them with one of their fingers'. Although not one of the more often quoted verses in the bible, it is the only New Testament reference employed by either man. It is particularly suited to the conspiracy thesis, insinuating that the family, like the biblical Pharisees, were cruel task-masters who stood to profit if their dictates were carried out. Playing on the clash of interests, Swift remarked upon 'the Style of Men at Ease, *who lay the heavy Burthens upon others, which they will not touch with one of their Fingers*':

> I have known some People such ill Computers, as to imagine the many Millions in Stocks and Annuities, are so much real Wealth

> in the Nation; whereas every Farthing of it is entirely lost to us, scattered in *Holland, Germany,* and *Spain*; and the Landed-Men, who now pay the Interest, must at last pay the Principal.
>
> (VI, 59)

The image was an apt one, but there is more than a chance that Swift borrowed it from Harley. 'Plaine English' was very brief compared to the *Conduct of the Allies*, but the concluding pages of Swift's pamphlet which dealt with 'No Peace without Spain' correspond to Harley's earlier offering. In his *exposé* of the malpractices that had been perpetrated to 'enrich an overgrown family', Harley had used a simile: 'Like their predecessors the Jewish zealots, they bind heavy burdens and hard to be borne upon mens shoulders, but will not touch them themselves with the top of their fingers; no wonder the Landed man is so hard pressed when our Task masters feel not the least part of it themselves' (p. 106). Both men emphasized the decline of the landed interest as a direct result of the activities of the family and its adherents: similarly they made the mental connection between the conduct of the Marlboroughs and the conduct of the Pharisees.

There are, then, indications that Swift had read the manuscript draft of Harley's 'Plaine English'. Furthermore, he knew enough about the Lord Treasurer to glean, from his conversation, that he felt a deeply-rooted anger against the late ministry. The sentiments expressed in the *Conduct of the Allies* did not owe their origin solely to the inspiration of St. John. Certain details could have come from no-one but Harley. Godolphin's stance on the question of war and peace in 1701, for instance, was known by only his associates at the time, and although Harley was one of them, St. John was not (VI, 11). The problems of revenue were also the province of the Lord Treasurer, not of the secretary of state. Swift offered to give 'the most ignorant Reader some Idea of our present Circumstances, without troubling him or my self with Computations in form'. He estimated a debt of 'about Fifty Millions' (VI, 54). Oxford shared the belief that there would be 'a heavy after Reckoning': 'Even the Civil List will produce a *Debt* that will startle . . . while a multitude of the greatest & most preferred Offices and Pensions together with the privy Purse *are* engrossed at Home, and an uninhabitable Palace [Blenheim] is erecting' (p. 105). Even the failure to make peace in 1706, when 'the General and the Ministry . . . refused to accept very Advantagious Offers . . . after the Battle of *Ramellies*' (VI, 43)—a charge which had been brought into the open by St. John in the *Letter to the Examiner*—had been anticipated by Harley in 'Plaine English'. He later dated his fall in 1708 from the time he stood out against continuing the war.[22] Swift observed that the family was 'forced to take in a Set of Men, with a previous Bargain, to skreen them from the Consequences of that Miscarriage'. Harley, the sacrifice, was none too happy about the situation in 1708. 'Whoever stands in their way must be removed at any expence', he explained, 'Even victorys are suffered by these Persons to be made no other use of but to subdue the enemies of their Enormitys at home, nor will they endure' (pp. 105, 108). There can be little doubt after reading 'Plaine English' that Harley was an ardent believer in the 'conspiracy thesis'.

Despite the success of the *Conduct of the Allies* in pinpointing the government line in parliament in the absence of party whips, it did little in the long run to promote Swift's career. True, he became something of a ministerial *chef de propagande*, editing and overseeing other writings. He was consulted on the composition of queen's speeches, and continued to be in close contact with the ministers. On the other hand he was rewarded with nothing tangible other than the deanery of St. Patrick's in Dublin—not the English bishopric he had coveted—and neither Oxford nor Bolingbroke displayed much enthusiasm for his projected history of the peace-making. He never met Queen Anne, who was also careful to stress that she had not been responsible for Swift's elevation as dean. The Irish deaneries, she remarked, were in the lord-lieutenant's gift.[23] On Oxford's dismissal in 1714, followed almost immediately by Queen Anne's death and the accession of the Hanoverians, Swift retired from the English political scene. He was never to return, apart from an occasional visit after the publication of *Gulliver's Travels*, and his subsequent political pamphlets were confined to Irish affairs.

But if St. John was the 'inspiration' behind Swift's attack on the conduct of the allies in 1711, there is more than enough evidence to suggest that Oxford provided the stimulus for the attack on the conduct of the Godolphin ministry. It is stretching credulity to argue that, after the harassments he had endured during the throes of the ministerial revolution of 1710, he wished to protect the Marlboroughs from Swift's printed attack. If anything, he was, no doubt, glad that at last the truth had been told three years and more after he himself had drafted an attack on the family. The suggestion that the publication of the *Conduct of the Allies* precipitated a crisis in the ministry, and that 'rather than face a recoil into Whiggery and war, Harley acquiesced in much of St. John's Tory programme',[24] appears to me to be unfounded. Even in the actual task of composition it is probable that the Lord Treasurer played a larger part than has often been conceded or imagined. Moreover, the question of influence must recognize the tradition in which the *Conduct* appeared: the country gentleman was suspicious of the power of courts and governments, and the suggestion that the family had simply acted in the corrupt manner in which 'Country theory' assumed all ministers would behave, merely served to bear out his thinking. Swift, at bottom, shared with his independent country audience an unshakable faith in the corruption of government, however much this conflicted with his relations with the Oxford ministry. His deep-rooted attitudes were to surface once more in *Gulliver's Travels* in the views of the King of Brobdingnag. Paradoxically Oxford also shared this distrust of the centre of political power, despite his position at the head of the government. Swift, however, accepted self-interest as normal human behaviour, and he did not disguise his own shortcomings. He recognized that he, too, was a Yahoo.

## NOTES

1 Jonathan Swift, *Journal to Stella*, ed. H. Williams (Oxford, 1948), 2 vols., I, 13, 46; *The Correspondence of Jonathan Swift*, ed. H. Williams, 5 vols. (Oxford, 1963), I, 173, 178.

2 *Journal*, I, 44.

3 See W. A. Speck, '*The Examiner* Examined: Swift's Tory Pamphleteering', in *Focus: Swift*, ed. C. Rawson (London, 1971), pp. 145–46.

4 *The Prose Works of Jonathan Swift*, ed. H. Davis (Oxford, 1939–68), III, 14. All quotations from Swift's prose writings are taken from this edition, and subsequent page references are given within the text in parentheses.

5 *Journal*, I, 91.

6 Viscount Bolingbroke, *A Letter to Sir William Windham* (1753), pp. 21–22.

7 *Journal*, I, 178.

8 From March 1711 onwards Swift gradually became aware that he was in the middle of the developing rivalry between Harley and St. John. He wanted to re-define his position as editor of *The Examiner*. A meeting with Harley on 19 May, 'where we talked through a great deal of matters I had a mind to settle with him', appears to have been the crucial date: less than three weeks later Swift published his last *Examiner*, after which he wrote to Stella: 'methinks in this day's *Examiner* the author talks doubtfully, as if he would write no more, so that if they go on, they may probably be by some other hand, which in my opinion is a thousand pities; but who can help it?' For some reason, Harold Williams relegates the last part of this sentence to a footnote: *Journal*, I, 273, 291 and n. 38.

9 *Ibid.*, p. 343.

10 A. D. MacLachlan, 'The Road to Peace, 1710–13', in *Britain after the Glorious Revolution 1689–1714*, ed. G. Holmes (London, 1969), pp. 210–11.

11 *Journal*, II, 397.

12 Richard I. Cook, *Jonathan Swift as a Tory Pamphleteer* (Washington, 1967), p. 31.

13 When he realized what Nottingham intended to do, Swift took extra steps to defend ministerial conduct by ridiculing the expected speech on 'No Peace without Spain'. In *An Excellent New Song, Being the Intended Speech of a famous Orator against Peace*, published on 6 December, Swift lampooned the 'Dismal' figure who, out of '*want of a Place*', had worked up an old speech '*to break the Queen's Peace*'. See *The Poems of Jonathan Swift*, ed. H. Williams, I, 142–3.

Significantly, in the Commons the motion on 'No Peace without Spain' was resoundingly defeated. The influence of Swift's *Conduct* in this triumph was accounted considerable by contemporaries. See *Journal*, II, 441.

14 *Ibid.*, pp. 480–82.

15 Irvin Ehrenpreis, *Swift: The Man, His Works, and the Age*, vol. 2, *Dr. Swift* (London, 1967), p. 484. Cf. *Journal*, ed. Williams, II, 408 n. 19: 'St. John chiefly supplied Swift with facts and suggestions'.

16 British Library, Portland Loan 29/266.

17 Bodleian Library, MS. Eng. Misc. e. 180, fo. 4, quoted in W. A. Speck, 'Conflict in Society', in *Britain after the Glorious Revolution*, p. 136. Dr. Speck's essay is a useful review of the clash of interests.

18 MacLachlan, *ibid.*, pp. 210–11.

19 *Journal*, II, 408, 421, 422.

20 *Ibid.*, p. 423.

21 '"Plaine English to all who are Honest, or would be so if they knew how": A Tract by Robert Harley', edited with an introductory note by W. A. Speck and J. A. Downie, *Literature and History*, no. 3

(March, 1976), 105–6. All references to 'Plaine English' are from this edition. Subsequent page numbers are supplied within the text in parentheses.

22 H.M.C. *Portland*, v. 647.

23 Cf. *The Diary of Sir David Hamilton 1709–14*, ed. Philip Roberts (Oxford, 1975), p. 54.

24 MacLachlan, *op. cit.*, p. 211.

# III

# 'GULLIVER'S TRAVELS': TEXT AND MEANINGS

# 6

# Swift's Copy of *Gulliver's Travels*: The Armagh *Gulliver*, Hyde's edition, and Swift's earliest corrections

by DAVID WOOLLEY

The modern traveller to Armagh seeking its diocesan library encounters the first of some puzzles even as he approaches the city. He looks for the Cathedral, and he sees not one but two. As a Victorian guide expressed it, 'two conspicuous objects strike the eye and arrest the attention. Two summits, one to the left and the other to the right of the small city which lies in the valley between, are crowned with noble cathedrals.' For this is the ecclesiastical metropolis of Ireland, established in the fifth century by St. Patrick himself. Each is denominated—the old and the new—the Cathedral Church of St. Patrick, and enthroned in each is an Archbishop, who is also Primate of all Ireland. This particular traveller recollects that he is to head for a small spot of ground, 'lying and being upon one of the two tops of the hill [*Parnassus*]', and having decided (on ecclesiological grounds) which, he starts his ascent. Half way up, in Market Street, he calls at the public library and enquires the way to the Public Library; which he learns is in Abbey Street, near the Infirmary, just below the Cathedral. And there he is confronted by a handsome eighteenth-century edifice of cut stone, whose large windows on the first floor lighten an elegant book-lined reading room—the foundation of Primate Robinson, completed in 1771, for the use of the clergy of the Diocese and the residents of the town. To this admirable Public

Library came years ago, in circumstances still the subject of conjecture, the celebrated 'Armagh' copy of *Gulliver's Travels* whose marginal inscriptions and markings are said by some, and denied by others, to be in the autograph of the author himself.[1]

In brief this enquiry into the authenticity and significance of these marginalia will proceed first with a description of the book and its manuscript additions; followed by an account of the few examinations known to me by earlier scholars, and their conclusions; then a section on the search for the earliest Irish printing of *Gulliver's Travels*, a book of the utmost rarity, whose significance in the history of the text has not been recognized, and only now is established by comparison with the Armagh corrections; next a discussion of the stylistic appearance of the manuscript additions and of the more numerous mnemonic marks; then some observations on Swift's handwriting and its variant forms; and finally an attempt to evaluate the corrections as a whole in the textual history of *Gulliver's Travels*.

### *The Book and Its Marginalia*

The Armagh *Gulliver* is a copy of the first London edition, on large paper with the portrait in the first state. It is bound in two volumes in a style which suggests a standard trade binding, being calf with a single gilt rule about one-quarter inch from the edge of each cover, the spine panels gilt around a diamond lozenge filling each panel, with red edges, and both spine labels original and intact reading 'GULLIVER'S | TRAVELS | Vol. I. [II.]'. This binding resembles closely the remaining original binding, much restored, of the first volume of Charles Ford's copy in the Forster Collection at the Victoria and Albert Museum.[2] It also resembles that of the surviving second volume of Swift's own duplicate copy, which appeared as an odd volume at the end of the 1745 Sale *Catalogue*, and is now in the Eugene Kaufmann Swift Collection at Cornell University Library.[3] Both of these copies are on large paper. A bibliographical description of the first edition of *Gulliver* is readily to hand in H. Teerink's *Bibliography of Swift* and in Harold Williams's Bicentenary edition of the *Travels* (1926), for the First Edition Club.[4] The Armagh copy exhibits one peculiarity of physical description: the final signature M of Part III, in the second volume, a quarter sheet of two leaves, occurs in the small paper printing and its edges remain uncut by the binder's plough. For some reason, when the sheets were assembled for this copy of the book, the large paper printing of sig. M in Part III (the final sheet of a unit from one printing house) seems not to have been selected. It is possible to infer from this that the Armagh *Gulliver* was one of the earliest large paper copies to be bound. In the first place, its portrait is of the earliest state. When Benjamin Motte visited Stationer's Hall on 29 November 1726, a whole month after publication day, and entered 'for his copy Travels into several Remote Nations of the World in four Parts by Lemuel Gulliver', he signed the Register with his own hand, paid his fee of vj$^{d}$, and was obliged to deposit by the provisions of Queen Anne's Copyright Act nine copies upon the best paper, in sheets.[5] These copyright deposit copies, so far as it is possible to tell from the examples remaining (at the British Library, Bodleian Library, University Library Cambridge, Sion College Library,[6] and Glasgow University Library) all had the portrait in its first state—and sig. M of Part III in the L.P. printing. And the same is true of those late copies of the large paper edition which have the portrait in the third state (Roths. 2106 and Pierpoint Morgan Library). It is at least a possible inference that only the small paper sig. M. was yet available when the Armagh copy was sewn for binding (cf. note 4).

There is reason to believe that Swift, from his liking for special copies of his own works, may have suggested to Motte the printing of 'a few on a Royal Paper', or at least, that he would have opted for the generous margins on which to enter his corrections or improvements. Temple's *Letters*, 2 vols. (1700), edited by Swift, were printed for the public at large on paper of rather poor quality which has turned brown in most copies today.[7] But because the work was dedicated to King William there had to be a special printing of a few copies on a fine paper to provide the dedication copy, those copies which the editor needed for presentation to influential persons, and a few for wealthy bibliophiles.[8] There were some large paper copies of the 1710 edition of *A Tale of a Tub*.[9] When printing Swift's *Miscellanies in Prose and Verse* of 1711, Tooke or Morphew arranged for some large paper copies, which are also to be found today in some copyright libraries.[10] *Gulliver* appeared in large paper, and there were also some large paper copies of *Polite Conversation*, printed for Motte in 1738.[11] Perhaps most significant of all, George Faulkner in 1735 printed some copies of Swift's *Works*, in four volumes, on large and thick paper, and matched them again in 1738 for Vols. V and VI, and for Vol. [VII] in 1741—all in octavo, but the large paper copies looking as formidable as small quartos.[12] It is difficult to conjecture the number printed on large paper of the first edition of *Gulliver*, called 'a few' in the advertisement, but for a normal edition of the time, varying between 750 and 2,000 copies, if we allow for the trouble of resetting the margins and the deduction of nine deposit copies, it could not well be less than fifty copies.[13] That Charles Ford should have had two large paper copies[14] specially in which to note Swift's formal revisions and corrections, which merited particular notice in the 'Advertisement' to Faulkner's printing of *Gulliver*,[15] makes it seem more likely that the author would have treated himself to the luxury and the wide margins of a large paper copy too, in which to take stock of his achievement.[16]

For these reasons it seems to me initially that the Armagh *Gulliver* was perhaps a very early copy of the book and could well have belonged to the author.

The marginal inscriptions, both of words and marks, are in ink and pencil, predominantly the latter, and by far the larger number occur in the second volume containing Parts III and IV. Of the total number of points showing editorial intervention one quarter are in Vol. I, and three quarters in Vol. II. In Vol. I all but two of the words are in ink, whereas in Vol. II all words and marks are in pencil, except one instance of each in ink. Within a month of publication in London Swift wrote from Dublin to Pope complaining, twice in the same letter, about the faults 'in the second volume particularly'.[17] From the pattern of these alternations between ink and pencil and from the similarities of script within each category, it looks as if the inscriptions were made at more than one session, possibly at considerable intervals of time.

I shall discuss the words first, and then the marks. To begin with the words, the grand total throughout both volumes is—after one's expectations have been raised—disappointingly not to say ludicrously small: a mere twenty-two words in a book of nearly 700 pages, of which curiously five appear a second time. Seven individual letters of the alphabet also occur at various points in the margins, as well as two instances of the symbol for deletion, and two commas. Of all these, the ones in ink include fifteen words, two letters, and a comma (all but one, in Vol. I); these are written in a fairly uniform, bold, quasi-printing upright script of detached letters unlike the familiar cursive hand of Swift reproduced so many times in biographies and editions of this century. The words in ink[18] were clearly written rather deliberately and carefully, perhaps as a procedure for subsequent recopying. The twelve *pencilled* words (all but two in Vol. II) are written very differently, the size of lettering not uniform with those in ink or as between themselves, also tending to slope to the right, more like cursive though with some element of separation, and executed for the most part carelessly and some even awkwardly (as if writing downhill). These pencilled words show an unmistakable similarity to some examples of Swift's familiar hand. But the difference in style between the ink and the pencil series is striking and the impression persists after detailed comparison of the two together.

To turn now to the markings: these are far more numerous, appearing at over fifty points in the two volumes, again unequally distributed for only eight are in the first volume. The marks (in descending order of frequency) take several forms: a short diagonal or vertical stroke in the margin, a saltire cross in the margin, some repeated short vertical strokes in a single column beside a passage, a long vertical stroke beside a passage, two vertical strokes close together, like a printer's parallel 'reference', and a tilted cross of Lorraine. There are also carets in the text, obliterations, and two deletion symbols in pencil in the margin. The short stroke, slanted or vertical, accounts for three quarters of the marks. Comment on all these features can be deferred until the discussion below of Swift's marginal inscriptions in other surviving texts.

A further distinct series of twenty-two deliberate markings promises to add to the stock of Swiftian enigmas. They are large crosses, or strokes, executed with a blunt instrument (almost certainly a broken pencil in the opinion of Andrew Carpenter), situated for the most part in the space between Motte's paragraphs, and leaving merely an impression in blind which carries through, in many cases, onto the leaf below. They elude normal photography and are therefore listed here. What they represent and indeed who was responsible for them does not appear.[19]

## *Earlier Opinions*

We can accept that at the time of Swift's death there existed a large paper copy of *Gulliver*, 1726, bound in two volumes, and containing his autograph in some form. 'A Catalogue of Books, the Library of the late Rev. Dr. Swift, to be sold by Auction . . . N.B. The Books marked thus * have Remarks and Observations on them in the Hand of Dr. Swift. Dublin: Printed for George Faulkner, in Essex Street MDDCCXLV.' lists this copy on p. 13, '*492 Dr. Swift's Gulliver's Travels in 2 vols. large paper. Lond. 1726', and this lot follows immediately upon two other copies of his own collected writings, both starred * as annotated.[20] Both survive today. The four volumes of *Miscellanies* (1727–32), (lot * 482), are now Rothschild 1422,[21] and the liberal editorial marginalia undoubtedly in Swift's hand have provided the illustrations accompanying this essay. The six-volume set of Faulkner's edition of the *Works*, 1735–38 (lot * 486), is at Lough Fea in the Shirley Library.[22] The compilation and printing of the auction catalogue were overseen by two men who knew Swift well in his last years and are not likely to have been mistaken about his handwriting —John Lyon,[23] and his printer and publisher George Faulkner. At Winchester College is Swift's copy of Herodotus (Geneva, 1618) bearing sixteen lines of comment in Latin opposite the title page, and immediately under this is written 'I do hereby certify that the above is the Hand Writing of the late Dr. Jonathan Swift, D.S.P.D. from whom I have had many Letters, and printed several Pieces from his original M.S. Dublin, August 21, 1762. George Faulkner'.[24] We do not know who bought the annotated *Gulliver* (lot * 492) at the sale of Swift's library. But Colin McKelvie has identified the Armagh *Gulliver* in a Dublin auction a hundred years later, 'Catalogue of the Library formerly belonging to the late Colonel Howard of Castle Howard . . . to be sold by Auction, by Charles Sharpe . . . Feb. 11, 1847'; lot 543 is 'Gulliver's Travels, 2 vols royal 8vo London. 1726'.[25] On this occasion the purchaser was Jonathan Osborne, M.D., who wrote in the beginning of vol. I 'This copy of Gulliver's Travels with marginal emendations (both ink and pencil) in the handwriting of Dean Swift was bought by me this day the 12th Feby 1847 at the Auction of the Hon. Colonel

Howard of Castle Howard. Jon$^{n}$ Osborne'. The price he paid, which might have reflected the auctioneer's view of the handwriting, is not known. Dr. Osborne[26] died at Blackrock, Co. Dublin on 22 January 1864, but his son-in-law the Rev. Dr. Thomas Jordan who died in 1908, was a canon of Armagh.[27] No entry was made of the *Gulliver* in the Public Library 'Register of Books donated and purchased' (commences in 1862), nor in Dean Reeves's magisterial complete Library catalogue (finished 1867). It remained uncatalogued until a twentieth- century marginal entry was made in the hand of James Dean.[28] Therefore, given the meticulous professional accomplishments of Reeves both as scholar and archivist, we may well doubt that Osborne was the direct donor.[29] In the absence of firmer evidence[30] we turn to the personal reminiscence of James Dean himself, who was Deputy Librarian from April 1911 to early 1948. Writing on 16 April 1929[31] he said 'No other literary worker has investigated the book [the Armagh *Gulliver*] as far as I know, certainly not since my appointment to the Library eighteen years ago. When I first took up my duties I found the book stuck away in a corner and not even catalogued'.

The investigation of the handwriting which has proved most influential to date, took place between 1929 and 1933. The three men concerned all had a scholarly interest in Swift. They met in Dublin or London, and inevitably were influenced by their exchanges of opinion. They were M. J. Ryan of Dublin, Harold Williams living then in Hertfordshire, and H. Teerink of Arnhem, Netherlands, at work on his bibliography of the printed editions of Swift.[32]

Ryan wrote to the Armagh Library in March 1929, asking to have the marginal notes copied into a *Gulliver* he sent for that purpose, a task which was duly performed by Dean. Ryan also sent, as a specimen of Swift's hand for comparison, the *Handbook of the Dyce and Forster Collections* [1880], which reproduces on p. 88, as examples of Swift's autograph, some alterations to the text of *Gulliver* in Forster 8551, the celebrated large paper first edition. As the hand is in fact that of Charles Ford,[33] Ryan clearly cannot have had much experience of Swift's autograph. Dean replied that 'the emendations in ink, which I have tried to copy, are written in a kind of printed hand, consequently it would be hard to tell who wrote them; but those in pencil certainly would pass for

Swift's writing, and are in a different hand altogether to the one on p. 88 of the Handbook'.

On 1 October of the same year (1929) the Keeper of the Library reported, at the Annual Visitation, 'I would like to draw the attention of Your Grace and the other Governors to a very valuable possession which we have in a first edition and possibly a proof copy of "Gulliver's Travels" with marginal corrections in Swift's handwriting', and again on 27 May 1930 James Dean read a paper at the Quarterly Meeting of the Library Association of Northern Ireland mentioning the book, 'worth thousands of pounds'.[34]

In the same month, March 1929, Ryan wrote to Teerink in Holland on the subject of *Gulliver*, and part of Teerink's reply on 9 April reads 'the last part of your second letter (regarding alterations in Swift's own hand in Parts I, II of Gull. Trav.) is a very important piece of news indeed! I long to hear more about it'. In the summer of 1932 Teerink visited Ireland and met Ryan. Having returned home he reported to Ryan on 29 August, 'I saw the copy of Gull. Trav. in Armagh Library, but the majority of the M.S. notes (I mean those in *ink*) being in block letters, I thought it rather disappointing. As to the others (in pencil) I certainly consider them as written by Swift himself; at least in my opinion they have all the characteristics of his handwriting. They are, however, very few'.[35]

Williams had been in touch with Ryan since 1927, for the publication of his *Gulliver* in 1926 had induced Ryan to write about the early Irish editions. In May 1933 Williams came to Dublin to further his work on Swift's *Poems* (1937), and sent a note to Ryan from the Shelbourne Hotel, on the 18th, proposing a meeting, to which he added a postcript 'I think you met my Dutch friend Teerink?' On 29 August 1933 Williams signed the Visitor's Book in the Armagh Public Library, and he then made a detailed entry of his examination of the *Gulliver* in his notebook. He recorded inter alia that there were 'a number of corrections, not in Swift's hand'. And he noted the words or marks on thirty-seven pages of the *Gulliver*, in a neat list on two pages of his exercise book labelled 'Library Notes and Jottings, 1933'.[36]

When undertaking the Shakespeare Head *Swift* for Blackwell in 1937 Herbert Davis consulted Williams at many points[37] and as early as April 1938 invited him to contribute an Introduction to the *Gulliver* volume. At this time Davis was deeply enough concerned about problems in the canon of Swift to suggest altering the scheme of publication. He proposed following vols. I–III with X (the Drapier) and XI (Gulliver), which would be relatively straight-forward to prepare. For the former he could use his 1935 edition, and for the latter—the outbreak of war, soon after, marooned him at Cornell and then Smith College—Williams offered the use of his own file of textual material, including that on the Armagh *Gulliver*, which was typed up with slight formal revisions, and its receipt acknowledged by Davis, in August 1940. This typed list is reprinted in Appendix II, at the end of the present article, and it will be seen that the notebook entry 'not in Swift's hand' became in the typescript 'in a hand I cannot identify'.[38] This in turn was rendered by Davis 'by an unknown hand' in his listing of the Armagh copy on p. 286 of the Shakespeare Head *Gulliver, Prose Works*, Vol. XI, when it appeared in 1941 (in the revised edition of 1959 and subsequent reprints the repagination makes it p. 302). So that from this rather obscure chain of events it will be seen that the editor of the present standard text of *Gulliver's Travels* appears to have cast his formidable vote *against* the handwriting being Swift's; although, of course, Williams's specific assistance is duly acknowledged in the headnote to the collations.

It is important not to underestimate the respect which Williams commanded from 1926, and especially after 1937, for his work on Swift. His first marriage brought him independent means. From 1921 onwards he applied fanatical industry, great skill, and ample leisure to the task of preparing *Gulliver* and the *Poems*, which upon publication far out-classed all previous editions. As a specialist he really knew most of the answers. By temperament he aspired to the leading position, and after giving an opinion he did not like to have it challenged.[39] When in 1948 the Armagh *Gulliver* was brought to Dublin for exhibition, the entry in the Exhibition Catalogue[40] dealt with the handwriting cautiously, for the corrections are said merely to be 'traceable back to Swift's authority', and 'more than one hand may be involved'. Dr. Maurice Craig has recalled that in arranging and cataloguing the exhibition he had the help of the late John Hayward, who visited Dublin for the purpose.[41] The Nonesuch *Swift*, 1934, diligently edited by Hayward, included a full text of *Gulliver* using Ford's corrections. Hayward would have known of Davis's 1941 text and certainly of Williams's expressed opinion. On arrival in Dublin he saw the contradictions in the handwriting that others had seen[42] and stood firm.

Finally, for the Swift Tercentenary exhibition in November 1967 at the Ulster Museum in Belfast, the Armagh *Gulliver* was lent, displayed and catalogued as Swift's own copy with his autograph corrections.[43]

### *The Search For Hyde's Edition*

Just as textual scholarship has flourished in the field of Anglo-American first editions, so the attention of collectors and editors fifty years ago was directed to searching out and examining the early Irish editions of *Gulliver's Travels*. Two were listed in 1908 by W. Spencer Jackson in his Bibliography which appeared as part of vol. XII (see p. 146) of Swift's *Prose Works*, ed. Temple Scott: the first[44] was printed in Dublin 'by and for J. Hyde, Bookseller in Dame's Street, 1726' but Jackson gave no location for the copy he described; the second[45] was 'Printed for G. Risk, G. Ewing, and W. Smith in Dame Street, MDCCXXVII', and the B.M. copy was cited. An editor could conceivably find that Swift, in Dublin during the winter of 1726–7, had taken a hand in the earliest republication of his book at home. The difficulty for Williams, preparing his Bicentenary edition, was to find one copy of Hyde to examine. So he wrote in April 1925 to G. Ravenscroft Dennis, editor of the volume (VIII, 1899) devoted to *Gulliver* in Temple Scott's collected *Prose Works of Swift*, in which the Hyde edition was mentioned (pp. xxxi–xxxii). Dennis replied that he had indeed owned the copy described by himself and by Spencer Jackson in his Bibliography, but that it had been sold to Francis Edwards Ltd in 1918. In the same month Williams also wrote to the American businessman who collected Imaginary Voyages (including *Gulliver's Travels*), and who proved to be the purchaser of Dennis's copy of the Hyde edition printed in Dublin, Lucius L. Hubbard of Houghton, Michigan.[46] A full bibliographical description of the Hyde volume was sent to Williams in August for use in his edition, and in October Hubbard forwarded a brief sample collation of twelve variants to show that Hyde's text was set up from Motte's first edition and not a later one. He commented 'The coincidences pointed out in a few cases, between these editions [Hyde, and Stone's abridgement of 1727] and Ford or Faulkner are interesting'. Williams asserted in his 1926 edition of *Gulliver* (p. lxxxi): 'None of these pirated editions [Hyde, and three others] has any authority, nor is their text of any value', but he noted one verbal change of significance in Hyde; and left it at that. Not till eight years later did Williams see the Armagh *Gulliver* (in August 1933).

This accounts for the first of four copies of Hyde known to me. Another is my own (bought in 1955 from P. J. Dobell, Cat. 145/195);[47] and the other two belonged in 1927 to M. J. Ryan (mentioned above [note 32]). After the appearance of Williams's edition late in 1926, Ryan wrote to Williams to say that he had a copy of Hyde, complete with the portrait frontispiece lacking in the Dennis–Hubbard copy. And in 1928 Ryan posted both his copies to a London firm of photographers to have the unique portrait, some plates, and the preliminary gathering expertly facsimiled,[48] in order to make good his second and defective copy. Williams failed in his attempts to persuade Ryan to sell these rare volumes at the time, but they arrived—both copies—unexpectedly in the post at Aspenden in July 1937, with a covering letter from Ryan to say that they were a gift, and both[49] are now with the rest of Williams's Swift collection in the University Library, Cambridge.

The vital importance of the Hyde edition of *Gulliver* for us is that a comparison of its text with the words and marks in the Armagh copy of the first London edition, shows unmistakably that there is a direct connection between the two. Unfortunately Williams seems not to have made the comparison in the years 1937 to 1940, when he could have told Herbert Davis; and Davis—who was permitted to borrow the Hubbard copy—reported in April 1940 to Williams, 'I have used the Hyde copy [*sc.* edition], but as far as I can see, it is a very poorly printed edition, full of misprints, and the corrections it contains are of no account. It is only rather curious that a good many of them are the same as those that appear in the 1727 London edition', words echoed in his Textual Notes to his *Gulliver* (*Prose Works*, XI, 285/301). He there added 'I find it difficult to believe that Swift could have had any interest in it'. By August he had received Williams's typescript of his report on the Armagh *Gulliver*, but since Davis gave no variants from Hyde in his own apparatus perhaps he did not compare them himself.

Turning now to the career of John Hyde[50] we find that it coincides, over twenty years, with the years of Swift's maturity in Dublin, ending in 1728. One aspect of it can be followed in the records of the Irish equivalent of the Stationers' Company, the Guild of St. Luke the Evangelist,[51] of which he was sworn free in 1707, after service, being elected to the Council within a year, and Master in 1718. He married the daughter of a printer, Joseph Ray, and was in business as a stationer (supplying Trinity College) and book-seller from 1708. His imprint as a 'publisher', from 1709 till his early death, is always 'in Dames Street'. But in 1725, the year before his edition of *Gulliver*, he commenced printer. His connection with Swift can be dated almost at the outset of his career. Miss Pollard, to whom I am indebted for the most generous communication of her researches, has found that on 24 August 1711 Hyde obtained leave from the Guild to go to England (while still holding office as Warden). Swift's *Conduct of the Allies* was first published in London (during his residence there) on 27 November of that year, and the first Dublin printing, which incorporates authorial revisions and was later to become Faulkner's copytext in 1738, appeared in 1712, 'Re-printed for *John Hyde* Bookseller in *Dames-Street*'.[52] One may note, in parenthesis, as a parallel to the situation later in the case of the earliest revisions to *Gulliver*, that the Dublin revisions to the *Conduct*, originating in the Hyde edition, form a stemma distinct from the series deriving from the successive London editions. In a letter to Charles Ford, of 16 February 1719, Swift reports that in undertaking to distribute Prior's folio *Poems* of 1718 in Ireland 'I think the Method must be to consign them to a Bookseller here, and I am sending for one Hide, who has dealt that way already and is recommended to me as an honest man'. These arrangements dragged on for three years,[53] first with Prior himself and then his executors, Swift acting as intermediary for Hyde who was ill with 'rheumatism'. Late in 1723 the first edition of Swift's *Some Arguments Against enlarging the Power of Bishops, in letting of Leases* appeared with the imprint

'Dublin: Printed for *J. Hyde*, 1723'. For the publication of the *Drapier's Letters* in the following year Swift turned to John Harding, who was a printer and perhaps a convenient screen as well. All of Hyde's imprints to date had read 'printed for' J. Hyde, but from 1725, in Stephen Radcliffe's *A Letter to Edward Synge*,[54] we find 'printed by and for J. Hyde', the imprint as it appears in his *Gulliver*, and indeed in the last of his books connected with Swift, the Dublin edition[55] of Voltaire's *An Essay upon the Civil Wars of France* (1728), to which was prefixed 'A Short Account of the Author'. Hyde's will was proved early in January 1729, but Sarah his widow carried on the business in Dame Street, as a printer till 1734 and stationer until 1746.

For the day of publication of Hyde's edition of *Gulliver's Travels* so far no advertisement has been found. His title-page is dated 1726. A rival edition, that bearing the imprint of Risk, Ewing and Smith (see note 45) proclaims 'MDCCXXVII', but this is likely to be the anticipation regularly practised at the time; for its advertisements have been found in *The Dublin Weekly Journal*, 26 Nov. 1726 as 'In the press, and will be published next week' (p. 342), 3 Dec. 1726 'Just Published' (p. 348), continuing through to 14 Jan. 1727 (p. 372).[56] Swift's corrections and revisions do not appear in this rival edition, which is a commoner book than Hyde's and was reset for a second edition with the same date. It may even have appeared first and seized the market from Hyde and Swift. At all events, though both rival editions relied perforce on Motte for their basic copy, there is evidence that Hyde dealt in business with Motte in the years following his *Gulliver*. Swift wrote to Motte about proposed subjects for illustration in the *Travels*, 28 Dec. 1727—'I had yours of the 16th from Mr. Hyde, and desire that henceforth you will write directly to me without scrupling to load me with the Postage'. And after Hyde's death he wrote to Worrall, his cathedral vicar, 18 January 1729, 'My bookseller, Mr. Motte, by my recommendation, dealt with Mr. Hyde; there are some accounts between them, and Mr. Hyde is in his debt . . .'[57]

Hyde's *Gulliver* was set up from Motte's first edition and carries, in those few instances where the large paper printing varies, the readings of the standard paper printing. It is a duodecimo, with two volume titles (following Motte) but paginated through as one volume, in which it is bound. The text is crowded onto the page in forty-one to forty-two lines of Long Primer, reducing Motte's 666 pages to 274. Despite the numerous typographical errors (perhaps caused by haste) noted by Herbert Davis, each title page proudly proclaims '*In this Impression, several* ERRORS *in the* London *Edition are corrected*'. True enough, and when eight years later Faulkner set up the title page to *Volume III. of the Author's Works*, containing *Gulliver's Travels* (much revised), he used exactly the same words with a significant addition: 'In this Impression several Errors in the *London* and *Dublin* Editions are corrected'. Although Hyde's sprinkling of original readings was so quickly forgotten that Faulkner ignored them, his slips made a selling point for the later edition.

## *The Marginalia*

In order to place the Armagh marginalia more precisely in the corpus of Swift's amendments to *Gulliver*, it is convenient to recognize broadly three consecutive stages of correction—Ford's manuscript changes (three versions), the Motte 1727 octavo, and Faulkner's 1735 octavo—broadly, because the divisions are not absolute, nor is the progression of change orderly. The earliest of Ford's three versions is his list of just over 100 changes, written out on the same double leaf as his letter to Motte, dated 3 Jan. 1726[–7], but omitted from all editions of Swift's correspondence.[58] It is probable from its substance and phrasing that this letter, though in Ford's autograph, was entirely composed by Swift, and similarly the list.[59] At all events this stage of revision can be placed within two months of the arrival of Motte's first edition in Dublin. The second stage, Motte's corrected fourth octavo edition, was published on 4 May 1727 (*The Post Boy* advt.), and the third, Faulkner's edition, on 7 Jan. 1735.

Of all the eighty-three points[60] in the Armagh *Gulliver* which show authorial intervention, whether by word or by mark, twenty-three can be located as emendations in the Hyde text; and six of these are *unique to that edition*, never reappearing. A further twenty-five instances from Armagh, which did not for some reason find their way to Hyde, are to be found on Ford's list of 3 Jan., to which should be annexed without counting in the total, five common to Hyde and Ford's list. Nine of the Armagh points reappear first in Ford's 'Book', his annotated large paper first edition in the Forster Collection (No. 8551);[61] four in Motte's 1727 octavo; and seven in Faulkner's 1735 octavo. This totals sixty-eight 'points', leaving fifteen ignored or overlooked. Before examining the marginalia as a whole, in some detail, those appearing first in Hyde's edition can be enumerated. (Throughout, the references will be to *Part* | *Chapter* | *Page* of Motte's first edition, facilitated by the recent line facsimile printing[62] from Scholars' Facsimiles & Reprints, of New York.)

(1) *Armagh–Hyde Emendations* (23)
(Lemma = Motte; Variant = Hyde)

| *Pt.* | *Ch.* | *p.* | |
|---|---|---|---|
| I. | 2. | 39 | (mark) *Ranfu – Lo*] *Ranfu – cess* This is certainly authorial, being a deliberate substantive change. It is noteworthy in offering potentially our first key to unlock any system that may underlie the contrived foreign languages[63] in the *Travels*, for we are apparently given two synonyms for the English word 'Breeches'. Unique to Hyde. |
| | 5. | 80 | (mark) bold] boldest A necessary correction made in Hyde, noted by Ford, and printed by Motte *1727*, and Faulkner, *1735*. |
| | 7. | 127 | (mark) perpetually] the most violent[ly] Undoubtedly an intention to vary the earlier of two proximate 'perpetual's has been frustrated by printing-house error; conjecturally emended here in square brackets. Unique to Hyde. An alternative and preferable emendation, proposed by Professor Ehrenpreis, retains Hyde's variant lection as it stands, assuming an instruction (overlooked by the compositor) to delete the next four words, 'instigated by her Majesty'. |
| | 7. | 132 | (mark) the] our A passage dealing with the two Emperors of Lilliput and Blefuscu ends, in Motte, with a possible ambiguity as to which of them 'discovers' the secret of Gulliver's disgrace, and indeed as to whether it is revealed (in one sense) or merely detected (in the other). Neatly resolved by emending one word. Unique to Hyde. |

| *Pt.* | *Ch.* | *p.* | |
|---|---|---|---|
| II. | 8. | 146 | (mark) Hunger!] Hunger? The change of terminal punctuation is unique to Hyde. |
| III. | 6. | 93 | (mark) who] they An unsatisfactory half-measure, to remedy an awkward construction, and producing a failure of grammar in Hyde. However, 'they' in fact adumbrates the recast passage as given in Ford's book, where it survives, grammatically correct. Reprinted in *1735*. |
| | 7. | 101 | (marks) an Assembly] a Convention Ford's list explains (perhaps in Swift's words) '. . . this must have been altered, for the word Assembly follows immediately after'. Varied again in Ford's Book to 'a modern Representative', reprinted thus in *1735*. Both forms conflated in the Carrol Wilson copy[64] to read 'a modern Representative of a Convention', validating Hyde's variant. Unique to Hyde. |
| | 8. | 114 | (mark) ngular] singular Misprint in Motte corrected in Hyde, unnoticed in Ford's list and Book; but noted in his second copy of Motte now in the Pierpont Morgan Library, New York. |
| | 8. | 114 | bis (mark) this] the At line 20 Motte's reading sounds awkward, but persists through four octavo editions. Rectified in Hyde, reappears in Faulkner's octavo, *1735*. |
| | 8. | 115 | (mark) *Libertina*] a *Libertina* Omission of the article a printer's error in Motte, corrected in Hyde, uncorrected by Motte through *1727*, corrected in Faulkner *1735*. |
| | 8. | 115 | bottom line (cross) Uncertain significance of mark here; but commas added around 'perhaps' following, only in Hyde. |
| | 10. | 144 | (cross, *through which is written* 'despised') deprived] despised Motte's error unnoticed by Ford; corrected in Hyde, Motte *1727*, and Faulkner *1735*. Williams (in ed. 1926, p. 483) discounts the authority of Hyde's reading, as 'the obvious emendation'. |
| | 10. | 146 | (mark) rallied] raillyed The distinction, reflecting the French spelling, was one insisted upon by Swift and is made elsewhere in Hyde's edition. Also corrected by Faulkner, *1735*. |

| Pt. | Ch. | p. | |
|---|---|---|---|
| IV. | 3. | 45 | (deletion symbol and 'to' deleted in text) not to] not Misprint in Motte; corrected in Hyde, Motte *1727*, and Faulkner, *1735*. |
| | 4. | 58 | (mark) making of . . . heard of] making of . . . heard In dealing with the propinquity of two 'of's within four lines (which one might hesitate to diagnose from the mark), Swift removed the *second* for Hyde, but the *first* for Faulkner, *1735*. Reading unique to Hyde. |
| | 5. | 60 | (mark) of which] which The compositor of Motte's first edition, perhaps, inadvertently repeated 'of' from the preceding phrase. Removed from Hyde, noted by Ford, corrected in *1727*, *1735*. |
| | 5. | 65 | (letter 'e' substituted for 'o') those] these Improvement effected in Hyde, noted by Ford, appears in *1727*, *1735*. |
| | 6. | 88 | ('posterior' *added in margin*) inferior] inferior posterior Whether restoration or revision this successful change appears in Hyde, Ford, and Faulkner, but not in Motte *1727*. |
| | 8. | 130 | (mark) were] are Motte's reading in 1. 19 a slip; the correct reading appears in Hyde, and in all three stages subsequently. |
| | 11. | 166 | (cross, and 'a' inserted) mong] among Misprint in Motte corrected in Hyde, *1727*, *1735*. |
| | 11. | 172 | (mark, 'as' *underscored* ,'or' *added*) A slip in 1. 17 is rectified in Hyde, but not noticed by Ford or by *1727*. Correction reappears in *1735*. |
| | 12. | 185 | ('were' in margin) was] were This after-thought, possibly unintentionally, produced two 'were's in three lines; not noted by Ford, or observed by *1727*. Revision reappears in *1735*. |
| | 12. | 198 | (*deleted*) 'Whore-master' in Motte disappears, censored from Hyde's text.[65] Unnoticed by Ford, ignored by *1727*. Motte's reading becomes 'Whoremunger' in Faulkner, *1735*. (NB. at IV 6. 83 'Whoring' is struck out in Armagh, but stands in all texts including Hyde.) |

It will be seen that three quarters of these emendations in Hyde are represented in the Armagh volumes simply by a marginal stroke of the pencil; and that six are unique in not being carried over, by any means, to later texts. Without Hyde we should probably be at a loss for their meaning, but since we can see the author's hand here—and the other Hyde readings corroborated elsewhere—we are in a better position to make an informed guess about the status of the Armagh *Gulliver*.

Hyde's edition as a whole is matter for a separate enquiry. Certainly it is strange that it ignores the remaining two-thirds of the Armagh marginalia, and yet other glaring corrigenda. But if one can legitimately assume that Hyde's venture demanded the utmost haste, that he was setting up his type as fast as he could get copy,[66] Swift may well have sent off to him his very earliest corrections, to be printed immediately, and only later garnered the collection sent by Ford to Motte on 3 Jan. 1726[–7]. The pattern of what he sent to Hyde is very like that of his later efforts, namely a far heavier concentration in Parts III and IV than in Parts I and II. The full extent of his task may only gradually have become apparent, for it seems clear that Swift did not have a manuscript at hand to consult, to judge from the wording of Ford's list and the system of marking in the Armagh copy. Thus, evidence of a November publication of Hyde's edition, if it ever turns up, would tend to support this theory.

The remaining marginalia can be dealt with more expeditiously, since they are partly covered by Williams's typed account reprinted below (Appendix II), which was employed by Davis in devising his apparatus of textual variants for the Blackwell edition. In Davis (pp. 302–22) variants can easily be located using the Part | Chapter reference employed here. The twenty-five 'points' appearing on Ford's list (annexing five also appearing in Hyde), nine from Ford's Book, four from Motte's 1727 octavo, and seven from Faulkner's 1735 octavo, are all listed individually below, and include also those overlooked or unspecified by Williams. Those fifteen 'points' never subsequently used by Swift form the final category. Since these lists have been compiled after minute examination of the Armagh volumes with the aid of a strong magnifying glass, I have aimed to make them definitive, by excluding certain marks which appeared to me to be flaws in the paper, or a flick of printing ink, and distinct from the stroke of Swift's pen or pencil; though these are impossible to distinguish, working from a photographic image.

(2) *Armagh–Ford's list* [headed 'Errata'] (25)

| *Armagh* | | *Ford's list/Davis edn. 1959* |
|---|---|---|
| I.2.36 | His | 33.25 |
| 8.145 | Blefuscu | 79.21 |
| II.1.9 | However, | 86.21 |
| 3.47 | perhaps | 102.24 |
| 3.48 | and | 103.14 |
| 3.65 | Insects | 110.4 |
| III.5.71 | Books | 182.2 *f.b.* |
| 5.74 | (mark) | 184.4 *f.b.* |
| 5.77 | (mark) | 186.1 |
| 5.78 | (mark) | 186.15 |
| 7.94 | is | 193.5 |
| 7.101 | into | 195.30 |
| 9.119 | (mark) | 203.14 [year change] |
| 9.121 | (mark) | 204.9 |
| 10.140 | (mark) | 212.4 |
| 10.144 | to | 213.25 |
| IV.1.8 | (mark) | 223.6 *f.b.* |
| 4.50 | s[old]t[ill] | *not in Davis*; see Williams ed. 1926, p. lxii |
| 5.68 | his | 248.8 |
| 5.69–79 | (marks) | 248.24–249.5 *f.b.* [noted on Ford's list] |
| 6.90–91 | (marks) | 255.3 [*noted* on Ford's list] |
| 6.97 | (marks) | 257.2 *ff* [*noted* on Ford's list] |
| 7.113 | last | 263.28 |
| 8.121 | (mark) | 266.22 |
| 10.147 | (mark) | 277.2 |

[*Also on Ford's list are the following which had appeared in Hyde's edition*]

| | | |
|---|---|---|
| I.5.80 | (mark) | 52.22 |
| IV.5.60 | (mark) | 245.7 |
| 5.65 | these | 246.2 *f.b.* |

| | | |
|---|---|---|
| 6.88 | posterior | 254.12 |
| 8.130 | (mark) | 270.4 |

(3) *Armagh–Ford's Book* [Forster 8551] (9)

| | | |
|---|---|---|
| I.3.50 | Blue Red Green | 39.19–20 |
| 3.51 | Blue Red Green | 39.4 *f.b.* |
| III.6.90 | (cross) | 191.3 *ff* |
| 6.90 | (mark) | 191.7–8 |
| 6.91 | (mark) | 191.17 |
| 6.92 | (mark) | 191.20 |
| 6.92 | (mark) | 191.26 |
| 6.92 | (mark) | 191.5 *f.b.* |
| IV.6.80 | (mark) | 251.2–3 |

(4) *Armagh–Motte's octavo, 1727* (4)

| | *Armagh* | *Motte's 8vo 1727/Davis edn. 1959* |
|---|---|---|
| I.5.79 | bending | 51.4 *f.b.* |
| 6.93 | (mark) | 57.19 |
| II.1.1 | (mark) | 83.11 |
| III.8.110 | (mark, and *comma inserted*) | (*not in Davis*) *1727*, III.8.110, l.20, 'history,' |

(5) *Armagh–Faulkner's octavo, 1735* (7)

| | *Armagh* | *Faulkner 1735/Davis edn. 1959* | |
|---|---|---|---|
| I.7.125 | (mark) | 71.10 | |
| II.2.30 | [toward]ly | 95.6 | |
| III.5.74 | (mark) | 184.6 *f.b.* | |
| 9.119 | (mark) | 203.14 | |
| IV.1.9 | (cross) | *Inadvertent transposition of corrections probably here in 1735 between 'the' and 'a' 'tree'* | 224.19 |
| 1.10 | (cross) | | 224.21 |
| 10.147 | (mark) | 276.8*f.b.* | |

(6) *Unused Marginalia in Armagh* (*15*)
(Lemma = Motte; variant = Swift)

| *Pt.* | *Ch.* | *p.* | |
|---|---|---|---|
| II. | 2. | 16 | (mark) 'thickness' underscored in text. Unused. |
| | 2. | 36 | *Green Eagle*] Horn and Crown Unused. |

| *Pt.* | *Ch.* | *p.* | |
|---|---|---|---|
| III. | 2. | 32 | (mark) signalling repetition of 'allowed' within four lines. Unused. |
| | 4. | 60 | (mark) against line 18. Unexplained. |
| | 6. | 87 | (mark) signalling unsatisfactory plural 'Natures'. Unused. |
| | 8. | 108 | (mark) signalling 'Family' (*underlined*), following on 'Families' three lines before. Unused. |
| | 9. | 121 | (mark) unless relating to a change six lines later (*Davis edn. 1959*, at 204. 15), this was unused. |
| | 9. | 121 | (mark) This, as proposed by McKelvie, may signal 'ways', repeated in Hyde, Motte *1727*; printed 'Ways' in *1735*, – *or* a fault of greater substance, unexplained. |
| | 9. | 124 | (mark) Unexplained. |
| | 10. | 141 | Memories] Understandings Unused. |
| IV. | 3. | 45 | (mark) signalling repetition of 'would'. Unused. |
| | 5. | 79 | (mark) The final sentence of Chap. V has an ink mark in the margin, midway, signalling a fault, but *which* (of the many inflicted on it by Andrew Tooke)[67] it is hard to say. Ford's Book, and Faulkner *1735*, restore the original, as in Davis edn. p. 250. (Note that the preceding ten pages consisted of Tooke's extraordinary rehandling of Swift's original, and consequently earned more than thirty repeated pencil strokes in the margins of the Armagh copy). |
| | 6. | 83 | Whoring (*deleted*). The word continues, unabashed, in all editions despite the deletion. |
| | 7. | 104 | Cause] Causes Unused. |
| | 10. | 164 | (mark, and underscored *o* in text) '9 *o*'clock' Another tiny clue identifying Swift, who spelled this with an 'a'. (See *Journal to Stella*, ed. Williams, p. 493, 'one a Clock', from MS portion; *Corresp*., II, 150, to Vanessa; and M. Shinagel, *Concordance to the Poems of Swift*, 1972, p. 1, s.v. 'A–CLOCK'.) Not used. |

Since the primary function of these static lists is to establish, in detail, Swift's responsibility for all the marginalia, words and marks, the movement of amendment between successive stages is only incidentally treated for reasons of space. What we undoubtedly discover is that virtually all the marginalia can be accounted for in the early textual history of *Gulliver's Travels*, that most of the seemingly inarticulate *marks* have a precise and demonstrable significance, and that nearly one third of the total number of points—twenty-three out of eighty-three—of textual intervention actually appeared in print, in Dublin, within weeks of London publication, in a rare edition which claimed, on its title pages, special textual amendment, and which provides inter alia six new substantive variant readings *which otherwise only occur in the Armagh volumes.*

Taken together this evidence may fairly be said to point to the author as responsible at least for its content, but there is, in addition, very good further evidence that all the words and all the marks, in ink and in pencil, are in the author's holograph and conforming to his system of correction and revision.

### *Swift's Handwriting*

Swift's handwriting has been illustrated in many books, in engraved facsimile and later photographically, since the early nineteenth century. But beyond many scattered references, and a somewhat random essay, there seem to be only two brief notes by modern scholars[68] which aim to deal with the subject. There is room for a methodical study, of which an outline is suggested below.

In order to distinguish a man's hand from those of his contemporaries, and also to reconcile the modifications and variations within his own practice, a useful first step is to identify if possible the model employed by him in his formative years (which he will share with others), and then the unique individual characteristics can be plotted and isolated by examining single letters and different combinations, as well as other features. In his elliptical account of his earliest years,[89] written very late in life, Swift recalled that his nurse took him when he was a year old to Whitehaven, 'where he continued for almost [two *erased*] three years'. 'The nurse was so carefull of him that before he returned he had learnt to spell, and by the time that he was three years old he could read any chapter in the Bible. After his return to Ireld, he was sent at six years old to the School of Kilkenny, from whence at fourteen he was admitted into the University of Dublin'. If we knew who in fact instructed Swift's class in handwriting at Kilkenny it would perhaps only support our conclusions drawn from the copy-books, or exemplars, of the time. Basically Swift's hand is well-controlled and legible, so that taking account of its later development one can compare its *earliest and neatest forms* with the range of authorities listed and illustrated in Sir Ambrose Heal's great survey *The English Writing Masters and their Copy-Books 1570–1800*, Cambridge 1931.

It is fortunate that today scores of pages survive from the decade of Swift's residence at Moor Park, when he copied out texts[70] with great care for Sir William Temple and his sister Lady Giffard, Swift being then in his twenties. Two examples have been published. A page of his transcript of Lady Giffard's translation of some songs from the *Diana* by Montemayor is illustrated in *Martha Lady Giffard*, ed. Julia G. Longe (1911), at p. 218. And a page from the Temple letterbook appears as frontispiece to *The Script of Swift and other Essays* by Shane Leslie (1935). The design of these cursive letters is very clear, as to both alphabets of minuscules and capitals, and virtually all of Swift's letter forms will be found in the tradition expounded by Louis Barbedor 'M$^{e}$ Escrivain Juré a Paris pour la verification des Escritures et Signatures', and published in Paris c.1650 in an ornate and handsome copy-book *Les Ecritures Financière et Italiane-Bastarde* (copy in the National Art Library, Victoria and Albert Museum),[71] see the series of alphabets on (pencilled) p. 55. According to Stanley Morrison[72] the Bastard Italian was Barbedor's favourite hand, who claimed it was the actual writing favoured not only by the Court and Persons of Quality but men of letters. The English writing master John Ayres was credited,[73] soon after his death, with having 'introduced the bastard Italian amongst us', and indeed all the letter forms[74] in these Moor Park manuscripts, with the occasional survival of secretary 'reversed' *e*, are present amongst others in the copy-books produced by Ayres from 1680 for the next twenty years.

The modifications made by Swift to this cursive Italian script, which Heal says came into vogue in England towards the end of the seventeenth century, can be seen in the many plates illustrating his hand. Two points can be noted, which serve to distinguish manuscripts *not* by Swift. He used the secretary 'reversed' *e* in his Moor Park period, and then he dropped it altogether in favour of the familiar Italian form used today. If one may judge from his holograph letters, he can be said to have commenced the regular use of the latter form in writing to John Winder on 1 April 1698 (*Corresp.* I, 25). The Greek form 'ε', much used at the time, he did not employ at all for normal text writing, but curiously for 'display' purposes, occasionally when inscribing in larger separated letters the address on the cover of a letter.[75]

Any discussion of the variations in Swift's hand will benefit from quoting, at the outset, a recent statement of general principles, delivered with the greatest authority and based on wide experience: 'Once a mature hand has been formed, as has usually happened by the time a writer is in his mid-twenties, it rarely undergoes any drastic change: its essential character normally persists throughout the writer's life, though it will be subject to gradual modification. This modification may afford clues to dating, but rash deductions about date have sometimes been made from the evidence of handwriting. In general, the variations of a mature cursive are attributed to changes in the writer's mood and the conditions under which he is writing more often than to any purely chronological development' (P. J. Croft, *Autograph Poetry in the English Language*, London, 1973, I, xvii).[76] Bearing this in mind we can examine some features of Swift's hand through the examples of forty years. They have been chosen from illustrations in modern books available in most large libraries, and in addition to the two examples given earlier of his meticulous performance as professional amanuensis, thirty specimens are chronologically listed in four broad categories, each reflecting a combination of distinct style and of varying care in execution. The mutation of different elements can thus be examined. From such scattered sources unfortunately no uniform measure can be given to indicate relative size, since nearly all are reduced, and to different scales. There is in reality a good deal of variation in size, partly affected by his eyesight and partly by the occasion, or the state of his quill or pencil. It is clear that as a young man he had good sight and a firm, sensitive hand, for he could and occasionally did write very small,[77] in which minuscule script his punctuation marks must be verified with a magnifying glass because of their delicate execution (commas are like the finest hair). He wrote small after his sight deteriorated, in haste, eliding words and syllables, often a barely legible mess.[78] Because of his eyesight in later years he also wrote larger than usual, and also perhaps when feeling unwell and therefore less able to control his pen. The writing in pencil is usually larger than normal and clumsy, because it seems always to have needed sharpening. An 'unmended' quill caused him to write larger, and sometimes merely the formality of the occasion or the person he was addressing. The leisurely, careful writing is nicely rounded out, following the writing master Edward Cocker's advice. But hurry produced a rapid, angular zig-zag, up and down, very unlike that.

The four broad categories have been labelled: FAIR, meaning *both* beautiful and free from blemish; AVERAGE, meaning unstudied but tidily executed; HASTY, in which there is a marked deterioration of letter forms, words do not adhere to a uniform base line, appearance is sloppy; and FOUL, where these factors begin to produce illegibility.

FAIR

*1* Inscription to Marsh, 1703. S. S. Smith, *Dean Swift* (1910), p. 18. *2 Baucis and Philemon*, 1706. P. J. Croft, *Autograph Poetry in the English Language* (1973), I, 62. *3 The History of Vanbrug's House*, 1706. *Poems of Swift*, ed. H. Williams, I, frontispiece. *4* Marginal addition to text of *History of the Four Last Years*, after 1712. Swift's *Prose Works*, ed. H. Davis VII, frontispiece. *5* Marginal memorandum in *Some Free Thoughts*, after 1714. Swift's *Prose Works*, ed. H. Davis, VIII, xxiv. *6 The Bubble*, 1720. *The Rothschild Library* (1954), II, 614. *7* Comment on Herodotus, 1720. Swift's *Prose Works*, ed. H. Davis, V, 243. *8 A Letter to a Young Lady*, 1723. G. P. Mayhew, *Rage or Raillery* (1967), p. 38 (and see *Prose Works*, ed. Davis, IX, 83, xxviii). *9 Directions to Servants*, c. 1724–5. Swift's *Prose Works*, ed. H. Davis, XIII, xii (N.B. *not* pp. xvii, xix.) *10* Document re copyright, 1732. Sotheby Sale Catalogue, 6 Nov. 1951, lot 424 (illustration).

AVERAGE

*1 A Dialogue in the Castilian Language*, 1707. S. Leslie, *The Script of Swift* (1935), p. 18. *2* Letter to Vanessa, 1712. *The Book Collector* (1953), II, 69(a). *3 Journal to Stella*, 1712. S. Leslie, *The Script of Swift* (1935), p. 2 (very small). *4 Some Considerations*, 1714. Swift's *Prose Works*, ed. Davis, VIII, 101. *5* Letter to Vanessa, ?1714. S. Leslie, *The Skull of Swift* (1928), p. 206. *6* To Charles

Ford, Esq. on his Birth-day, 1723. *Swift's Poems*, ed. H. Williams, III, frontispiece. *7* Letter to Mrs. Howard, 1727. *The Book Collector* (1953), II, 69 (b). *8* Letter to Motte, 1727. S. Goulding, *Swift en France* (1924), p. 84.

HASTY

*1 When I come to be old*, 1699. Swift's *Prose Works*, ed. H. Davis, I, xxxvii (actual size). *2 Journal to Stella*, Letter I, 1710. *Journal*, ed. H. Williams, p. 4. *3 An Enquiry*, after 1715. Marginal endorsement. Swift's *Prose Works*, ed. H. Davis, VIII, frontispiece. *4* Letter to Charles Ford, 1725. *The Rothschild Library* (1954), II, 618. *5 Directions to Servants*, c. 1724–5. Swift's *Prose Works*, ed. H. Davis, XIII, xvii, xix. *6* Memoranda in the *Holyhead Journal*, 1727. Swift's *Prose Works*, ed. H. Davis, V, 334. *7 Some Free Thoughts*, endorsement dated 1737 (doubtless intended to be 'Fair', now uncontrolled) *ibid.*, VIII, xxv. *8 Family of Swift*, c. 1737, *ibid.*, V. 192.

FOUL

*1* An early draft of a Will, c. 1727. Swift's *Prose Works*, ed. H. Davis, XIII, 199. *2* On his deafness, 1734. G. P. Mayhew, *Rage or Raillery* (1967), p. 39 (recto of unnumbered leaf preceding). *3* Notes for *Polite Conversation*, 1734–6. *Ibid.*, p. 39.

Anyone with the stamina to read through this list against the reproductions will note that these four categories are not mutually exclusive, that one style will appear in several, that they do not take systematic account of the degree of linking or separation which varies according to the occasion, and that there is no example of Swift's 'printing' hand (considered in due course). Broadly, however, they do demonstrate the range of variation in Swift's manuscript. But they also demonstrate the precise difficulties encountered by the first scholars who examined the Armagh *Gulliver*.[79] For, as we have seen, the bulk of the marginalia there occur in pencil (of which I have not been able to cite any published illustrations); and the 'printing' hand, employed by Swift on certain occasions, must be specially sought out.

The place to look, of course, is in the margins of other books annotated by Swift, particularly any work of his own bearing his comments or preparations for revision or corrections.

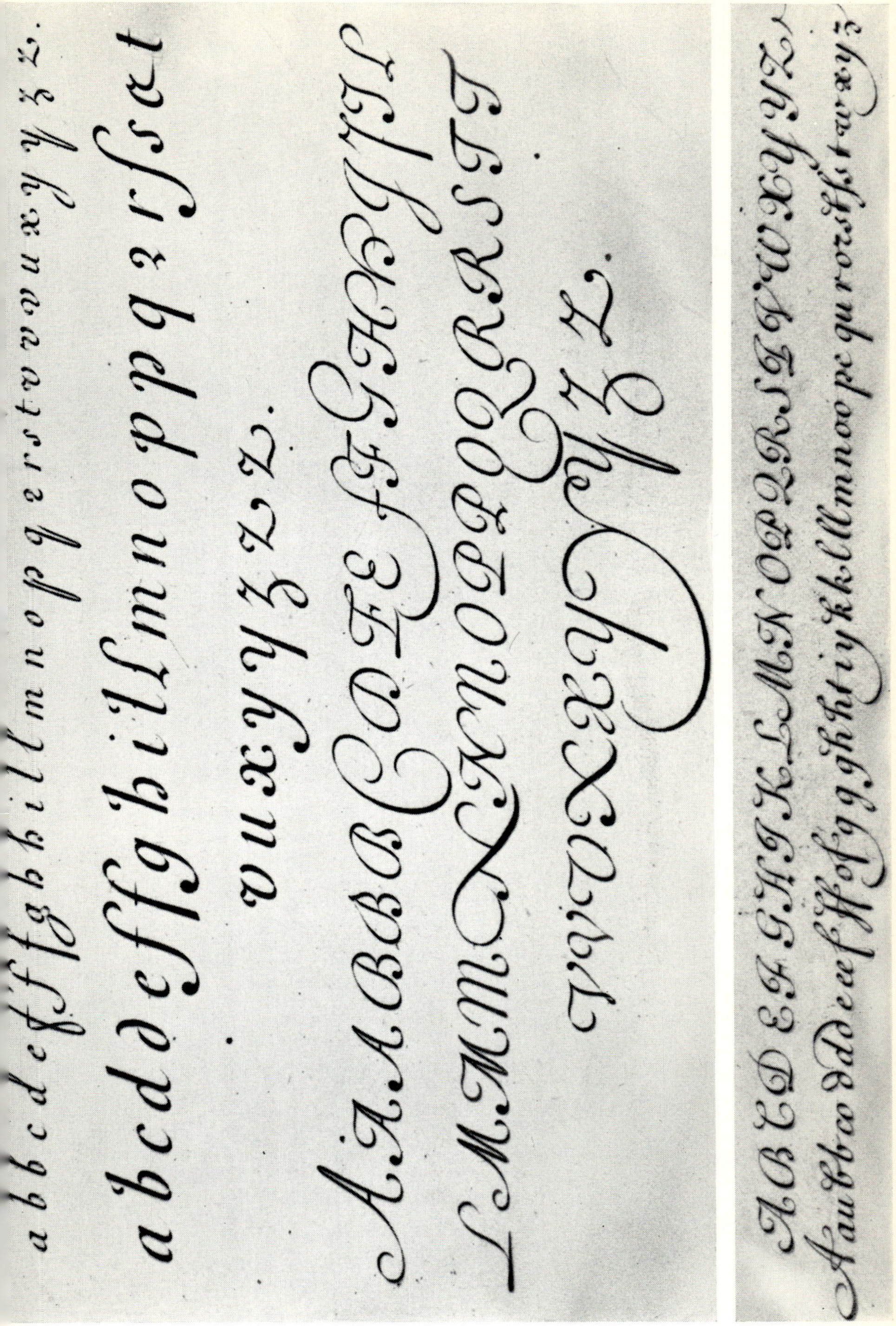

A B C D E

PLATE I: 17th Century Copy-Books

(*by courtesy of the Victoria and Albert Museum*)

A, B, C } L. Barbedor, *Les Ecritures*, Paris [c. 1650], p. 55 Excerpt

D, E } J. Ayres, *A Tutor to Penmanship*, London [1697–8], f. 11 Excerp

PLATE II: Marginalia in The Rothschild Library

(*by courtesy of the Librarian, Trinity College, Cambridge*)

1 *Miscellanies* (1727), I, 14. *Contests and Dissensions*
2 *ibid.*, I, 194. *A Project*
3 *ibid.*, I, 194. *A Project*
4 *ibid.*, I, 118. *The Sentiments*
5 *ibid.*, I, 116. *The Sentiments*
6 Scribal MS. of *An Enquiry*, fol. 39
7 *Miscellanies* (1727), I, 24. *Contests and Dissensions*
8 *ibid.*, I, 46. *Contests and Dissensions*. Pencil corrections
9 *ibid.*, I, 24. *Contests and Dissensions*. Two pencil corrections

Ex.

1 a — vantage, I look upon as a greater Evil than *Anarchy* it ſelf, as much as ^ *Savage* is a happier State of Life, than a *Slave*

2 this — Fear of ill Uſage from the Laity, have not a greater Share in ~~the~~ miſtaken Conduct, than their own Inclinations: How-

3 choqued — ſation, when once they were out of Fear of being ~~choaked~~ by Ribaldry or Prophaneneſs.

4 that ^ — that is uſually ſuppoſed to be a Thing ~~which~~ no Man can help in himſelf; which however I do not conceive

5 Beſt ✕ — generally by the Corruption of Manners, againſt which the ^ Inſtitution is no long~~er~~ Security, and without which a very ill one may ſubſiſt and flouriſh:

6 She therefore — of the Constitution eith[er] State; ~~And~~ determine all just and proper

7 although — wiſe while ſuch Hands were at the Helm,) ~~tho'~~ *impeach'd for high Crimes and Midemeanors*, ſuch *as Bribery, Arbitrary Proceedings, miſapplying or im-*

8 although — other Authors; ~~tho'~~ I do not think it neceſſary to deduce this Matter any further, ſo very particularly as I have ~~hither~~ done. — hitherto

9 ·|A| though — the *Fleet*, and being no ways a Match for them, ſet Sail for *Athens*; ~~a~~t his Arrival he was *impeach'd* by the Commons for Treachery, ~~tho'~~ not able to appear by reaſon of his Wounds, fin'd 30000 Crowns, and died in Priſon. Tho'ugh the Conſequences of this Proceeding upon the Affairs of *Athens*, were no other~~wiſe~~ than ~~by~~ the untimely Loſs of ſo

ſeveral further Acquiſitions. This however muſt be granted, that ('till about the Middle of the fourth Century) when the Senate appeared reſolute at any time upon exerting their Authority, and adhere cloſely together, they did often carry their Point. Beſides, it is obſerved by the beſt Au-

untill

to

*Dionyſ. Hal. Plutarch,* &c.

leſs than to make uſe of the whole Power, that is, to declare an Opinion to be Law, which has always been conteſted, or perhaps never ſtarted at all before ſuch an Incident brought it on the Stage. Not to conſent to the Enacting of ſuch a Law, which hath no View beſides the general Good,

: T

hath

nouriſh up a dormant Power, and reſerve the Privileges in *petto*, to exert upon Occaſions, to ſerve Expedients, and

be inſtructed, may apprehend he is got into a wrong Opinion, although the whole Courſe of his Mind and Inclination would perſuade him to believe it true; He may be convinced that he is in an Error, though he does not ſee where it lies, by the bad Effects

ments. I will help you to enough of them, ſhall be ready to allow the *Pope* as little Power here as you pleaſe; and the

who

late in Lyes and Impudence than his *Presbyterian* Brother. The Reaſon why I mention him, is to have an Occaſion of letting you know, that you have

X

thing could suffer Her to defer it.
When this Promotion was made, Mr
Secretary St John whose Merits and

numerous

34

time, which

PLATE III: The Rothschild Library *continued*

10 *Miscellanies* (1727), I, 46. *Contests and Dissensions*. One pencil correction

11 *ibid*, I, 14. *Contests and Dissensions*

12 *ibid.*, I, 14. *Contests and Dissensions*

13 *ibid.*, I, 118. *The Sentiments*

14 *ibid.*, I, 227. *A Letter concerning the Sacramental Test*

15 *ibid.*, I, 219. *A Letter concerning the Sacramental Test*. Pencil cross

16 Scribal MS. of *An Enquiry*, fol. 34

17 Scribal MS. of *An Enquiry*, fol. 34

Ex.

18 not above a Foot diſtant, ſo that I could hardly ſqueeze my Body betwixt them. However, I made a ſhift to go forward till I came

19 my Veracity. I then ſhewed him the Gold given me by the Emperor of *Lilliput*, together with his Majeſty's Picture at full length, and ſome other Rarities

20 Field under the Window, where we ſtood. *Alexander* was called up in the Room: It was with great difficulty that — into

21 to — brought me at ſeveral times by ſome of my Friends; but although they were

22 to be thoſe who turn to Dotage, and entirely loſe their Memories; theſe meet with more Pity and Aſſiſtance, becauſe they want many bad Qualities which — Understandings

23 Kind from the Imputation of Singularity upon the Article, if there had been any *Swine* in that Country, (as un-

24 lids and Liquids, and the inferior for Ejection, theſe Artiſts ingeniouſly con-

25 large Chamber, and an Aſſembly of ſomewhat a latter Age, in Counterview in another. The firſt ſeemed to be an Aſſembly of Heroes and Demy-Gods;

26 ſhould ſpeak in *England*, as a *Yahoo* in *Houyhnhnm-land*. The honeſt *Portu-*

27 despised — THEY are deprived and hated by all ſort of People; when one of them

28 a Fool, a Lord, a Gameſter, a Politician, a ~~Whore-maſter~~, a Phyſician, an Evidence, a Suborner, an Attorney,

PLATE IV: The Armagh *Gulliver*

*(by courtesy of the Public Library, Armagh, N.I.)*

18 Part II, ch. 1, p. 9. Correction in ink
19 Part I, ch. 8, p. 145. Correction in pencil
20 Part III, ch. 7, p. 101. Pencil
21 Part III, ch. 10, p. 144. Pencil
22 Part III, ch. 10, p. 141. Pencil
23 Part IV, ch. 7, p. 113. Pencil
24 Part IV, ch. 6, p. 88. Pencil
25 Part III, ch. 7, p. 101. Pencil
26 Part IV, ch. 11, p. 172. Pencil
27 Part III, ch. 10, p. 144. Pencil
28 Part IV, ch. 12, p. 198. Pencil

Examples 18–28 are indicated by **bold** typeface in text references thus, Armagh II. **9**

### *The Armagh Handwriting and Marks*

THE PRINTING SCRIPT. For some reason the fair margin beside a column of printed text prompted Swift occasionally to write in a clearer, more formal style than his usual flowing cursive. In its most extreme form it approaches a simulation of print, being upright and without serifs. More relaxed, it leans very slightly from vertical, the letters still detached and formal in design; and this tendency eventually produces a pleasing, sloped italic, semi-cursive, which is however still a distinct 'printing' hand. The particular range can be illustrated readily from the similar practice of Alexander Pope, in two modern facsimiles: manuscript versions of *An Essay on Man*, Epistle II (in P. J. Croft, *op. cit.*, I, 69, 70, 71), and in his autograph transcript of Lady Mary Wortley Montagu's *Court Eclogs* (ed. Robert Halsband, New York: New York Public Library, 1977). Pope's workaday cursive in the foul copy of the *Essay* is transformed to a delicate and comely italic in the fair text, whose side notes are a sloped 'printing' script. In *Eclog I* the first and third pages show examples of the text proper as a calligraphic exercise in beauty and legibility, the footnotes of classical parallels in italic, followed by the citation in simulated roman print.

Swift's 'printing' hand is to be seen in the margins of his own copy of the Pope–Swift *Miscellanies*, 4 vols. 1727–32, now in the Library of Trinity College, Cambridge (Rothschild 1422), and in his copy of John Browne's *Essay on Trade* (1729), now in Cambridge University Library, Williams collection no. 538 (these latter marginalia are published in *Prose Works*, ed. Davis, V, 256–7). The former example shows scripts from cursive through sloped italic to upright printing, and examples of ink and pencil, clearly inscribed at different times (from which the present accompanying illustrations are taken);[80] while his comments in the latter are in the printing hand gently sloping to the right. Further, in the Houghton Library at Harvard his comments in the margins of John Putland's copy of Macky's *Memoirs* (1733), are indeed *autograph* and in this style, which may account for Davis's mistaken notice[81] of the volume in *Prose Works*, V, xxxv.

The photographic examples of Swift's marginal handwriting

*in other volumes* are given in the actual size of the original, to facilitate comparison with the Armagh handwriting. Examples 1–7 are arranged to show the 'printing' hand, in ink, becoming progressively less formal, leaning, and then linking, until finally there is the full running hand. Ex. 1 can be compared with the same letter in ink in Armagh II. 36, 47, 48. Ex. 2 is made up of the same letters, in the same order, as Armagh I. 36, IV. 68 (both in ink), and Armagh III. 94 (pencil). Ex. 3 terminal two letters, compare with Armagh I. 51, four *e*'s, *u*, and a straight-stemmed *d* in ink (varied in Armagh I. 50). The minuscule *d* is also rendered in *pencil*, rather differently, in Armagh III. **141**, **144**. The *h* is at Armagh II. 47 in ink, and see exx. 4, 11, 14 below; for cursive *h* in ink see exx. 6, 7, 11 (the second), and in pencil exx. 8, 9. Capital *H* is in ex. 13, l. 5 (cf. Armagh I. 36), interpolated. Ex. 4 provides two *t*'s against Armagh II. 65 in ink (and see exx. 5, 10). Ex. 5 in ink, italic style, reduplicates the pattern and tilting of 'last' at Armagh IV. **113**, even with different letters. Ex. 6 gives, in ink, the *style* of cursive employed in the pencilled words at Armagh III. 71, **144**, IV. **88**, in which not all letters are linked. Ex. 7 in full cursive does not find a counterpart in Armagh, but has been included to provide an instructive contrast with ex. 8, being the same word 'although', written by Swift in ink and again in pencil.

THE WORDS IN PENCIL. The difficulty of satisfactorily reproducing pencilled writing perhaps accounts for the absence of published specimens, but in fact many of Swift's marginalia are written in pencil of not very good quality by today's standard. We forget now that pens needed replacement and upkeep, requiring a sharp knife and some skill and that ink was a problem, so that a blunt old pencil was the easy way out when recording a chance revision or correction. We find a number of Swift's texts, printed and manuscript, with both ink and pencil marginalia from his hand in the same work. Thus the Armagh *Gulliver*, and thus the *Miscellanies*, 1727–32. The pencilled writing is always executed with a clumsy thick line, nearly always grey in tone and lightening here and there into illegibility. Consequently the writing is larger than in ink, not as well controlled, and the letters take on a related but rather individual shape; they tend to lean at different angles and to dispense with the tiny flourishes. Hence the very odd look of 'bending' at Armagh I. 79, and the clumsiness of 'Understandings' at Armagh III. 141; for Swift it was an awkward medium.

The first word in ex. 8 has been compared with its ink equivalent in ex. 7, both for style and size. The second word ends in 'to' *cursive*, with which compare pencil 'to' *disjunct* in ex. 10, and the termination of Armagh III. 101 also in pencil. A cramped isolated pencil *t* occurs at Armagh IV. 50. Ex. 9 includes two rather faint versions of the same word, the first showing an exaggerated spread (cf. Armagh III. 141, a word overrunning); the second, in the pattern of amending a printed word by cobbling it in manuscript (cf. Armagh II. 30) instead of rewriting, a procedure employed also by Charles Ford in his two *Gullivers*. See two other examples interpolated in the text of ex. 13, ll. 2, 5. Ex. 10, compare the same word in pencil in Armagh III. 144. In ex. 8 *er* of 'hitherto' may be compared with Armagh IV. 185, both in pencil.

MARKS, DELETION SYMBOL, CARET, PUNCTUATION, SCORING OUT, OVERWRITTEN CROSS. The following comparisons are valid for both ink and pencil. The diagonal slash, a single stroke, is the commonest mark,[82] see ex. 13: it seems to have served as an advance signal to locate a desideratum and then as a flag *after* this had been attended to; there are about forty in the Armagh *Gulliver*. Two parallel strokes (tramlines) occur four times there, once in conjunction with a recorded revision (Armagh I. 79). The saltire cross is more common, eight in Armagh, with two revisions present at III. 144, and IV. 166; see illustrated pencil cross in ex. 15, and ink in exx. 5, 16. The T-junction mark in Armagh at III. 115 is not apparently an incomplete cross because it can be found elsewhere, and similarly the tilted cross of Lorraine at IV. 9. The slash and St. Andrew's cross are quite common through texts[83] marked by Swift. Exx. 9, 11, 12 illustrate ink specimens of the deletion symbol on the same pattern as the two in pencil at Armagh IV. 45, 198. In exx. 6, 10 the *double* caret in the text, l. 6, is also not an aberration, but a variant symbol found in Armagh IV. 88 and in the holograph of *Apollo to the Dean*, at l. 50.[84] The single caret was standard for Swift, as the illustrations show. Punctuation added or changed was usually marked directly into the text, ex. 13, l. 5 (cf. Armagh III, 110), and the comma was often an enlarged hook, ex. 16, l. 2 (cf. Armagh II. 9, III. 110). In deleting a word from a text, Swift often used a vigorous lateral scrubbing technique, see exx. 2, 3, 4, 5, 11, sometimes a single horizontal line through the word, exx. 7, 8, 9, 12, sometimes a short line under the word; all of these are in the Armagh *Gulliver*, and not any other techniques. Ex. 16 gives the oddity of writing the revision actually *through* the marginal cross, observed also in Armagh *Gulliver* at III. 144, producing a basic ambiguity; this also occurs elsewhere.

Finally, ex. 17 gives a page number in Swift's hand, suggesting that the manuscript renumbering of p. 74 in Armagh III, misprinted 44, is the only intrusion of another hand than Swift's into the text of the Armagh *Gulliver*.

## *Conclusion*

To summarize, then, an extended argument: there is good evidence that such a copy as the Armagh *Gulliver* was in existence at the time of Swift's death, and in his possession. The second recorded owner of the Armagh copy, one hundred years later, for some reason correctly identified the marginal hand as the author's; an unknown earlier provenance could have provided a clue. No independent examination of the hand has so far come to light earlier than about 1929. A sceptical view based, as has been shown, on inadequate experience of Swift's manuscript and his editorial practice, has prevailed in the small scholarly literature on the Armagh copy for thirty-five years past. Swift's handwriting merits detailed examination, of which the outline here provides a minimum to validate the Armagh hand, by reconciling two very contrasting styles. In textual content the words and marks in the margins of this copy can be shown, in the established history of *Gulliver*'s text, to have a precise and extensive significance which is not apparent on casual inspection. Finally, the immediate publication of more than a quarter of the textual changes in the Armagh copy, in what must now be regarded as the first authorized Irish reprint of *Gulliver*, having in common six unique readings, establishes the authority and the priority of this stage of revision of Swift's masterpiece.[85]

Can we say more about the origins of the Armagh marginalia? Is it the first source for all these changes, or merely an abbreviated record? As much space again would be taken up in seeking the answers. For the moment we may celebrate the survival of that most desirable association copy of any book—Swift's own marked copy of *Gulliver's Travels*.

### Appendix I

*Charles Ford's letter to Benjamin Motte of 3 January 1727, Forster MS. 561*

The letter and list of errata are written consecutively on the first and third pages of a large folio sheet of paper (318 x 204 mm.), the second page left blank and the fourth (the 'cover') carrying the address and postmarks. The letter occupies the upper half of p. [1], and is written in a neat deliberate hand, the lines well spaced but curiously the words too are individually spaced out, suggesting a formal fair copy. In the first sentence the change from 'as well' to 'both' is probably stylistic improvement, not a mere correction. The list, headed 'Errata', commences straight after the signature and continues over onto three-fifths of p. [3], the rest of which is blank. Immediately, the spacing of lines and words is contracted, and a number of slips or mistakes are made and rectified in the course of writing. Ford seems to have been copying from a 'paper' listing page numbers, followed by the 'corrected' (i.e. sometimes revised) reading or alternatively a general stricture or critical observation; which however left *him* to retrieve from Motte's text, and to record, the faulty reading. Ford goes wrong at Part 4 page 8 when he inadvertently copies the correction first, has to score it out, resume with the corrigendum, and a second time transcribe the correction lying before him, leaving out and then inserting 'time', in his confusion. Towards the end these organizational slips increase: e.g. at Part 4 pages 130, 133, 134, 146. He starts his list using a 'should be' formula, changes quickly to 'for', reverts to 'must be' and 'should be', and twice at the end uses 'r.' [=read]. The crowded appearance and relative untidiness of the list, as against the clearly executed letter, suggest an element of improvisation and also uncertainty in estimating the demand he would make on limited space. He could not be sure how far notation of the corrigenda proper would expand the author's own list of corrections, so he started the list on a tighter spacing. It came out successfully short, for two-fifths of p. [3] remain unused. The following (*) argue for Swift's composition of the list: Part II, 140; Part III, 42, 90, 101 (bis); Part IV, *8* (*bis*), *67*, 69, 90, 91, 93, *97*. In three of them some words have been added after writing: III, 101 (bis), for clarification; IV, 8 (bis), a restoration; IV, 69, (i) for clarification, (ii) a restoration. The last instance is specially significant, being the longest single item, but also a peroration about Swift himself in which his words take wing characteristically. 'Candour,' *added* was I suggest a word in the examplar, omitted at first by Ford; for it is scarcely essential to clarify the meaning, while it is very much part of the *spiel*. Three times there are third person references to 'the Author', a *persona* routine habitual to Swift, used for example in nearly all chapter headings of *Gulliver*, in the prefatory matter provided for each of Faulkner's four volumes of Swift's *Works*, 1735, and even on their title pages (see *Prose* XI, 3; XIII, 181–7), the most absurdly thin of disguises. The editorial half-brackets in the present text show where another hand has clumsily scored a thin wobbly line through or under most of the items asterisked above (italicized are those which escaped)—one can only guess whose hand. All these asterisked items failed to appear along with the remaining errata in Motte's fourth 8vo edition (1727), being in each case a stricture without specifying a remedy—except one, *viz.* Part IV page 8 (bis), which accordingly did appear in 1727.

This document survived intact with others in the Motte–Swift archive, into the nineteenth century, cp. note 58 above. Among them too was another clearly pseudonymous letter *in Ford's hand* to Motte, signed 'Rich$^{d}$ Sympson', 27 April 1727, written within a week of Swift's arrival in London and relating to *Gulliver's Travels.*

In this transcription angle brackets ⟨ ⟩ enclose text deleted by Ford, diagonals \ / denote his insertions, half-brackets ⌜ ⌝ indicate text lightly scored over, or under, in ink of a darker colour, and different quill. The whole document, including the address, is in Ford's handwriting. Enough of the seal remains to show that it was Ford's, a shield displaying three lions rampant, the crest a demi-lion, the motto NOLI IRRITARE [LEONES].

Forster 561

*Charles Ford to Benjamin Motte*

*Address:* To | M$^{r}$ Benjamin Motte Bookseller | near the Temple in | London

*Postmark:* $\frac{10}{1A}$ *DUBLIN* *Seal*

Dublin Jan 3. 1726[–7]

Sir

I bought here Capt$^{n}$ Gulliver's Travels publish'd by you, ⟨as well⟩ \both/ because I heard much Talk of it, and because of a Rumor, that a Friend of mine is suspected to be the Author. I have read this Book twice over with great Care, as well as great Pleasure, & am sorry to tell you it abounds with many gross Errors of the Press, whereof I have sent you as many as I could find, with the Corrections of them as the plain Sense must lead, and I hope you will insert them, if you make another Edition.

I have an entire Respect for the Memory of the late Queen, and am always pleas'd when others shew the same; but that Paragraph relating to her looks so very much beside the Purpose that I cannot think it to have been written by the same Author. I wish you & your Friends would consider it, and let it be left out in the next Edition. For it is plainly false in Fact, since all the World knows that the Queen during her whole Reign governed by one first Minister or other. Neither do I find the Author to be any where given to Flattery, or indeed very favourable to any Prince or Minister whatsoever.

These things I let you know out of perfect good Will to the Author and yourself, and I hope you will so understand me, who am | S$^{r}$ your affectionate Friend & Servant | Cha: Ford

**Errata**

Part. 1. Page 22. Use should be Uses. P. 36. ⟨\it/ should be.⟩ of his Council 79. arrived to for arrived at. 80. bold for boldest. 144. Pledges I had left. 145 Lilliput ⟨s$^{d}$ b⟩ \for/ Blefuscu

Part 2. P. 9. However I made a shift. 30. toward for forward. 47. her Majesty perhaps. 48. Dominions, and had. 98. least his Honour for least his Courage. 108. Praise for Praises. 111. all Questions for several Questions. 120 were enobled, were advanced, for are enobled, are advanced. 133. ⟨s[d] be⟩ the Inclemencies ib. Species of Man for Species of Men. 140. ⸢not directly over, the Sense is imperfect.⸣ 156 his own Presence for his Presence 161. necessary for me while.

Part 3. P. 31. Spirits for Sprites. 34 Womenkind for Womankind. 42 ⟨*injury*⟩ Goodness. ⸢For this Advantage &c., the Sense imperfect.⸣ ib. the Discoveries for their Discoveries 44 Death for Dearth. 49 Abode here for Abode there 59 Act for act. 71 write both for write Books. 73 or the Square for as the Square. 74 in the Book for in Books. 77. Saddles for Sacks. 78 the Ambassadors for thus Ambassadors 83. Method of Cure for Methods of Cure. 85. dispose of them for dispose them. 87. Persons for Person's. 89. To take a strict View. ⸢P. 90. to the end of the Chapter seems to have much of the Author's manner of thinking, but in many places wants his Spirit.⸣ P. 94 was a part for is a part. 101. in the Room for into the Room. ib. ⸢Assembly of somewhat a latter Age, this must have been altered, for \the word/ Assembly follows immediately after.⸣ 102. Ancestors for Ancestor 110 Faction for Factions. 119 Apr. 1711. for Apr. 1709. P. 119. a Passage for the Passage. 121 had never heard. 133, Languages, Fashions, Dress for Language, Fashions of Dress, 134 Choice for choice. 137 these Kingdoms for those Kingdoms 138 eldest for oldest 140 they were too few. 141 come for comes to be fourscore. 142 continuing for continue. ib. forgot for forget. 144 brought to me. ib. sort of People for sorts of People. 152 conver for convey 154 petformed for performed ib. arrived safe to for arrived safe at.

Part 4. P. 8. sharp points, and hooked. ⸢ib. Hair on their Heads, but none on their⸣ ib. P. 8. long lank Hair on their Faces, nor &c. This Passage puzled me for some\time/, it should be long lank Hair on their Heads, but none on their Faces, nor 17. before them for before him. 31. fare for fared. 42 Secret of my having 49, Oats, when for Oats, where. 50 treasted for treated, old for sold, ill for till. 51 meanest Servant for weakest Servant. ib. rouling for rolling. 53. Office for Offices. 54 one of my Forefeet 56.

Trade it is. ib. called a Queen. 60. Points of which for points which 65 For those Reasons for For these Reasons ib. likewise another Kind for likewise a Kind. 67. Seafights. is there no mention of Land fights? 68 my Hoof for his Hoof. P. 69. ⸢\towards y$^{e}$ end/ &c. manifestly most barbarously corrupted, full of Flatnesses, Cant Words, and Softenings unworthy the Dignity, Spirit,\Candour,/ & Frankness of the Author. By that admirable Instance of the Cow it is plain the Satyr is design'd against the Profession in general, and not only against Attornys or, as they are there smartly styl'd, Pettifoggers. You ought in Justice to restore those twelve pages to the true Reading.⸣ P. 85. and Conveniencies for or Conveniencies. 86 operated contrary d. the one. 88. it must be inferior posterior to answer to anterior superior. ⸢Part of P. 90 and 91 false & silly, infallibly not the same Author 93. at last by an Act of Indemnity, abrupt.⸣ P. 97. a great Man. Nonsence. the Author is not talking of great Men, but of Men highly born. I believe it should be ⸢*of a Noble Birth,*⸣ or rather *Marks of Noble Blood.* ⸢I take this Page to be likewise corrupted, from some low Expressions in it.⸣ P. 99 enlightened for enlarged. 109 produced in them the same Effects. ib. ⟨for⟩ taken my self, it should be, This I have since often known to have been taken with success, 112. with the Females as fiercely. 113 upon the last Article ib. nor could the Servants for nor did the Servants. could follows. 121 scratch about for search about. 127 be[stow] him one. 130 hard, and stony for hard stony. 130 ⟨for⟩ were immediately for are immediately 133. Oooze ⟨and⟩ \or/ for Oooze ⟨or⟩ \and/ 134 ⟨for⟩ old ones for elder. 138 Mem[ory] for Memorys. 141 several covered for certain covered 144 cut their for cuts their 145 Room to be made for me 146. Of these I made. for Of these I also made. 147 Splenatick for Splenaticks. 149 for the Thoughts r. their Thoughts, and for their Discourse r. the Discourse 152. my Friends, and my Countrymen for my Friends, my Countrymen. 157. an unnatural 182. became for had become 186 temptations for Temptation. 192 in some modern for in modern ib. Discovery for Discoverys. 194 a Desire for any Desire 195 may concern for more concerns.

## Appendix II

*Collation sent by H. Williams to H. Davis, August 1940 (from the typescript in the Davis papers, Bodleian Library, Oxford)*

*Note:* At I. 79, 'turning' is a misreading of Swift's 'bending'.

### COPY OF 'GULLIVER'S TRAVELS' IN ARMAGH PUBLIC LIBRARY

In the Armagh Public Library is a large paper copy of *Gulliver*, portrait in first state, which was bought by Jonathan Osborne at the auction of the Hon. Colonel Howard of Castle Howard, 12 Feb. 1847.

Dr. Osborne was a medical man of Dublin, and a book-collector. Dr. Jordan of Armagh married Osborne's daughter, & the volume probably came through them to the Armagh Library.

The two volumes contain a number of corrections in ink or pencil, in a hand I cannot identify. The corrections are tabulated below. Those in pencil are specified; otherwise they are in ink.

| *Pt.* | *p.* | *l.* | |
|---|---|---|---|
| I. | 36. | 12 | His (in margin before 'Council') |
| | 50. | | Blue, Red, Green |
| | 51. | | Blue, Red, Green |
| | 79. | 8 | turning (in margin for 'binding' (*pencil*) ) |
| | 80. | 23 | (Pencil ticks in margin) |
| | 145. | 8/9 | Blefuscu (in margin for 'Lilliput' (*pencil*) ) |
| II. | 9. | 13 | However (in margin to follow 'them') |
| | 30. | 7 | ly (in margin to follow 'toward') |
| | 36. | 19 | Green Eagle (struck through, and, in margin 'Horn and Crown') |
| | 47. | 2 | perhaps (in margin to follow 'Majesty') |
| | 48. | last | and (in margin to precede 'had') |
| | 65. | 22 | 'Creatures' (struck through, and, in margin 'Insects') |
| III. | 71. | 23 | Books (in margin for 'both' (pencil) ) |
| | 87. | 9 | Natures (double line, in pencil, follows, and pencil strokes in margin) |

| | | | |
|---|---|---|---|
| | 90. | 3 | (The para. beginning 'I told' has a pencil x in margin, and, on the next page, a pencil tick at "Custody." There are also pencil ticks on pp. 92, 93) |
| | 94. | 7 | Is (in margin for 'was' (pencil) ) |
| | 101. | 5 | ('in' underlined in pencil, and 'into' written in pencil in margin. There are also some pencil ticks at the foot of the page, one below 'Assembly' in the last line) |
| | 119. | 4 | (A pencil tick in margin, and below 'in') |
| | 141. | 10 | Understandings (in margin for 'Memories' (pencil) ) |
| | 144. | 1 | to (in margin to precede 'me' (pencil) ) |
| | 144. | 13 | despised (in margin for 'deprived' (pencil) ) |
| | 108. | 19 | (pencil tick in margin, and below 'Family') |
| | 114. | 20 | (pencil tick in margin, and below 'this') |
| IV. | 45. | 13/14 | ('to' is struck through, and marked (pencil) for deletion in margin, and 'would' in the next line is underlined in pencil) |
| | 50. | 10/11 | ('s' and 't' supplied in pencil) |
| | 65. | 6 | ('e' in pencil in margin, and 'o' of 'those' struck through) |
| | 68. | 16 | his (in margin, and 'my' struck through) |
| | 83. | last | (pencil tick in margin, and 'whoring' struck through) |
| | 88. | 12 | posterior (in margin to follow 'inferior' (pencil) ) |
| | 104. | 7 | s (in margin to follow 'Cause' (pencil) ) |
| | 113. | 2 | last (in margin to precede 'Article' (pencil) ) |
| | 164. | 10 | (Pencil tick under 'o' of 'o' Clock') |
| | 166. | 18 | (a pencil x in margin before 'mong') |
| | 172. | 17 | or (in margin, and 'as' underlined (pencil) ) |
| | 185. | 20 | were (in margin for 'was' (pencil) ) |
| | 198. | 3 | ('Whore-master' struck through, and marked for deletion in margin (pencil) ) |

There are also ticks or lines in pencil against passages amended or restored by Ford.

## NOTES

1 Since 1930, *pro*, the Public Library authorities, H. Teerink, the present writer; *contra*, Harold Williams, Herbert Davis, John Hayward, amongst others. Two recent editions of *Gulliver's Travels* have declared unequivocally in favour of authenticity—ed. Angus Ross (London, 1972); ed. Colin McKelvie (Belfast, 1976). In the standard text of *Gulliver* in vol. XI of Swift's *Prose Works*, ed. H. Davis, the editor denies the hand to be Swift's. See Andrew Carpenter in *The Irish Times* 25 Sept. 1976, C. L. McKelvie, *ibid.*, 5 Oct.; and further 8 Oct., correspondence in 2, 18, 23 October 1976.

2 See *Travels*, ed. H. Williams (London, 1926), p. xxxvi, n. 1. This is no. 8551 in *A Catalogue of the Printed Books bequeathed by John Forster* (1888), pp. 479–80.

3 *A Catalogue of Books the Library of the late Rev. Dr. Swift* (1745), p. 16, lot 657. See Sotheby's auction catalogue, 15 July 1929, property of G. W. Panter, lot 369. For a description of the volume now at Cornell I am much indebted to Dr. Donald Eddy, Rare Books Librarian. That this is indeed the same book, subsequently mated (or immediately reunited) with a matching first volume, can be proved from the contemporary inscription on the title of Vol. II 'Bought at Swift's Auction. Praeti. 0–2–0'; for this one-off price is recorded in the margin of John Putland's priced copy of the 1745 *Catalogue* (Forster FD.10.97) as ': 02: —'. A similar verified inscription is to be found in Forster 361 (lot*627 Baconi *Fran.* Opera omnia, priced '—: 05: —' by Putland in his 1745 *Catalogue*) which has on the title in a contemporary hand 'Bought at Swift's Auction, Praeti [£]0.[s]5.[d]0.' Possibly the same purchaser in each case.

4 Teerink 289, ed. A. Scouten (1963), pp. 195–7. *Travels*, ed. H. Williams (1926), pp. lxxxv–vi. In sig. M of Part III, pp. 153–5, a number of typographical errors—turned letter, foul case, wrong fount—stand uncorrected in those large and small paper copies seen. But one error, on p. 155, l. 1, '*Guiuea*', is correctly '*Guinea*' in some small paper copies, suggesting that these were last to be printed. In the Armagh copy the reading is '*Guiuea*', uncorrected.

5 I am grateful to the Master and Wardens of the Worshipful Company of Stationers and Newspaper Makers for permitting inspection of the original entry.

6 Sold, among valuable gifts and bequests, 'The Property of Sion College', at Sotheby's on 13 June 1977. The only copyright title in the sale, its disposal may presage the destruction of a precious national archive of deposit copies, 1710–1836.

7 Including the handsomely bound set, vols. I and II, in blue Turkey leather accompanying Swift's presentation copy of Temple's *Letters to the King* (1703), to Lorenzo Magalotti (British Libr. C. 28. f. 5).

8 For example, Forster 8718 (with the bookplate of Charles, Lord Hali-

fax, 1702); British Libr. G. 14841, 42 (the Duke of Shrewsbury's copy) —both in handsome contemporary red leather bindings.

9 *A Tale of a Tub*, ed. Guthkelch and Nichol Smith, 2nd edn. (corrected, 1973) p. lxviii. *The Library of William Congreve*, ed. J. C. Hodges, 1955, no. 554.

10 British Libr. 838. g. 1; Bodleian Libr. 8°. Y. 24. Jur.; Sion College ARC/K12. Also Rothschild 2015, 2016, 2017 (possibly Congreve's copy, listed in Hodges, *op. cit.*, no. 553), all at Trinity College, Cambridge. Another large paper copy is in the Rare Books collection at Smith College, Northampton, Mass. The British Library copy has been reproduced in facsimile, correctly margined, by the Scolar Press, with an Introductory Note by C. P. Daw (1972).

11 Teerink no. 761 (ed. 1963, p. 368). Copies on large paper: Rothschild 2158, 2159 at TCC.

12 Teerink, ed. 1963, pp. 22–3. Copies on large paper of the original editions of vols. I—[VII] are in Rothschild 2151, 2172 at Trinity College, Cambridge, and in the Teerink Collection at Pennsylvania University Library. The seventh volume was published in 1741 as *Letters to and from Dr. J. Swift* (Teerink no. 62B, ed. 1963, p. 143) and the presentation copy, on large paper prettily bound, inscribed (not in Swift's hand) 'Doctor Swift's gift to Doc[r] Wilson' on the flyleaf, is at ULC, Williams 218. (Cf. Dobell's Catalogue no. 105, item 21.) John Hayward's set of Faulkner's large paper vols. I—[VII] was sold at Sotheby's, 15 March 1966, lot 349. Vols. I–IV (1735) are at the Huntington Library, no. 81494, on large paper.

13 I am obliged to Philip Gaskell for this estimate.

14 Forster 8551 (see n. 4 above); and the Pierpont Morgan Library, New York. See *The Dickensian*, vol. 70 (1974), pp. 194, 201 n. 18.

15 It appears immediately after the title-leaf of *Works* (1735), vol. III, on the recto of $\pi$2 (see Teerink no. 41), and is reprinted by Davis in *Prose*, XI (ed. 1959), 3.

16 The correction of printing errors in Part IV, p. 50, lines 11, 12 is relevant only to large paper copies (*Travels*, ed. H. Williams [1926], lxii). If Ford's list of errata is simply a transcript from an original compiled by Swift, as maintained in Appendix I, this suggests that Swift too was working from a large paper copy. The particular correction is made, in Swift's hand, in the Armagh copy on large paper.

17 Pope's *Corresp.*, ed. Sherburn (1956), II, 417–18; Swift's *Corresp.*, ed. Williams (1963), III, 189–90. Letter dated [27] Nov. 1726.

18 The publisher of Colin McKelvie's edition of the *Travels* (Belfast, 1976) has conveniently provided reproductions of four pages from the Armagh *Gulliver* showing seven words in ink (three repeated), subject to slight technical distortion. A curious reader will observe, from their unique foxing patterns that the same background of old paper has been used for both facsimile pages 50 and 65, and another for both pages 51 and 36; while yet other paper is backing these same pages on the lower cover, or dustjacket. None of this paper is from the

Armagh *Gulliver*. The technical processes involved have distorted areas of the print on these pages and subtly affected the handwriting, making it altogether more gross than the original. No cautionary note to this effect appears.

19 My own examination of the volumes at Armagh in the minimum light conditions of late November was followed up independently by Andrew Carpenter eight months later, in July 1977, when the Armagh *Gulliver* was in Dublin briefly for expert repairs to the bindings by John F. Newman and Son. For this second opinion, the discovery of the blind crosses, and many other kindnesses I am greatly indebted to Dr. Carpenter. In the following list of locations the Part and page numbers are followed by super-script line numbers indicating position in right or left margin.
I. $52^{1\text{-}3L}$ $59^{1\text{-}2R}$ $68^{9\text{-}11L}$ $102^{11\text{-}12L}$ II. $5^{\text{headline-}5R}$ $40^{19\text{-}21L}$ $114^{13\text{-}14L}$ $119^{8\text{-}9R}$ $132^{4\text{-}6L}$ $136^{6\text{-}10L}$ $156^{11\text{-}14L}$ III. $51^{10\text{-}11R}$ $61^{13\text{-}14R}$ $62^{\text{chapt. summary}L}$ $71^{3\text{-}5R}$ $76^{8\text{-}10L}$ $83^{17\text{-}19R}$ $87^{22\text{-}23R}$ $92^{17\text{-}20L}$ $122^{10\text{-}13L}$ IV. $98^{\text{chapt. summary}L}$ $108^{17L}$ (*doubtful*).

20 Williams's monograph, *Dean Swift's Library* (1932), which reproduces in facsimile the 1745 *Catalogue*, was researched, written and published *before* he had seen the Armagh *Gulliver*. His conjectures on pp. 56–7, connecting lot *492 with Ford's annotated copy, though consistent with his subsequent view of the handwriting, can be treated with proper reserve in the light of later research. At the sale on 3 Feb. 1746, lot *482 fetched 8s. 1d., lot *486 £1 5s., and lot *492 (the *Gulliver*) 7s.—all annotated by the author—less than their new prices on publication. Cf. note 3.

21 Described in remarkable detail in the formal entry, under 'Miscellanies', in *The Rothschild Library*, 2 vols. (Cambridge, 1954; repr. London, 1969), I, 367–72. The majority of examples of Swift's hand, in ink and pencil, illustrated here in plates II and III are from this source. For comparison, mainly pencilled examples are given from the Armagh *Gulliver* in plate IV, because the ink specimens are shown elsewhere, and line facsimile fails to convey the subtle distinctions in medium. See note 18.

22 *Catalogue of the Library at Lough Fea in Illustration of the History and Antiquities of Ireland* (London: privately printed at the Chiswick Press, 1872). [Bodleian Libr. shelfmark: 259. a. 42.] p. 318: 'Swift (Jonathan) *The Works*, 6 vols. 8vo. Dublin, 1738. This copy belonged to the Dean himself, and was purchased at the auction of his effects in 1745–6. Inside the cover of the fifth volume is this inscription, "Read thorough", in the Dean's well-known autograph'. And see Shane Leslie 'The Shirley Library at Lough Fea, Carrickmacross in Co. Monaghan, Ireland' in *The Book Collector's Quarterly*, no. VI (April 1932), at p. 7. Williams records his opinion of the set in his edition of Swift's *Poems*, 2nd ed. (1958), p. l, formulated before 1937 and clearly meriting reconsideration.

23 John Lyon (1702–1790), clergyman and antiquary, noticed in *DNB*.

See Alan R. Eager, *A Guide to Irish Bibliographical Material* (1964), p. 323, no. 3645. He is footnoted by F. Elrington Ball in his ed. of Swift's *Corresp.*, V, 383 nn. 2, 3; and by H. Williams in his ed., *Corresp.*, IV, 534 n. 2. Lyon's detailed work on the inventory of Swift's library in 1742 and 1744 can be seen today at Abbotsford, cf. H. Williams, *Dean Swift's Library* (1932), pp. 10, 13. Further, Lyon owned for nearly forty years the set of Burnet's *History of my Own Time*, which bore in its margins the copious marginalia inscribed in pencil by Swift, *ibid.*, pp. 61–2. The connexion of Lyon with the 1745 auction *Catalogue* is established from salvaged waste paper in an article in *N & Q*, First Series, V, 292 ff. His competence as a judge of Swift's autograph can scarcely be questioned.

24 Swift's *Prose Works*, ed. H. Davis, V, plate opp. p. 243.

25 See *Travels*, ed. C. McKelvie (1976), p. 16 and n. 16. Part I of Sharpe's *Catalogue* (the main series) is followed by Part II, an additional series headed 'Books omitted', in which the *Gulliver* occurs, as Mr. McKelvie kindly informs me. The RIA copy is unpriced.

26 Jonathan Osborne (1794–1864): a biographical sketch of him by James Little M.D., and chronological list of his published writings (in medical research) by T. P. C. Kirkpatrick M.D., appears in *Dubl. Jo. of Medical Science*, March, 1915.

27 Thomas Jordan, D.D., Rector of Magherafelt (co. Derry), inst. 5 Dec. 1878. Prebendary of Loughgall, 1886–1900; Treasurer of Armagh Cathedral, from 1900 until his death on 7 Feb. 1908. He married, as his second wife, Florence d. of Jonathan Osborne M.D. on 14 June 1866, who died 12 Jan. 1868. See James B. Leslie, *Armagh Clergy and Parishes* (1911), pp. 45, 72, 365; corrected by the same author's *Supplement to Armagh Clergy and Parishes* (1948), p. 135. Jordan was a member of the Library Board.

28 From information kindly given by the present Keeper of the Public Library, Armagh, the Very Rev. H. A. Lillie, Dean of Armagh.

29 William Reeves (1815–1892): see Lady M. C. Ferguson's *Life of the Right Rev. William Reeves, D.D.* (Dublin, 1893), including a list of his published writings. Reeves sent John Forster accurate transcripts, in his own hand, of Swift's letters to Archbishop King at Armagh, 8 Feb. 1860 (Forster 48 E.26, item 16). His name is revered to this day in the Public Library, where he spent twenty-five years as Keeper, 1862–1887.

30 In the *List of Books selected from the Catalogue of the Public Library of Armagh, with a Catalogue of its Manuscripts* (Belfast, 1892), 67 pp., there is no entry of the *Gulliver* in the printed books or manuscripts categories. Forde Tichborne, *St. Patrick's Cathedral, Armagh, A short history* (1932), p. 22, specifies the *Gulliver* in an account of the Public Library, contributed by James Dean.

31 Letter of J. Dean to M. J. Ryan, in my possession. He added 'Of Jonathan Osborne I know no more than that he was a Dublin M.D., and the father-in-law of the late Rev. Dr. Thos. Jordan, a former

canon here, which last fact I expect accounts for the gift of the book to the Library. Canon Jordan died twenty-one years ago.' See n. 27 above, for Jordan's connexion with Armagh Cathedral over a period of twenty-two years.

32 Ryan was a Dublin solicitor and book collector, whose special interests included the earliest Irish reprints of eighteenth-century authors. He died in 1937. See *The Irish Times* 13, 14 July 1937 (*ex inf.* Andrew Carpenter).

For Harold Williams, knighted in 1951, see the memoir by Geoffrey Tillotson 'Harold Herbert Williams 1880–1964', in *Proc. of the Brit. Academy*, LI, 455–66.

The first edition of Teerink's *Bibliography of Swift* was published at The Hague in 1937. He died in 1961. A long-overdue tribute to Teerink's achievement is to be found in G. P. Mayhew's review of the revised edition (*PQ*, XLIII, 1964, 395), edited by A. H. Scouten (Philadelphia, 1963).

33 The mistaken view that these manuscript changes were in Swift's hand perhaps found confirmation in the ambiguity of Forster's reference, *Life of Swift* (1875), p. viii, repeated in the Forster collection *Catalogue*, 1888, p. 480. Cf. *English Letters and Letter-Writers of the 18th Century* (1st Series, Swift and Pope), ed Howard Williams (1886), plate opp, p. 272—a full page from the interleaves in Ford's autograph, tacitly shown as Swift's. The error was demonstrated by G. R. Dennis in *The Athenaeum*, 19 Jan. 1898, pp. 153–4, by the simple expedient of comparing Ford's holograph signed letter to Motte, Forster MS. 561, and the *Gulliver* marginalia, side by side.

34 Information from the Public Library, by favour of the Keeper.

35 The letters from Teerink and Williams to Ryan, and from Ryan and Davis to Williams, are quoted from the originals in my possession. Ryan also visited Armagh Public Library at some time, for among his notes are a marked sheet of paper measuring the dimensions of the *Gulliver*, and hasty jottings in his hand relating to their other Swiftiana.

36 University Library, Cambridge, Add. MSS. 7788 (Box 14); the notebook is not paginated. Entry on leaf 6, r. and v.

37 See *University Review* [Dublin], IV, 1967, pp. 89–90: 'The Shakespeare Head *Swift*' by Sir Basil Blackwell. Davis's letters to Williams bear this out. And see the memoir by Helen Gardner, 'Herbert John Davis 1893–1967' in *Proc. of the Brit. Acad.*, LIV, 289–99.

38 Like the rest of us Williams had to acquire his skills. On handwriting he continued to be fallible. In 1929 he came to the conclusion that Stella's word-book (sold at Sotheby's, 22 June 1976, lot 252, and plate) was in Swift's hand, though he changed his mind the next year. Before 1932 he saw Swift's hand in Macky's *Memoirs* apparently without recognizing it (see note 81 below). However, as late as 1952, in his Sandars Lectures he reprinted 'Richard Sympson's' letter to Motte, 17 April 1727 (original now in the Pierpont Morgan Library)

with a footnote 'I agree with Dr. Teerink that it does appear to have been written by Swift himself in a deliberately disguised hand' (*The Text of Gulliver's Travels*, p. 16. n. 1). In 1963 this information reappears 'The Letter and address are in Swift's hand with a clumsy attempt at disguise' (*Corresp.*, III, 206, n. 1). But without doubt the hand is that of Charles Ford, undisguised. See note 33 above.

39 See J. J. Stathis, *A Bibliography of Swift Studies* (1967), p. 103, nos. 650, 651, for Williams's reply to reviews of *The Text of Gulliver's Travels* (1952).

40 *The Legacy of Swift, A Bi-Centenary Record of St. Patrick's Hospital, Dublin* (1948), ed. M. J. Craig, p. 65, no. 60. The exhibition was held in the Royal College of Physicians in Ireland, in connection with the Swift Bi-Centenary and the Dublin meeting of the Royal Medico-Psychological Association, May 1948. This volume also includes six important essays on Swift's hospital through two centuries.

41 See correspondence in 'Points', *The Sunday Times*, 22 August 1976. Nearly thirty years later Dr. Craig has been able to detail Hayward's references to the Armagh *Gulliver*. Hayward wrote from England on February 20, 27 and 29 (1948) expressing disbelief in the claims that the handwriting was authorial. On 4 March he wrote 'It is known to Williams and Davis . . . The annotations are *not* in Swift's hand, but the Armagh copy is well worth exhibiting all the same. You should write a note on it based on Davis's description of it and the other annotated copies [He then goes on to berate the Armagh Librarian and the Armagh Curator for their ignorance, in typically Haywardian vein.]' Maurice Craig concludes 'I am positive that when he saw the book at the exhibition he found no reason to change his opinion one way or the other. In other words he regarded my catalogue-entry as going as far as the evidence warranted.' I warmly thank Dr. Craig for this information.

42 Without doubt Hayward knew very well the annoted copy of the Pope–Swift *Miscellanies*, 4 vols., 1727–32 (see n. 21 above), the source of the present accompanying illustrations, which had been in Lord Rothschild's collection since 1935, at his house, Merton Hall, Cambridge (see *The Book Collector*, 1965, p. 473), and which is described in the catalogue, where his assistance is acknowledged, I. ix, x. A year after the Dublin exhibition the Cresset Press published *Selected Prose Writings of Swift*, ed. J. Hayward (1949), including some 'Thoughts on Various Subjects' from the second volume of the set (see *The Rothschild Library*, I, 368, n. 4). These 'Thoughts' however are by Pope, as Spence was told in 1735 (*Observations, Anecdotes*, ed. Osborn, 1966, I, 60, anecdote 144). Hayward regrettably failed to notice, or to accept, the similarities in the marginal scripts and marking between the Armagh *Gulliver* and the set of *Miscellanies*. I feel that he deferred excessively to Williams on Swift.

43 Item 11 in the exhibition, the title opening illustrated at p. 8 of the printed catalogue, 1967. The Dolmen Press of Dublin issued a Ter-

centenary Tribute collection of essays, *Jonathan Swift*, ed. R. McHugh and P. Edwards (1967), the illustrations after p. xx including photographs of two annotated pages from the Armagh *Gulliver*, *viz.* Part I, pp. 50, 51.

44 Teerink no. 297 (1963 ed. p. 204).

45 Teerink no. 298 (1963 ed. p. 205).

46 The replies of Dennis and Hubbard to Williams are in my possession. Hubbard was a Regent of the University of Michigan from 1911 until his death in 1933. In 1922 he presented to the University Library, at Ann Arbor, his collection of Imaginary Voyages numbering about 2,600 volumes, half of it devoted to Defoe's *Robinson Crusoe*. Some 600 volumes constitute the section on *Gulliver's Travels*, being editions, translations, and some complete editions of Swift's *Works*. Hubbard's *Contributions towards a Bibliography of Gulliver's Travels to establish the number and order of issue of the Motte Editions of 1726 and 1727, their relative accuracy and the source of the changes made in the Faulkner Edition* (Chicago: Walter M. Hill, 1922), is a pioneer work of considerable merit acknowledged by Williams (*Travels*, 1926, p. vii). He had trained as a geologist.

47 A poor thing, it lacks pp. 75–94 and 256–74, there is no portrait, and only the upper cover survives. Of the portrait I salvaged the lower right corner, enough to prove that the unique surviving example in Ryan's copy was original (see H. Williams '*Gulliver's Travels*: Further Notes' in *The Library*, fourth series, IX, 188). This is now ULC, Williams 235. It is to be hoped that more copies will come to light.

48 Ryan's invoices from R. B. Fleming and Co., and duplicates of the facsimiles, were sent by Mrs. Ryan to Teerink in August 1939, who in turn gave them to me in January 1958.

49 Classmarks: Williams 235, 236. Unfortunately the perfect copy, the former, has suffered extensive 'restoration', having been disbound, the portrait and sigs. A. B. C washed and re-sized, re-sewn and re-cased in the original covers, and pressed. The spine label seems original. The made-up copy has been re-backed after insertion of the modern facsimiles.

The covering letter, dated 12 July, is pathetic in the extreme. Ryan died the same day, knowing that he would never complete his work on *Gulliver*.

50 Published sources include: *A Dictionary of the Printers and Booksellers 1726–1775* (1930), p. 390. *A Catalogue of the Bradshaw collection of Irish Books* (1916), I, 105–7. D. Foxon, *English Verse 1701–1750 A Catalogue* (1975), II. Index of Imprints, s.v. Hyde, John and ——, Sarah.

51 See Robert Munter, *The History of the Irish Newspaper, 1685–1760* (1967), pp. 19–30. Joseph Ray's immediate successor in business was his widow; Munter, p. 34.

52 See *Prose Works*, ed. H. Davis, VI, 207.

53 Swift's *Corresp.*, II, 313, 318, 324, 329, 347, 379, 416–17, 419–20,

421. A reprint of this collection in small format was published in Dublin soon after. 'POEMS ON Several Occasions. By MAT. PRIOR, Esq; *DUBLIN*: Printed for *J. Hyde* in *Dame-street*, *R. Gunne* in *Caple-street*, *R. Owen* in *Skinner-Row*, and *E. Dobson* in *Castle-street*, Booksellers, 1719.' See Prior's *Literary Works*, ed. H. B. Wright and M. K. Spears (1971), I, xxxvii, n.

54 ULC, class-mark: Hib. 7. 725. 7.

55 Swift's *Prose*, V, 109 and plate, 351. This first Dublin edition is not in Teerink's *Bibliography of Swift* (1937–1963), and the copy used by Davis is at Trinity College, Dublin, shelfmark 54. T. 102. no. 4.

56 ULC, class-mark: Hib. 3. 725. 3. Ryan also noted the same edition advertised in *The Dublin Intelligence or Weekly Gazette* no. 2525, Tues. 29 Nov. to Sat. 3 Dec. 1726; repeated Tues. 6 Dec. to Sat. 10 Dec., 1726; also no. 2529, Tues. 13 Dec. to Sat. 17 Dec., 1726. The second edition is advertised as 'just published' in *Faulkner's Dublin Post Boy*, 2 Feb. 1726–7; as 'also published' in *The Dublin Journal*, no. 185, Sat. 28 Jan. to Wed. 1 Feb. 1726–7, and no. 186, Wed. 1 Feb. to Sat. 4 Feb., 1726–7. Teerink's discussion of some of these advertisements seems mistaken (1963 ed., pp. 204–5): in Teerink no. 299, the second edition, the printer appears in the imprint 'Printed by S.P. for G. Risk, G. Ewing, and W. Smith in *Dame's-street*'.

57 *Corresp.*, III, 257, 310.

58 Reprinted in Appendix I, from Ford's holograph in Forster MS. 561. Both the letter and list were printed in the *Gentleman's Magazine*, Feb. 1855, pp. 148–50. The letter alone, not quite accurately, is in *Corresp.*, III, 194. Ford's slips in writing, noted in my transcription, suggest that he was copying out both letter and list from a composed text lying before him.

This holograph, with three letters from Swift to Motte, and receipts from Swift to Tooke, was sold at Puttick and Simpson's, 20 July 1855, lots 69–70, having descended in the family of Motte's partner and successor Charles Bathurst (Forster 48.E.26, items 91–2). It is therefore unnecessary to speculate that it 'may probably' have been returned to Ford (H. Williams, *The Text of Gulliver's Travels*, 1952, p. 26). 'Sympson's' letter to Motte, 27 April 1727, *also in Ford's hand*, was in this archive (see note 38 above). And see *Travels*, ed. W. Cooke Taylor [1840], pp. 5–7.

59 Clauston Jenkins, 'The Ford Changes and the Text of *Gulliver's Travels*', *PBSA* 62 (1968), 1–23, indicates that his study was based on modern printed accounts of the Ford changes (see p. 2, n. 6), from which of course all the manuscript clues have been effectively edited out. (See Appendix I.). His conclusions rest upon the unquestioned premise that letter and list represent Ford's independent judgement.

60 'Point' is slightly rule-of-thumb: very occasionally more than one mark, used to denote a short or long repair, counts as one (Armagh III. 101), and two localized adjoining repairs count as one (IV. 50).

61 See H. Williams, *The Text of Gulliver's Travels* (1952), p. 23.

62 Advertised in *The Scriblerian* IX/1 (Fall, 1976), p. 66, and distributed in early 1977, the first printing omits Maps I and II and the text of pp. 154–5 of Part III; enlarges the text size and some marginalia; transposes Swift's corrections at I. 50; diminishes to absurdity those at I. 145, II. 36, III. 141, 144, IV. 88; shows a blank margin, without Swift's notations, at II. 47, IV. 65, 104; and wholly omits the significant marginal marks at fifty-four points. The publisher advises (30 June 1977) his intention to replace all copies of the defective edition with a new printing in which the various faults are corrected, to be ready in late 1977.

63 Compare the commentary, and digest of earlier attempts to decode these words, in *Travels*, ed. Angus Ross (London, 1972), pp. 286–294. And see the Note and glossary in Swift, *Oeuvres*, ed. E. Pons (Bibliothèque de la Pléiade), 1965, pp. 9–24.

64 Identified in Davis's apparatus by siglum W (*Prose*, XI, 301); see Carroll A. Wilson, *Thirteen Author Collections* (New York, 1950), I, 430–2, and Bernard Quaritch's Catalogue no. 432 (1930), pp. 21–3, item 216, at Cat. p. 22.

65 Deleted from the Carroll Wilson copy ('with the author's own Amendments'), see note 64 above. Quaritch cat. 432, p. 23.

66 Not to venture far in deep waters, a straightforward text of 274 pages in Long Primer, 22 ems by 41 lines, would over a period of four weeks require each of four compositors to average an output of 30,893 ens per week, which is well within the upper limits given by D. F. McKenzie, *The Cambridge University Press 1696–1712* (1966), I, 120 (Table 13). To reduce the number of weeks, or of men, by one an average weekly output of 41,191 ens would be required, and indeed two exceptional, higher figures are given in the Table. On the earlier figure a daily average of 5,148 ens compares with 5,700 and 5,603 given by McKenzie, p. 119, or an hourly rate of 429 ens comparing with 'seldom more than [500 ens]' (Philip Gaskell, *A New Introduction to Bibliography*, 1972, pp. 54–5).

67 Andrew Tooke, brother of Swift's 'bookseller' Benjamin Tooke Jr., is noticed in *D.N.B.*, and was named by Swift in his letters to Charles Ford, first published in 1935 (ed. D. Nichol Smith), as the inserter of 'a good deal of trash contrary to the Author's Manner and Style, and Intention' (9 Oct. 1733), see *Letters of Swift to Ford*, pp. xliv, 154, 162. Faulkner added an editorial footnote to his 1756 printing of *Gulliver's Travels* in 18mo (Teerink no. 309), sig. Aa2$^{r}$, which first publicly identified him as '**The Reverend Mr.* TOOKE, *who left out some Paragraphs, and put in others of his own, which were set right by the Author in all the Editions printed by* GEORGE FAULKNER *in* Dublin.' The asterisk refers to '*a Person* since deceased*' (in *Prose* XI, 3, line 5).

68 (i) T. J. Brown, 'English Literary Autographs: V Jonathan Swift' in *The Book Collector*, II (1953), p. 69 and plate. (ii) P. J. Croft, *Autograph Poetry in the English Language* (1973), I, 62. Mr. Croft's

commentary is central to the study of post-mediaeval English handwriting.

The essay was originally a lecture delivered by Shane Leslie at the University of Pennsylvania, on a foundation by Dr. Rosenbach, in 1933–4 and published with excellent plates in 1935 as *The Script of Swift and other Essays*, referred to later.

69 *Prose*, V, 192. For its date of composition, see I. Ehrenpreis, *Swift* (1962), I, 30, n. 5.

70 see *The Rothschild Library* (1954), II, 609–10; items 2251–5. From the Temple letter-book, nine lines in Swift's formal copy-hand are illustrated by A. C. Elias Jr., 'Stella's Writing-Master', *The Scriblerian*, IX/2 (1977), 136.

71 Shelfmark: RC. T. 6. Three alphabets from (pencilled) p. 55 are illustrated in plate I.

72 In 'The Development of Handwriting: An Outline': Ambrose Heal, *op. cit.*, p. xxxiv. See also Herbert C. Schultz, 'The Teaching of Handwriting in Tudor and Stuart Times', *HLQ*, 1943, p. 416.

73 See the account of Ayres in *D.N.B.* Heal's comment on this qualifies the statement to mean 'the later, and more cursive, form' of Italian Bâtarde (*The English Writing Masters*, p. 8). Two alphabets from *A Tutor to Penmanship* [1697–8] by Ayres, fol. 11, are illustrated in plate I from the V. & A. copy, shelfmark 86. K. 17. A fine copy is at ULC, classmark LA. 8. 94.

74 The specimen alphabets illustrated from the copy-books of Barbedor and Ayres in plate I establish the tradition within which Swift's hand was formed, but they are only a starting point (as noted above) to determine the details of execution and combination of variant forms, which make up his particular hand in its different manifestations. For example, his early *W*, both capital and minuscule, is not shown at all, which in his fair hand was made up in effect from *v* and *u*, linked, and often thereafter reflected that imbalance between the limbs. Closer study will reveal the sequence of pen-strokes in writing letters, both singly and in combination.

75 The address on the cover of Letter XLIII of the *Journal to Stella*, in March 1712, is reproduced by A. D. McKillop, *English Literature from Dryden to Burns* (1948), p. 137, in which Greek ε is used for 'Ireland', written large.

76 Quoted by permission of the author and Cassell and Co.

77 Examples are: 'When I come to be old 1699', *Prose*, I, xxxvii and plate. Many of the unpublished Account Books, see *Corresp.*, V, 222 (Appendix II), of which a meticulous edition has just been completed by Paul V. Thompson. And parts of the surviving manuscript of the *Journal to Stella* in the British Library (ed. H. Williams, 1948, I, xlviii, n. 3).

78 An extreme example showing all these features is Forster MS. 533, *The Dean to himself on St. Cecilia's day* (*Poems*, II, 521–2), first printed by Deane Swift in 1765, and brilliantly deciphered. Line 3 is

metrically incomplete in the MS, and conjecturally restored by editors; in line 4 *read* 'blowers' *for* 'players', Swift's revision *currente calamo* and a better description of trumpets and hautboys.

79 It is opportune here to record a tribute of affection and respect to Teerink, Williams, and Davis, whose sustained labours made possible the present essay.

80 By permission of the Master and Fellows of Trinity College, Cambridge.

81 Confusion persists through all accounts of the various manuscript texts of Swift's marginalia on Macky. The *holograph original* is that at the Houghton Library, the gift of Donald and Mary Hyde, seen by Williams before 1932 (*Dean Swift's Library*, p. 63, n. 1), who failed to recognize the handwriting. Putland, who owned this volume, then in his own hand transcribed the notes into another copy of Macky (sold in 1974 by Paul Grinke, Catalogue 10, item 161) which became the immediate source of Nichols's printed text of 1779 (*Supplement to Swift's Works*, in three formats: see large 8vo. vol. XXV, pp. 429, 462).

82 This was also used in the margins of books he was reading, e.g. Clarendon's *History* (*Prose*, V, see p. xxxviii), sometimes in conjunction with an underline in the text.

83 Examples are: MS. of *Some Free Thoughts* (Roths. 2263), at pp. 27, 29, 30, 33. Both MSS of *An Enquiry* (Roths. 2264), with ink slashes throughout, and pencil crosses in the scribal copy, autograph corrections or revisions by Swift in both. The scribal MS. of *Directions to Servants* (Forster MS. 528) has crosses (St. Andrew's *and* St. George) on fifteen folios, and changes, some in Swift's hand.

84 In the Pierpont Morgan Library, call number MA 1207, p. 2 of the manuscript. The corresponding double caret stands at the head of twenty-three lines, in Swift's holograph, on a separate smaller leaf, being part of the Morgan Library MS of this poem, in the form of an insertion. This leaf is in the Dreer Collection of Autographs (*Catalogue*, 1890–3, II, 150) at the Historical Society of Pennsylvania in Philadelphia. At the sale of J. W. Croker's collection, Sotheby, 6 May 1858, the complete manuscript was lot 165: 'Swift. Lines to Appolo (sic)', occupying 3 folio pages and an addition as a correction for insertion; the whole in the autograph of Swift. On the basis of the completed holograph it is now possible to show that this *was* in fact the source for Stella's transcript at Woburn (*Poems*, I, 260).

85 For advice and assistance over the last ten years, and for permission to publish, I am deeply grateful to the Academic Division of Oxford University Press, particularly to John Bell and Dan Davin.

# 7

# Gulliver's Glasses

by PAT ROGERS

Lemuel Gulliver is perhaps the first bespectacled hero in English literature. Very early on we learn (I, ii) that he held back from the Lilliputians the contents of 'one private Pocket which escaped their search'.[1] These 'little Necessaries' were 'a Pair of Spectacles (which I sometimes use for the Weakness of mine Eyes) a Pocket Perspective, and several other little Conveniences . . . I apprehended they might be lost or spoiled if I ventured them out of my Possession'. From the start, then, Gulliver associates his glasses with secrecy, privacy, ownership, identity. I shall argue that this is connected with the mixed feelings about *sight* which Swift reveals, and that such a concern lies at the centre of the *Travels*. There will be three stages in the argument: a brief consideration of the psychology of spectacles; a discussion of attitudes to the faculty of vision in Swift's day; and then, at greater length, an application of these ideas to *Gulliver's Travels*.

## *1*

Spectacles were not known to the ancients, which might suggest they would conveniently serve as a symbol for the moderns. (In *The Battel of the Books*, as a matter of fact, Descartes is killed by an arrow through his right eye owing to 'a *Defect* in his *Head-piece*'.)[2] Optical aids began seriously around the fourteenth century, but the major development came in the seventeenth. Charles I granted a charter to the guild of Spectacle Makers in 1629, and with the need for more accurate scientific lenses there was a steady improvement in the techniques of grinding glass—although Newton still had to cut his own prisms. By the eighteenth century portraits commonly show sitters equipped with reading glasses, perched on inquisitive or acquisitive faces. Benjamin Franklin invented bifocals around 1760 and claimed that he understood French better with the help of his spectacles—presumably for lip-reading.

It is an elementary observation that spectacles flourished after the invention of printing, and indeed they have always been connected in people's minds with intellectual enquiry. They stand for a certain masterful negotiation of the external world. In popular writing they are often an emblem of vulnerability or retreat from the physical; the school swot is always duly equipped, whilst in Western movies the schoolma'am removes her glasses as she shakes down her hair in a well-understood gesture of sexual awakening. The presence of spectacles is often a clue to character in more serious literature, however: Mr. Pickwick or Widmerpool would scarcely exist without this vital personal effect, and indeed we contemplate 'the bald head, and circular spectacles' of Pickwick before we learn anything at all about him—in the Phiz illustration they are the nearest thing to us in the entire scene, as Pickwick inclines forward at an angle. There is a feeling that someone who wears spectacles is not quite himself when bereft of them—yet a man who drops his glasses is comic, whereas a girl rooting about on the floor for a missing contact lens is merely embarrassing. (The glasses are separate from the self, whereas the contact lens is like an intimate part of the body itself.) Though they are intended to supply a defect of nature, spectacles can be *used*, as props in a lecture or as agents of a steely implacable gaze. They are allotted a special status, quite implausibly, as a mark of intelligence or curiosity. This is perhaps clearest with devices such as a lorgnette or quizzing-glass; it is interesting to note that (many productions of Restoration comedy notwithstanding) the quizzing-glass did not come in until about 1800, and in fact the word *quiz* with its associations of close interrogation dates from the same period. *OED* gives no usage earlier than the 1780s and reports a story that the word was invented by an Irish theatre manager as late as 1791. Whatever Lady Wishfort and her kind did, it cannot have been quizzing.

## 2

Poor eyesight abounded in Swift's day, and no-one can have been unaware of visual defects. There were many inherited conditions, with glaucoma sadly in evidence; total blindness must have been very much more common than today, although there are of course no firm statistics. Reading in semi-darkness cannot have improved things in a number of cases, and the obstinate Augustan determination to hold everything by candle-light, from funerals to auctions, seems like a perverse reinforcement. In 1710—the very year when Defoe left his glasses in Newcastle[3]—one of Swift's missions in London was to obtain two pairs of spectacles for Mrs. Dingley: later he had to get a pair for Stella herself. A cargo sent back to Dublin finally included 'four pair of spectacles for the Lord knows who.'[4] The *Journal to Stella* also records Swift's concern with the failing sight of his friend Congreve, by now almost blind with cataracts on both eyes. He mentions that Congreve can no longer read without a magnifying-glass.[5] One recalls that by the age of forty Pope was unable to read by candle-light; though he enjoyed the friendship of the great surgeon William Cheselden, his last years were badly affected by eye troubles. Various afflictions beset Dr. Johnson, Burke and Horace Walpole (who acquired a pair of green glasses); Lady Mary Wortley Montagu at sixty-one was surprised enough to thank God that her sight served her yet without glasses.[6] Then there are the cases of musicians such as Bach, Handel and the blind composer John Stanley; Handel went more than once to Cheltenham and Bath to assist in his treatment, and it is not generally recognized that the valetudinarians at any spa included a large proportion of people with eye trouble. Of course, ophthalmic science was not very advanced; the princely Duke of Chandos asked his wine merchant amongst others for advice and was recommended to put Portugese snuff in the corner of his eye. The merchant supplied a recipe involving first washing the eye in urine and then anointing it with viper's fat. Chandos got a second opinion from his doctor, who suggested confining the regimen to the viper's fat.[7]

Swift himself was subject to eye disorder. In the birthday poem he wrote for Stella in 1725 we get one of the few direct admissions:

> 'Tis true, but let it not be known,
> My eyes are somewhat dimmish grown;
> For Nature, always in the Right,
> To your Decays adapts my Sight,
> And Wrinkles undistinguish'd pass,
> For I'm asham'd to use a Glass;
> And till I see them with these Eyes,
> Whoever says you have them, lyes.

Characteristically, Swift's ostensible subject is the fact of *Stella's* ageing. Sir Harold Williams comments, 'Even in old age Swift refused to adopt spectacles.'[8] This may be put down to simple vanity, but there seem to be deeper worries at hand. We have heard a good deal about the progress of Ménière's disease, the deafness and the giddiness; perhaps Swift felt just as acutely about the loss of his visual powers, though he was less open about the subject. It was generally agreed at this period that (in Locke's words) sight was 'the most instructive of the senses'. As well as Newton's *Opticks*, writers like Molyneux and Swift's friend George Berkeley had erected a whole psychology of perception around the faculty of vision. The importance for Swift of developments in the microscope has been shown before now; it is interesting to see him in a lighter mood, idling away the moments until Harley falls in the summer of 1714, professing detachment in the not-very-remote vicarage at Letcombe, as reported by Pope in a letter to Dr. Arbuthnot:

> As for the methods of passing his time, I must tell you one which constantly employs an hour about noone. He has in his window an Orbicular Glass, which by Contraction of the Solar Beams into a proper Focus, doth burn, singe, or speckle white, or printed Paper, in curious little Holes, or various figures.[9]

Could a man with such a hobby speak innocently of the 'Glass' of satire?

## *3*

Meanwhile, back in Lilliput, Gulliver is hanging on to his optical aids. He is, we notice, prepared to give up to his captors his money, his watch, his guns, his razor, his handkerchief, his knife and even his 'Journal Book'. Contrast with this the reactions of Robinson Crusoe on his arrival at the island. When Crusoe lands, he has neither clothes nor weapon on his person: 'I had nothing about me but a Knife, a Tobacco-pipe, and a little Tobacco in a Box.' However, he makes twelve trips to the wrecked boat, bringing back a variety of stores and provisions. Among these things, though 'of less Value', he lists 'three or four Compasses, some Mathematical Instruments, Dials, Perspectives, Charts, and Books of Navigation, all which I huddel'd together, whether I might want them or no.' In point of fact it is nearly eighteen years before he apparently thinks to make use of his telescope, and takes a resolve 'to go no more out without a Prospective Glass in my Pocket.'[10] Crusoe has been too busy doing, making, creating. His daily life is organized around the objects he can see with the naked eye. There is no occasion for prying into the centre of things, for looking below the surface. Gulliver's trouble is that he is always trying to peer and peep.

One of the very few critics to have taken any account of Gulliver's spectacles, W. B. Carnochan, reaches the conclusion that he is 'the myopic hero' whose lack of understanding is symbolized by the weakness and vulnerability of his eyesight.[11] I think almost the opposite—that the glasses represent visual over-development, hypertrophy of the sight. Gulliver lives through his gaze and his traveller's *curiosity* rather than through any settled principles or inner resources. His spectacles are, so to speak, bionic eyes, probing everywhere, hoarded lovingly like sexual attributes, secret, self-directed, protective. His 'insatiable Desire to see the World' is fed by his bespectacled competence as an observer. A common mistake, in my view, is to suppose that the narrator of the *Travels* is a mere victim of circumstance: a neutral patient rather than a constructive agent of his own fate. It is true that he is a man without qualities; but that is precisely the point. He has travelled so much, studied and applied himself—he measures everything down to the Brobdingnagian hailstones that fall on him—he is always *computing* (a favourite verb)—yet he has very little moral identity. He has been too preoccupied by watching to receive any direct impress from life. His character is an extension of that of Addison's *Spectator*—whose social background is closely allied, too.

> Thus I live in the World, rather as a Spectator of Mankind, than as one of the Species: by which means I have made my self a Speculative Statesman, Soldier, Merchant and Artizan, without ever medling with any Practical Part in Life. I am very well versed in the Theory of an Husband, or a Father, and can discern the Errors in the Oeconomy, Business and Diversion of others, better than those who are engaged in them; as Standers-by discover Blots, which are apt to escape those who are in the Game. I never espoused any Party with Violence, and am resolved to observe an exact Neutrality between the Whigs and Tories, unless I shall be forc'd to declare my self by the Hostilities of either Side. In short, I have acted in all the Parts of my Life as a Looker-on, which is the Character I intend to preserve in this Paper.[12]

Ironically, it was a character not very remote from this self-dramatization which Pope was to build into the portrait of Atticus. In each case 'neutrality' becomes a matter of withdrawal.

Now Gulliver's typical mode of withdrawal is through retreat into observation. The word *observe* and its derivatives occur some 140 times in the work: the frequency increases steadily from twenty-five in the first voyage, thirty-four in the second, thirty-eight in the third, to forty-five in the fourth. And, as in *The Dunciad*, the most horrific features of the satirist's world are beheld as a staged spectacle:

> All these, and more, the cloud-compelling Queen
> Beholds thro' fogs, that magnify the scene.[13]

Observation is generally delusive or futile. The Lilliputians who draw up an inventory of Gulliver's belongings, and mistake the purpose of all, speak of 'observing' (I, ii). The three great scholars ordered by the King of Brobdingnag to inspect Gulliver's person, likewise misleadingly, report in terms of observing, examining, viewing (II, iii). Gulliver himself, delightedly imagining the blessings of Struldbrugg existence, draws up a prospective list of 'Observations' and 'Discoveries' he would make if granted an extended term of life (III, x). *Discoveries* similarly carries malign overtones; it occurs in connection with gunpowder, when the King of Brobdingnag protests he would 'rather lose Half his Kingdom than be privy to such a Secret' (II, vii), and again where the Yahoos dig for the shining stones (IV, vii). Gulliver's role as looker-on, rather than participant, is emphasized at points where he witnesses events as a scene or tableau. He speaks of 'the whole Scene of this Voyage' (II, i); he dilates upon the 'Prospect' of Balnibarbi (III, iv), and indeed he climbs hills in order to gain a better prospect, like an eighteenth-century landscape painter. There is a fanciful or poetic quality to this viewing at times: the 'entertaining Prospect' of Lilliput strikes Gulliver thus:

> The Country round appeared like a continued Garden; and the inclosed Fields, which were generally Forty Foot square, resembled so many Beds of Flowers . . . I viewed the Town on my left Hand, which looked like the painted Scene of a City in a Theatre.

Though he claims to be averse to such 'Spectacles', he visits an execution in Brobdingnag, and the spouting up of the blood reminds him of 'the great *Jet d'Eau* at *Versailles*' (II, v). He tells us he has 'often seen' the parade of the militia in Lorbrulgrud: 'Imagination can Figure nothing so Grand, so surprising and so astonishing. It looked as if ten thousand Flashes of Lightning were darting at the same time from every Quarter of the Sky' (II, vii). Small wonder that Swift recalled the book as a succession of graphic episodes and not as a bare allegory, a fact amply confirmed by his letter to Motte of 28 December 1727.[14] A favourite formula is 'I have seen . . .', used of such prominent episodes as the rope-dancers (I, iii), or the Houyhnhnm mare threading a needle (IV, ix).

All this amounts to what might be called the drama of perception. The basic technique is to control the narrative through sense impressions; passages are introduced with verbs indicating Gulliver's awareness of what is happening to him. Thus in Lilliput, when he first awakes in his bound condition, we have *I found my Arms and Legs were strongly fastened / I likewise felt several slender Ligatures across my Body / I could only look upwards / I heard a confused Noise / I felt something alive / I perceived it to be a human Creature / I felt at least Forty more*—all within fifteen lines of print. Similarly the narrative of his being carried off by an eagle (II, viii) is shaped by the perceptual verbs: *found, felt, looked, could see, heard, began to perceive, observed, heard, felt, could see, perceived*, and so on. When he visits the

Grand Academy of Lagado, virtually every paragraph begins with a brief introductory formula (*I saw / I visited*) which fix our attention on Gulliver as observer or receiver (III, iv–v). An identical technique is found in the passage describing the parade of ghosts at Glubbdubdrib (III, vii). It would be natural to find some such usages, but their density goes far beyond the functional requirement of keeping the sights passing before us.

The most striking motif Swift employs is that of associating vision and surprise, usually pained surprise. There are many such episodes, with one or more characters (often but not necessarily Gulliver) gawping in disbelief at some unexpected sight. This happens when the Blefuscudians 'perceive' Gulliver pulling the fleet and begin to scream in despair (I. v). Or when he is taken home by the farmer in Brobdingnag, and shown to the farmer's wife: she screams 'as Women in *England* do at the Sight of a Toad or a Spider' (II, i). Or when Gulliver himself is 'confounded at the Sight of so many Pigmies', as are the sailors who have rescued him (I, viii). Or when the first Yahoo and first Houyhnhnm encounter Gulliver 'with manifest Tokens of Wonder' (IV, i). Or when the Portugese sailors gaze 'in Admiration' at his strange appearance (IV, xi).[15] Sight has come to express the ordeal of consciousness. Moral outrage is preceded by some affront to visual expectation; contrary to the popular view, most outbursts of negative feelings in *Gulliver's Travels* occur when something nasty is *seen*, not smelt.

It is in this context that we should take account of the many explicit references to the faculty of sight. I mean such events as the arrow which narrowly misses Gulliver's left eye in Lilliput; the use of his glasses as protection against the Blefuscan fusillades (I, v); the plan to put out Gulliver's eyes, an 'Operation' which might easily be interpreted as castration (but not by Gulliver, who is less worried about sexual prowess than decency); the sight of the nurse's breasts in Brobdingnag, where the defects are apparent as though they have been viewed through a magnifying glass (II, i); the old man with his eyes behind their spectacles 'like the Full-Moon shining into a Chamber at two Windows' (II, ii); the lice-ridden beggars, viewed again as through a microscope—another sight/nausea connection (II, iv); the problems of readjustment to the smallness of everything, after Gulliver has returned from Brobdingnag (II, viii); the absurd astronomers in Laputa, with their superior telescopes (III, iii); Gulliver's horror at his own reflection in Houyhnhnmland (IV, x); or his ability to see a remote island through his pocket-glass, where the sorrel nag can distinguish nothing (IV, x). These episodes serve different rhetorical ends, but in each case seeing brings either pain or unwelcome news. It is as though looking too hard were an aggressive act for Swift, liable to shift into physical piercing of the object beheld. And in the passage at the close of Book II we have a dislocation of visual function used to point up a moral confusion.

*4*

My argument has been this. Gulliver's quasi-objectivity as Spectator, the one who *observes*, represents the intrusive intellect; the over-intent scrutiny of what is better left unexamined, because it causes pain and revulsion when pried into by the modern empiricist. He basically wishes to peep, as from the back window of Don Pedro's house, but not be peeped at (as he is by the monkey during Glumdalclitch's absence). The glasses are the badge of his meddling and inquisitive nature. Thus far Gulliver is a satiric butt, standing for curiosity as against purposeful, spiritually directed living. But on another level Swift shares Gulliver's instincts, to hide and to peer out, to avoid bodily contact which squeezes and pains us. He wants to do this while at the same time negotiating at a safe distance with the physical world, through his sight. It is instructive that Swift has made Gulliver reliant for his very survival on spectacles, an aid which (as Swift admitted in his poem to Stella) he needed but was too proud to employ. The desire to transcend the body—that is, to ignore the inescapable limitations of human existence—was a proper object of satire for Swift. But the desire to escape from the body—to conceal its frailties and repress its urges—was Swift's very own, and its expression in *Gulliver's Travels* should call out our pity and not our scorn. We do not share Gulliver's pride but we are accomplices in his shame.

## NOTES

1 Textual references follow Volume XI of *The Prose Works of Jonathan Swift,* ed. Herbert Davis (Oxford, 1941, reptd. 1959): page references are not given but the number of books and chapters is supplied. This paper is based on a lecture given under the Winston Churchill Foundation at the University of Bristol in 1976; I am grateful to some of those who heard it, now my colleagues, for useful criticism and comments.

2 *A Tale of a Tub,* ed. A. C. Guthkelch and D. Nichol Smith (Oxford, 1958), p. 244.

3 *The Letters of Daniel Defoe,* ed. G. H. Healey (Oxford, 1955), p. 305.

4 *Journal to Stella,* ed. Harold Williams (Oxford, 1948), I, 81, 88, 95, 97, 149; II, 389–90, 402.

5 *Journal to Stella*, I, 69, 305; II, 455. For Pope's relations with Cheselden, see M. H. Nicolson and G. S. Rousseau, *This Long Disease, My Life* (Princeton, 1968), pp. 58–61.

6 *The Letters of Lady Mary Wortley Montagu,* ed. Robert Halsband (Oxford, 1965–67), II, 474. Lady Mary is commenting on the case of the Duke of Montrose, who had gone blind before reaching the age of forty. I have of course omitted the names of many less important writers such as Dennis, Gildon, and Oldmixon, who suffered extremely severe ailments of the eye.

7 C. H. Collins Baker and Muriel I. Baker, *The Life and Circumstances of James Brydges First Duke of Chandos* (Oxford, 1949), p. 424.

8 *The Poems of Jonathan Swift,* ed. Harold Williams (Oxford, 1958), II, 757–58.

9 *The Correspondence of Alexander Pope,* ed. George Sherburn (Oxford, 1956), I, 234.

10 *Robinson Crusoe,* ed. J. Donald Crowley (Oxford, 1972), pp. 47, 64, 164.

11 W. B. Carnochan, *Lemuel Gulliver's Mirror for Man* (Berkeley and Los Angeles, 1968), p. 135. See also Denis Donoghue, *Jonathan Swift:* A *Critical Introduction* (Cambridge, 1969), pp. 59–85, on the optical 'perspectives' of satire.

12 *The Spectator,* ed D. F. Bond, 5 vols. (Oxford, 1965), I, 4–5.

13 *The Dunciad*, ed. James Sutherland (London, 1963), p. 275.

14 *The Correspondence of Jonathan Swift*, ed. Harold Williams (Oxford, 1963–65), III, 257–58. I have discussed this letter in *The Augustan Vision* (London, 1974), pp. 195–96.

15 There are many other examples, including the reaction when Gulliver fires his pistol (I, ii); when he eats a sirloin bones and all (I, vi); when he arrives at the port of Blefuscu (I, viii); and when the Houyhnhnms conduct a general inspection (IV, iii). All these link sight and surprise: 'observation' is commonly in evidence.

# 8

# Gulliver and Other Heroes

by JENNY MEZCIEMS

> Thro' School and College, thy kind Cloud o'ercast,
> Safe and unseen the young Aeneas past:
> Thence, bursting glorious, all at once let down,
> Stunn'd with his giddy Larum half the Town.
> Intrepid then, o'er Seas and Lands he flew:
> Europe he saw, and Europe saw him too.
>
> (*The Dunciad*, IV, 289)

Pope's modern Aeneas, in spite of the vulgarity of his European Grand Tour, is an epic hero in direct descent from the original.[1] Though the theme of *The Dunciad* is the debasement of literature and life (or of literature *by* life) Pope's method of heroic allusion illustrates the general decline by means of an ironic pretence that he has not noticed it. Like the superior steward to a household impoverished through folly he keeps his own uniform impeccable and polishes away at the brass to show us how inferior it is to silver. His authority as a poet is maintained by the assumption of a role which is in fact subversive. He celebrates the birth of a new age and the beginning of a cultural reign in terms of a tradition and a form which require them to be more glorious than any before. His heroes, his eulogies, his ceremonies, the machinery of language, and the poetic faith match the occasion with unhesitating vigour and élan. In his pose as poet of the day his epic allusions are wings on which the upward soaring of literate man in civilized society should continue unchecked, and also our means of seeing that this particular bird does not measure up to the flight offered.

*Gulliver's Travels* is a literary occasion of a very different kind, but it, too, celebrating half-consciously the conception, if not the birth, of the novel, is dependent on tradition for its treatment of the same theme: both works chastise the modern world, mocking its pretensions to greatness through satiric literary allusion. *Gulliver's Travels* is itself a 'modern' work in a way that *The Dunciad*, however nearly contemporary with it, is not. Comparison of the two is appropriate, bearing in mind Swift's part in the earlier version of *The Dunciad* and Pope's involvement in the sketch for the travels of Martinus Scriblerus, so that each contributed to drafts of the other's masterpiece while the later finished achievements are those of single, separate, but complementary talents. In this discussion, however, I shall use the comparison as an approach to the problem of Swift's use of allusion, so indirect where Pope's is direct, taking his attitude and method of reference to the concept of the hero as an example on which to focus. Swift's satire, like Pope's, depends on the exact placing of a central figure within a formal literary context, within a genre which in turn has a relationship to society (the reading public), and the satire works by exploring these relationships, passing to and fro, using allusion all the time to point up risible incompatibilities. Pope's satire is easier, because he names names and provides references,[2] but Swift leaves his reader to do this work, to guess a range of targets and to draw from his own literary experience, without authorial guidance, the models by which they are to be judged. The identification of 'sources' for *Gulliver's Travels* is comparatively straightforward: the difficult part is in assessing Swift's attitude to them, since what Swift usually does with borrowed material is to weave it silently into his narrative without comment.[3] Pope's reader may appreciate discrepancies between form and material pointed out to him by the poet's skilful treatment of those discrepancies, but Swift almost becomes a discrepancy himself, making his own work not just parody but example, and butt for the criticism which the reader, having made certain necessary discoveries of flawed joints, must level.

*Gulliver's Travels* is not Swift's *Dunciad* (*A Tale of a Tub* is a nearer equivalent) but it can be regarded as Swift's *Robinson Crusoe*. Here, again, comparison shows how indirectly Swift works: any allusion to Defoe is a matter not of parody or imitation but of a particular kind of involvement. The tales of Gulliver and Crusoe are parallel examples of the popular literature of their time, to be set on the same shelf in the childrens' library (as has been their fate, to prove Swift's point). Swift acknowledges no debt to Defoe, nor does he mock him.[4] His book, like Defoe's, is simply part of the modern reader's experience and belongs equally to the modern world, much to Swift's knowing discomfort. Pope, as Epic Poet, self-consciously anachronistic, can hold the banal world at arm's length, shielded by his sublime and dutiful gift to it of its own image, but Swift is close enough to Gulliver to be hurt, as it were, by Lilliputian arrows, and Gulliver is closer still to Crusoe. It is because of this dangerous proximity to his own and other modern heroes, contrasted so easily with the distance between Pope and *either* of the Aeneas figures referred to in *The Dunciad*, that I have taken the figure of the hero as centre not only of the narrative but of the allusive satire on form and function.

Swift stands between Pope and Defoe: his sympathies are with the poet but he insists on performing alongside the prose hack. Swift and Pope are equals in their gentlemanly support of classical literary standards, fighting the eternal losing battle against the modern world.[5] But in their shared views on the decline of civilization they differ from each other in the choice of a root cause for the dishonesty which separates the modern from the ancient and affects the relationship between literature and life in one age as opposed to another. Pope's perceptions are not necessarily shallower than Swift's, but they are of a different order, and his attitude to ancient models is more conventional and less disturbed. By using the epic form, even by using generally the heroic couplet and an elevated style, Pope reasserts the values of classical literature and insists on their permanence as a constant standard from which departure is a falling-off. Dishonesty is a matter of not recognizing those standards, of allowing a blunted judgement to mistake distortions for the real thing and emulation for achievement.[6] For Swift, however, emulation is itself dishonest, not because men are worse than they used to be but because it is increasingly irresponsible to take refuge in illusions about what they ever could be or have been. The comparatively straightforward retreat back into imitation of models and forms suited to a previous less sophisticated age would be for Swift a perverse abdication, especially in an age of so-called rational enlightenment. His own way of expressing a sense of responsibility is to align himself deliberately, in his fiction, alongside Defoe, who is as proudly modern as they come. Defoe presents us with a hero, Robinson Crusoe: allowing for some adjustment of concepts there is really no way of claiming that he is *not* a hero, on his own terms. Gulliver stands alongside him, his background is strikingly similar, and his adventures begin in a way that suggests direct imitation. Yet there is no heroic concept which will allow us to juggle the parts around so that we can call this figure a hero, in spite of various and really quite frequent heroic allusions pervading the narrative. It is part of Gulliver's *literary* perversity (to be compared with the much more heavily stressed but quite *un*-literary perversity of Crusoe) and part of the unease of the whole book.

In contrast to *Gulliver's Travels* there are no heroic allusions in *Robinson Crusoe*. Defoe, in the new world, with its own novel genre, forges his own hero who needs no background or frame of reference beyond the local and immediate, except of course for the Christian scheme of grace and salvation which is, in itself, enough to ensure independence of the classical world whenever such a thing is desired. Nevertheless, the substitution of new heroes for old, and new genres for old, is a matter of modification and not of total honest rejection. Titles play their part, in this important switch from epic to novel, from high poetry to low prose aiming high. Two of the three most influential ancient epics, the *Odyssey* and the *Aeneid*, not only carry heroes' names for titles but, by doing so, imply complete social structures, which express themselves in the separate heroic concepts involved. It is hard to imagine that it is an accidental feature of the novel, or one unrelated to its epic ancestor, that, in its early stages, titles focused so commonly and characteristically on the names of individuals central to the narrative, whom we were obliged to regard as heroes even before Fielding made his self-conscious explorations of the transition and elevated the novel from the status of romance to that of comic epic in prose. Both epic and novel are 'about' the relationships between outstanding individuals and their own societies, and such titles stress the fact.[7] *Robinson Crusoe* heralds and justifies a concept of heroism common in the novel by showing an individual at first perversely at odds with society but generally, and in the terms of that new society rather gloriously, making out on his own as well as contributing to the spread of civilization.[8] Gulliver's alienation from society has an opposite effect: neither he nor it emerge or re-unite with anything like glory, and the Mr. Gulliver who retires to Newark to enjoy the good esteem of his neighbours does so by virtue of leaving his past and his papers behind on removal from Redriff. He has returned to his native county, but only by virtually casting aside the effect of his travels.

The experiences of Crusoe and Gulliver take place in a world where narrative credibility needs to be assured by an easy relationship with contemporary reality, and Gulliver's fantasy depends for acceptance at least in part on the verisimilitude of Crusoe which paves the way for it. Verisimilitude acts as a guarantee that the fiction does not belong to the category of romance, that its terms of reference are those of the real world, and that the real world is to be taken seriously as a literary context. Within such terms Gulliver is very soon in trouble. The framework for his adventures obliges him to be a hero of the Crusoe variety, while the adventures themselves prevent that. In his Defoe-like refusal to have anything to do with romance, however, Swift does have another literary form which backs up his criticism of that world in which Crusoe can be a hero and which gives him the support of tradition for the further discomfort of Gulliver, and that is the travel book. The travel book is traditionally 'low': moreover, even when elevated as literature by utopian ideals or as real experience by didactic aims, it has no hero because its narrator is at least temporarily cut off from his own society and cannot possibly represent the society he describes because he has no place within it. Swift apparently read all the travel books he could lay his hands on while writing or preparing to write *Gulliver's Travels*: his failure to comment upon *Robinson Crusoe* is evidence only of his feelings about Defoe as a writer generally unworthy of being named (or copied, or parodied).[9] However *Gulliver's Travels* stands in relation to *The Dunciad* (by theme) and to *Robinson Crusoe* (by form), the relationships I have suggested show the nature of the problems in Swift's use of allusion; in that allusion to either of these contemporary works is as understated as allusions to past models of greater stature are indirect. All we have to start with is an incompatibility between the concept of the hero and the genre of the travel book. We should note the difference, however, between the short title acquired by the book for common use and for later editions, which forces Gulliver into a quasi-heroic role, and Swift's original title, which presents him as an unknown author whose name needs the support of his qualifications. The irony is *imposed*, whereby the hero's name is coupled with that of a genre classification which has, by definition, no place for heroes.

If Swift's non-hero illustrates degeneration then we might feel justified in looking for signs of wistful backward glances at heroes worthy of their status in genres that can carry them, and particularly at the epic, to see what concept of the heroic we are to use as a model in measuring Gulliver's inadequacy and, by implication, the inadequacy of the narrative form in which he struts, or sails. The text helps us at one point in particular. There is a sad and awful finality, the sense of a gaping and bottomless chasm, in Gulliver's comment on that very small group of admired figures in the ghostly procession at Glubbdubdrib ('A *Sextumvirate* to which all the Ages of the World cannot add a Seventh') which seems, however silently, to demand investigation, in case there is someone behind the narrative who regrets the dearth of such heroic figures. The passage is especially striking for being one of those occasions, rare within a satire, where Swift (surely not Gulliver alone, here) indulges in a positive value judgement, and it brings us up short because we are used to ironic reversals, oblique thrusts, sudden sidesteps, or simple blank refusals at the fence of open commitment. The phrase 'All the Ages of the World' suggests that the survey encompasses an earlier past as well as a predictable future, and does not therefore imply the theory of steady degeneration which Swift is commonly supposed to have held. His heroes include one from the comparatively recent and local past, as well as those from antiquity, and all are figures who claimed to represent the interests of the state at moments when the public good was threatened by tyranny of one kind or another. It may be said that concepts of the heroic in literature describe, at least when viewed in retrospect, a progress towards civilization, from darker and more superstitious ages, when heroes were giants or supernaturally gifted but primarily physical beings (Herakles, for instance), to more enlightened times when heroes were governors and leaders of their people.[10] (The assumed upward climb is what makes *The Dunciad* a successful satire, because the fall seems so sudden and unnatural, with no precedent except that of Satan.) Swift, according to Gulliver's list, evidently favours the hero who is socially responsible and who makes private sacrifices to public principle, rather than the towering individual who scores through brilliant personal prowess. But if Swift's heroes are those of a late age, preceded by giant figures from dark ages of myth and superstition and followed by modern socially irresponsible individualists, then his ideal is found at the highest point on a curve and not at the beginning of a slope which has never allowed any direction except downwards. Darkness is both before and after, surrounding whatever isolated spots of light there are.

At this point, then, we have to remember that Gulliver, transported from the 'real' world into a fictional one, becomes first a giant, whose outstanding features are physical and associate him with the primitive Herakles alone among classical heroes, and that this is something of a jump from his initial narrative status as ordinary modern Englishman. The great heroes whom Gulliver lists are relegated to the Struldbruggian limbo. Since they are dead they belong obviously to points in historical time, as well as to that permanent timeless ideal which provides Swift's concept of the heroic. One of the difficulties, however, with Swift's allusions to the past is his strange use and seeming distrust of historical time, with which at certain points in *Gulliver's Travels* he appears to mock the reader's conceptions and expectations of history. I suggested earlier that Swift's view of decline and human failing was different from Pope's, and that this was a clue to his more complicated treatment of allusion. There have traditionally been a number of alternative theories of decline,[11] with or without beginning or end, but all are systems which perhaps foster illusions about the passage of time, giving tradition a stranglehold over thought and imagination. In *Gulliver's Travels* Swift engineers some curious time-slips which disturb and confuse the reader and which may serve as an attack on the latter's vulnerability to such systems. For instance, the argument for the steady degeneration of mankind, in the book in the Brobdingnagian library, is based on 'History and Tradition' which takes the evidence of 'huge Bones and Sculls . . . far exceeding the common dwindled Race of Man in our Days' as support for an assumption that there are 'Laws of Nature' by which men have degenerated down to the present size of the giants in Brobdingnag, a theory whose logical consequence (given the nature of those giants) places Gulliver ridiculously far down the scale and simultaneously makes nonsense of time as a factor (p. 137).[12] Similar dubious reasoning is used by the Houyhnhnms in their theories about the origins and development of the Yahoos (p. 272), again to the disadvantage of Gulliver, and perhaps the best-known instance of a peculiar slip in the handling of time (though one hard to prove deliberate) is that passage in Book I, Chapter 6, where Gulliver hastily asserts that while seeming to talk of the Lilliputian present he is in fact referring to 'the original Institutions, and not the most scandalous Corruptions into which these People are fallen by the degenerate Nature of Man' (p. 60).

It is this ambiguity about time, history, and theoretical systems which makes Swift's allusions to heroes in *Gulliver's Travels* hard to evaluate or to place on a meaningful scale, as more or less worthy of imitation, more or less to be regretted as representing concepts no longer upheld. An earlier and provocative reference to heroes illustrates the problem in a characteristic way. It is the passage from the 'Digression concerning Critics', *A Tale of a Tub*, Section 3, interesting enough for its discussion of particular heroes, their genealogies, and 'Heroick Virtue' in the abstract to be worth quoting at length.

> Every *True Critick* is a Hero born, descending in a direct Line from a Celestial Stem, by *Momus* and *Hybris*, who begat *Zoilus*, who begat *Tigellius*, who begat *Etcætera* the Elder, who begat *Bently*, and *Rymer*, and *Wotton*, and *Perrault*, and *Dennis*, who begat *Etcætera* the Younger.
>
> And these are the *Criticks* from whom the Commonwealth of Learning has in all Ages received such immense benefits, that the Gratitude of their Admirers placed their Origine in Heaven, among those of *Hercules*, *Theseus*, *Perseus*, and other great Deservers of Mankind. But Heroick Virtue it self hath not been exempt from the Obloquy of Evil Tongues. For it hath been objected, that those Antient Heroes, famous for their Combating so many Giants, and Dragons, and Robbers, were in their own

> Persons a greater Nuisance to Mankind, than any of those Monsters they subdued; and therefore, to render their Obligation more Compleat, when all *other* Vermin were destroy'd, should in Conscience have concluded with the same Justice upon themselves: as *Hercules* most generously did, and hath upon that Score, procured to himself more Temples and Votaries than the best of his Fellows. For these Reasons, I suppose it is, why some have conceived, it would be very expedient for the Publick Good of Learning, that every *True Critick*, as soon as he had finished his Task assigned, should immediately deliver himself up to Ratsbane, or Hemp, or from some convenient *Altitude*, and that no Man's Pretensions to so illustrious a Character, should by any means be received, before That Operation were performed. (*Works*, I, 57)

The problem of disentangling Swift's views from those of his narrator, where the irony is not always straight reversal, is a familiar one. 'True Criticks' are of course charlatans, the other kinds (like Gulliver's heroes) being now extinct. The points to note are: that the charlatan claims an unbroken lineage; that this lineage shows real degeneration in the transition from classical monstrosities to puny modern men; that the modern charlatan is seen as a hero; that the type of hero subsuming all other types in a generalized category is the primitive dragon-killer of heroic myth; that among the 'Pretensions to so illustrious a Character' particularly irrelevant in this type of hero are benefits to 'the Commonwealth of Learning' and 'the Publick Good of Learning' (by self-destruction), which place the 'True Critick' among the 'great Deservers of Mankind'. Swift does not mean to say that the only good hero is a dead hero, but he does manage to convey the idea, by the very remoteness of these most shadowy allusions to qualities which really matter, that there are heroes and heroes, just as there are critics and critics. If we want Swift's views straight we can take, as an easier formulation of opinions which are hardly personal or idiosyncratic, the definition given by Sir William Temple in his essay 'Of Heroick Virtue': 'the character of heroic virtue seems to be, in short, the deserving well of mankind'. The definition is reached after consideration that heroic virtue

> may be said to arise from some great and native excellency of temper or genius transcending the common race of mankind in

> wisdom, goodness, and fortitude. These ingredients advantaged by birth, improved by education, and assisted by fortune, seem to make that noble composition, which gives such a lustre to those who have possessed it as made them appear to common eyes something more than mortals, and to have been born of some mixture between divine and human race; to have been honoured and obeyed in their lives, and after their deaths bewailed and adored.

The mention of birth, education, and fortune may take us irresistibly back to Gulliver, who is not noble and is neither more nor less than mortal, in spite of his excitement at meeting Struldbruggs, Yahoos, and Houyhnhnms. Temple goes on to say that the talents and powers of heroes

> by the goodness of their nature, were turned and exercised upon such subjects as were of general good to mankind in the common uses of life, or to their own countries in the institutions of such laws, orders, or governments, as were of most ease, safety, and advantage to civil society.[13]

Gulliver's failure by such standards may be measured against the qualifications of the figures in the famous Sextumvirate. These qualities also belong to the most favoured kind of epic hero, in the prescriptive criticism of the eighteenth century: qualities for which Swift finds no living representative and which, if they live on in academic discussion of an already defunct form, are significantly absent in those lively narratives where Crusoe and Gulliver reign.[14] The essay 'Of Heroick Virtue' not only delineates for us a proper heroic figure but has further connections with the non-heroic Gulliver in that it surveys *four* great civilizations dependent for their power on the institutions of wise and strong individual founders, so that relationships are discussed which are in marked contrast to those obtaining between Gulliver and the four lands he visits but which, as a refugee from his own country, he hardly becomes fit to rule. The benefits he confers on Lilliput, where at least he has heroic *physical* stature, go unappreciated, as does his mere *advice* on military matters to the king of Brobdingnag. In Laputa Gulliver is appropriately ignored, and from Houyhnhnmland he is ejected, so that in the sense of being heroically useful to society he degenerates by nice degrees.

As an allusion to the heroic concept this regression is far from direct but, once thought of, cannot be ignored.

Swift's heroic ideal is not an extravagant or flamboyant one. Literary heroes rarely approach it and the modest men of the Sextumvirate are long since dead. From the high point on his essentially timeless curve up to and away from civilized perfection the ground falls back in both directions. The situation of Gulliver again throws light on the heroes of Pope and Defoe. The confidence in an upward climb must be there for Pope to demolish it by the sudden explosive tumble into chaos, and the same confidence enables Defoe to launch Crusoe, without literary roots, on seas which narrow their horizons for the trader who takes over from the Renaissance gentleman who followed the epic hero in the path of progress. Travel is traditionally part of the education or testing of a hero. Odysseus and Aeneas travel in order to arrive, to resume their home-life, to re-establish the old order in society. If Thomas More is one of Swift's heroes we should register the important fact that the travel aspect moves away from the heroic and noble in *Utopia*, where Hythlodaeus, freeing himself as Gulliver does from commitments at home, refuses to return to play a part in European society and is presented as a *romantic* figure in opposition to the domestically harassed and socially fettered More. Robinson Crusoe, freest of all, admits to his own perversity but also triumphs in spite of his moralizing sops to divine providence, gaining power and authority for himself, by himself. The same romantic individualism destroys Gulliver, as a parallel figure, from within—because he looks like Crusoe yet is obliged to act within the distant literary shadow of Odysseus.

What with the substance of Robinson Crusoe beside him, and the void out of which figures like Thomas More can never be recreated, we can hardly see, through the insubstantial Gulliver, those remote figures of earlier epic heroes whose actions he partly and unconsciously imitates. The reader is in the situation of Plato's cave-dweller. The analogy works well, since, for Swift, the fiction which entertains us does so by exploiting our culpable vulnerability to illusions about ourselves and our pride in what we are not. Gulliver himself, in spite of his leisure-time reading of 'the best Authors, ancient and modern', never observes any parallel between his own experiences and those of any literary hero, though there are occasions when he might do so (unlike Crusoe, who has no reading but the bible, which he uses frequently to find out where he is, morally speaking). Instead we have to rely on modern editors and source-hunters to point out to us the resemblances between Gulliver and other heroes. The fullest record seems to be that of Paul Turner, in the notes to his edition of *Gulliver's Travels* (London, 1971) and a brief summary of his citations will show how slight and shadowy, though unmistakable, the references actually are. The list includes some found by W. A. Eddy, whose purpose in the hunt for sources understandably does not lead him to make too much of this kind of allusion. The allusions themselves have often, in any case, to pass through intermediate literary 'screens' before reaching *Gulliver's Travels*. These screens are sometimes Eddy's 'sources' (Rabelais, for instance). Intermediate figures from more recent popular literature stand in relation to heroic models as the fire in Plato's cave stands to the sun, and it is their light we recognize first. For Swift's purpose, intentionally or not, this is as it should be: if we see Pantagruel where we ought to glimpse Hercules, so much the worse for us; the remoteness of the model is proof of our own rootless illiteracy.

First among the heroic allusions cited by Turner is Gulliver's awakening in Lilliput, 'possibly suggested by the account in Philostratus (*Eikones*, II, xxii) of an attack on the sleeping Hercules by pygmies' (p. 310, n. 12; with a reference also to Eddy, pp. 53, 76–7). The second reference (p. 314, n. 14) is to the soldiers marching between Gulliver's legs, as in *Julius Caesar*, I,2.134:

> Why, man, he doth bestride the narrow world
> Like a Colossus; and we petty men
> Walk under his huge legs, and peep about
> To find ourselves dishonourable graves.

Thirdly we have two references in the Articles of Impeachment against Gulliver (I, 7, 69–70): 'Some of your Servants were to have private Orders to strew a poisonous Juice on your Shirts and Sheets, which would soon make you tear your own Flesh, and die in the utmost Torture'; and 'the Loss of your Eyes would be no Impediment to your bodily Strength'. Turner cites 'the shirt smeared with the poisoned blood of the Centaur, Nessus, which made Hercules die in agony' (p. 321, n. 7) and the blinding of Samson by the Philistines (n. 10). The references are all to classical giants (Samson has an equal stature and distance) but they are not, except for Samson, the first parallels which would occur to a modern reader or to a contemporary one picking up a story he might expect to find on a par with *Robinson Crusoe*. Shakespeare, as an intermediary linking Julius Caesar *or* the Colossus with Gulliver, is a rather special case, but the giant who really acts as a screen or filter for the reference is Rabelais's Pantagruel. The ancient giants, when we recognize them, are obviously hugely superior to Gulliver, and all the more pointedly so in parallel situations:[15] they can hardly be emulated in any modern literary context, however fantastic. But Pantagruel, though from a more recent, popular, vernacular, and by comparison fairly absurd fable, is *also* greater than Gulliver. Rabelais's giant is as self-confident and as independent of emulatory anxieties as Defoe's hero, and when considering how Swift's allusions travel thus in so many directions, with such levels of silent evaluation of each figure on a scale that is not declared, the reader needs to look at Pantagruel not merely as a source for Gulliver but in a wider context which makes clearer the relationship between Gulliver and real heroes.

The bondage of the prostrate Gulliver by Lilliputian threads, and his awakening to a new world in which he must find a way to live, can be allegorized as a rebirth.[16] The bondage in his cradle of the infant Pantagruel is similarly an obvious allegory describing the birth of the humanist giant scholar-prince who is to use all the resources of fable to force the chains of medieval scholasticism. Interestingly, and in contrast to Gulliver among the Lilliputians, Rabelais gives Pantagruel direct claims not in emulation of Hercules but surpassing that hero: 'What Hercules did was as nothing, when in his cradle he killed two serpents, for those serpents were only small and weak. But Pantagruel, while still in the cradle, did quite astounding things.'[17] Swift's use of Rabelais as a source is not in question here, since we know from his numerous references elsewhere, as well as those of other writers, that he read and admired him enough to imitate. Gulliver's creator, however, within the narrative mentions neither Pantagruel nor Hercules, and where Rabelais insists on his giant's superiority by direct comparison Swift's reader must make his own comparisons.

The infant Pantagruel shows a voracious appetite and the strength to lay hands on what he wants, thus echoing his author's irrepressible hope and joy in seizing opportunities, wielding language and literature alike to his own ends in life. (Swift, equating himself with Gulliver, might well envy Rabelais.) In alarm at the infant's powers 'his attendants tied him down with stout cables' (p. 179), but 'he freed himself from those cables as easily as did Samson from the Philistines' (p. 180; again the direct reference contrasts with the indirectness of the Samsonian shadow discovered by Swift's editor or reader) and had to be tied again with 'four great iron chains'. After some strenuous tugging and banging Pantagruel escapes by tearing loose the whole cradle, carrying it on his back into the great hall where his father's household is feasting. 'When his father saw this he realized they had left him without anything to eat, and ordered that he should be loosed from those chains . . . When he was released they made him sit up, and he ate very heartily. Then he broke that cradle of his into more than five thousand pieces with a blow of his fist which he struck at the middle of it in his rage, swearing he would never go back into it' (pp. 180–81). Gulliver's situation is identical in the allegorical terms of the fiction. He wakes (or is born) in Lilliput to find himself bound by 'slender Ligatures' some of which he breaks without difficulty, though he does not persevere. Seeing the stature of the people who approach him, and the effect on them of his roar of astonishment, Gulliver recognizes that he 'might be a Match for the greatest Armies they could bring against' him, yet decides that 'the most prudent Method [is] to lie still' and wait to release himself, if at all, by stealth at night (pp. 21–2). He does not take up the opportunity to be a giant, even when the stature is forced upon him, but renders up his power to tiny people who can only *abuse* heroic potential in their demands. Though hungry, like Pantagruel, he must depend on the Lilliputians to calculate what food he needs and to bring it to him. Released from bondage he hastens to put himself in bondage again, as man offered enlightenment hastens back into the cave rather than look at the sun, or as Swift's reader prefers diversion to vexation in his reading.

Gulliver's size is chiefly an embarrassment to him, as is the copiousness of his flow of urine in at least two other Rabelaisian reminiscences where the effect on Gulliver is restraint or punishment rather than relief. And in the instance of the soldiers peeping up between his legs the emotion engendered is the 'Admiration' of laughter, not of awe, so that it is Gulliver who is diminished, not the onlookers as in the quotation from *Julius Caesar*. Heroic references in Brobdingnag, as listed by Paul Turner, are slightly more numerous than they are in Lilliput. The field of reference is somewhat narrower, and the Rabelaisian screen is not appropriate where Gulliver is no longer a giant and where the images he fails, on moral rather than physical grounds, are those of the more mature epic heroes. Here we have, at least, direct access to figures from Homer and Virgil, but in the first place the allusions are not particularly obvious and, secondly, they all show heroes at a particular kind of disadvantage, not quite living up to the heroic image (with Odysseus as specific model) or being proved in some way inferior, so that their failures cast a shadow over Gulliver himself as he constantly attempts to survive by adapting to alien surroundings. In contrast, Odysseus (and, later, Aeneas) not only escape but are obliged to rescue an entire company or society. The circumstances of Gulliver's arrival in Brobdingnag are associated with the occasion when Polyphemus wades out after a boat which has just rescued a lone straggler from Odysseus's crew (*Aeneid*, III, 662f.; Turner, p. 325, n. 29). The allusion is more interesting than Turner has occasion to suggest, and the threat of the Cyclopean savagery much more relevant to Gulliver's later plight. The passage begins at *Aeneid*, III. 588 (767 in Dryden's translation):

> . . . from the woods there bolts, before our sight,
> Somewhat betwixt a mortal and a sprite,
> So thin, so ghastly meager, and so wan,
> So bare of flesh, he scarce resembled man.
> This thing, all tattered, seemed from far to implore
> Our pious aid, and pointed to the shore.
> We look behind; then view his shaggy beard;
> His clothes were tagged with thorns, and filth his limbs besmeared;

At a later point in this Yahoo-like outcast's story he expresses a particularly Gulliverian sentiment:

> From Ithaca, my native soil, I came
> To Troy; and Achaemenides my name.
> Me my poor father with Ulysses sent;
> (*O! had I stayed, with poverty content!*)
> (*Aeneid*, III. 613; Dryden, 804; my italics)[18]

There follows a comparison between Gulliver's slipping on cow-dung (p. 124) and the similar experience of Ajax in the *Iliad* (XXIII. 774f.; Turner, p. 332, n. 24), which seems at first remote and even strained. The point of the analogy has to be provided by the Homeric context: the fact that Ajax falls because Athene favours a hero (Odysseus) more worthy as one 'born in better days' (Pope) or 'of an earlier race of men' (Lang, Leaf, and Myers), as Antilochus explains. Gulliver is not only muddied by the association but at the same time is proved degenerate. It may be evidence of some progressive moral decorum that Aeneas should rescue a man whom Odysseus left behind, but in a sense it is by wanting to *settle* among strange beings of another kind that the degenerate Gulliver becomes, eventually, a Yahoo. A more central passage on the diminution in size and degeneration in the nature of man, from Chapter 7, is traced by Turner (p. 336, n. 14) to the *Iliad* (XII. 447–9), though Swift presumably had more recent discussions of the theory in his mind, as Turner also suggests, referring to Eddy. (In any case, the reference seems an arbitrary choice from a number of possible instances.) Two remaining references are both to Calypso's island in *Odyssey*, V. 81–4, 149–58: Gulliver casting 'many a wistful melancholy Look towards the Sea' (p. 140; Turner, p. 337, n. 5) like Odysseus and, finally, in a single reference from Houyhnhnmland, Gulliver building a boat for his escape, which Turner likens to Odysseus's need to do the same. Where Odysseus is anxious to leave Calypso's superbly exotic bower, of course, Gulliver pleads against his dismissal from Houyhnhnmland (p. 280).

With this tailing off, the complete absence of heroic allusion in Book III (though Eddy (p. 165) refers us to the classical myth of Tithonus as a source for the Struldbruggian dilemma), and the remote nature of the allusions when they can be spotted, the list is disappointing, at least until one pursues the references into their original contexts in order to establish some real relationship with Gulliver which is never obvious. Eddy has some discussion of Gulliver's relationship with Ulysses and the beast fable in his chapter on Houyhnhnmland, but moves inevitably away from the classical Odysseus to Ulysses in his more modern forms. Plutarch, however, anticipated Swift in reversing the moral of the Circe story to make beasts superior to men. The slightness and remoteness of specific references does not matter; what is proved by investigation is that Swift's allusions are larger and more complicated and indirect than any simple imitation or occasional borrowings. If Gulliver reminds us of Odysseus in situations where the hero is at his most vulnerable or at his most anxious to make his way home, the purpose of the reminder can only be to make us think in larger terms of the differences between the two figures. Gulliver is not the kind of satiric butt that can bear direct contrast with heroic figures, such as we find in Pope's *Dunciad*. Swift reserves such treatment for his 'True Criticks' and other small fry, while Gulliver is quite another matter. It is by means of the barriers between him and a range of figures at various imprecisely measured distances from him, this penumbra of shadowy allusions which causes his silhouette to fade in and out of an uncertain outline, that Swift obliges us to take Gulliver so seriously, as seriously as he does himself.

The butt of Swift's satire is the 'gentle reader', whom Gulliver invokes just as Pope invokes the 'great Patricians' or 'the Great', to preside over offerings prepared to their several tastes. Satiric intent is established by the change in relationship between author and muse to one of irony (and Pope of course has, as it were in parenthesis, a further invocation to Swift himself, as a deeper irony rather in the spirit of the pun in the title of Erasmus's *Moriae Encomium*). Swift's invocation is not confined to the text but must include the prefatory letters from publisher to reader and from Gulliver to publisher, distant bastard offspring of the epic invocation but offspring nonetheless, showing as clearly as does the traditional poet where responsibility is to be placed. Defoe of course needs no such invocation, any more than he needs literary allusions. In addressing himself to the reader without introduction Crusoe asserts his individualism to such an extent that the reader is absorbed into the hero's mind and Crusoe in effect addresses only himself.

Swift carefully prevents his reader from going too far towards identification with Gulliver: the shadowy outline which gradually replaces the initial Crusoe-like substance, the fantasy which never allows us for a moment to confuse Gulliver's experiences with reality, however concrete the details, and the hovering presence of half-recognized heroic forms, all hold us off. Swift's attack, like Pope's is at the pretensions of modern man, including the pretension to heroic dimensions. He presents us with Gulliver as a mirror in which we are faced not so much with ourselves as with our wish for and insistence on illusions about ourselves. The reader, not Gulliver, is responsible for the creation of the figure of the giant, and when the common man becomes a fictional monster, to oblige the expectations of a reader who insists on being entertained with fantasy, things are bound to go wrong for him. Defoe romanticizes reality, in a regressive step which takes the literary form back into a culpable irrationality, but Swift, making fantasy horribly real, refuses ever to let 'a Man's Fancy get *astride* on his Reason'. He indulges the reader's desire for fantasy, and lets Gulliver fail in a fantasy world, only to teach us that the proper study of mankind is man, not giants, or horses. Swift's own progression, as a writer, through a long and varied sequence of literary poses, brought him to the reiteration, as an old man, of the simple phrase 'I am what I am'.[19]

## NOTES

1 Reuben Brower uses the passage quoted, in *Alexander Pope: The Poetry of Allusion* (London, 1968), and his comments on the debasement of the hero and the relationship between the ideal and the practice of travel as education first alerted my attention to the figure of Gulliver as travelling hero. See Brower, pp. 32, 347–8, and also Aubrey L. Williams, *Pope's 'Dunciad': A Study of its Meaning* (London, 1955; Hampden, Connecticut, 1968), pp. 121–2, for references to Ascham and George Turnbull modelling Renaissance humanist travellers on the figure of Ulysses.

2 The Variorum notes and commentary confuse the issue and increase the ambiguity of references in the poem which are otherwise clear enough, as is suggested by Williams, pp. 61–2.

3 W. A. Eddy's study of borrowings and influences, in *'Gulliver's Travels': A Critical Study* (New York, 1923), provided the basic material but did not go very far in the task of working out how Swift chose his borrowings or what relationships he saw between them, one work set against another in an undercurrent of silent comparisons.

4 See Nigel Dennis, *Jonathan Swift: A Short Character* (London, 1964), p. 123: 'To describe *Gulliver's Travels* as Swift's deliberate retort to *Robinson Crusoe* would be unwarranted, but if we amuse ourselves by considering it as such, the result is as informative as it is entertaining . . . Defoe embodies everything that Swift hates'. I believe Defoe is too small an adversary for Swift, though the attack is levelled at something that includes him, which is not to say that Swift does not take Defoe seriously.

5 See Williams, pp. 9–12, for a neat summary of the situation.

6 See Williams, p. 48: 'Since this aping of classic writings was so prevalent among the dunces, no more fitting punishment could have been devised for them than that by which they are forced to continue, in the timeless realm of art, their emulation of the epic figures of the past.' Pope criticizes emulation by the unworthy, but his own choice of form suggests that he himself is in a superior category and has no doubts about it.

7 Discussions of names in titles include the following: Harry Levin, 'The Title as a Literary Genre', *MLR*, 72, No. 4 (October 1977), xxiii–xxxvi; Steven G. Kellman, 'Dropping Names: The Poetics of Titles', *Criticism*, 17, No. 2 (Spring 1975), 152–67; J. Paul Hunter, 'Biography and the Novel' (lecture delivered at the University of Warwick, 9 November 1976).

8 Ian Watt, 'The Naming of Characters in Defoe, Richardson, and Fielding', *RES*, 25 (1949), 322–38, mentions Robinson Crusoe as the only one of Defoe's characters to be given full identity by means of a proper, real name, but he rather tantalizingly leaves the matter there.

9 Maximillian E. Novak states that '*Robinson Crusoe* was read by Pope and Swift' ('Defoe's Use of Irony', in *Irony in Swift and Defoe*, Papers read at a Clark Library Seminar, 2 April, 1966 (Los Angeles, 1966), p. 15). I do not know the source, if it is recent, for the certainty of this statement. Nigel Dennis describes Swift as reading 'all the travel books he could find' while writing *Gulliver's Travels*. John F. Ross, in *Swift and Defoe: A Study in Relationship* (Berkeley and London, 1941), went only so far as to 'conjecture that each read the other's masterpiece' concluding that 'what Defoe thought of *Gulliver*, or Swift of *Crusoe* we do not know'.

10 See W. B. Stanford, *The Ulysses Theme: A Study in the Adaptability of a Traditional Hero*, second edition (Oxford, 1963) and G. Karl Galinsky, *The Herakles Theme: The Adaptations of the Hero in Literature from Homer to the Twentieth Century* (Oxford, 1972). The kind of modification which commonly occurs is exemplified in the changing reputations of Ulysses and Herakles. Ulysses may be made

to seem an ever-restless traveller, irresponsible when measured against the virtues of Aeneas, for instance, and Herakles becomes a clumsy and rather tiresome boor among the company of the Argonauts of a later age. The qualities of a particular hero may be distorted or, at least, presented selectively so that he seems an anachronism among changed concepts in the literature of an age which thinks itself more civilized.

11 See C. A. Patrides, *The Phoenix and the Ladder: The Rise and Decline of the Christian View of History* (Berkeley and Los Angeles, 1964).

12 Quotations are from Herbert Davis's edition, Volume 11 of *The Prose Works of Jonathan Swift*, 14 vols (Oxford, 1939–68), referred to in the text hereafter as *Works*. Page references for *Gulliver's Travels* are to the revised edition, 1959.

13 'Of Heroick Virtue', *The Works of Sir William Temple*, 4 vols (London, 1770), III. 304–5.

14 In a period when so much literary criticism centred on the epic and when heroic definitions were a matter of interest Swift could expect an educated reader to look for, and recognize, the presence or absence of the necessary qualities in Gulliver, given the context of even a negative capability. See H. T. Swedenberg, Jr, *The Theory of the Epic in England, 1650–1800* (Berkeley and Los Angeles, 1944).

15 The Herakles described by Philostratus 'stands erect and laughs at the danger, and sweeping together the hostile forces he puts them in his lion's skin', a course of action which it is useful to be able to remember as we follow Gulliver's very different conduct (*Imagines*, II, 22, translated by Arthur Fairbanks, Loeb Classical Library (London and Cambridge, Mass., 1960), p. 231).

16 See W. B. Carnochan, *Lemuel Gulliver's Mirror for Man* (Berkeley and Los Angeles, 1968), pp. 133–4, for suggestions which seem far-fetched by themselves but less so when linked with the Rabelaisian background.

17 *The Histories of Gargantua and Pantagruel*, translated by J. M. Cohen (Harmondsworth, 1955), p. 179 (Book II, Chapter 4). Subsequent page references to this edition are given in the text.

18 Dryden's translation, edited by Robert Fitzgerald, Classics of Greece and Rome Series (New York and London, 1964).

19 According to the anecdote related by Thomas Sheridan in his *Life of the Rev. Dr. Jonathan Swift . . .*, second edition (London, 1787), p. 406. Compare, however, the notion in T. S. Eliot's essay 'Shakespeare and the Stoicism of Seneca' of an ultimate pride and self-dramatization in the statement of identity by various tragic heroes and heroines faced with death. If Swift's modesty is really pride after all it is at least not as obvious a target for mockery as Gulliver's, nor is there a literary audience to share the guilt. I owe the Eliot reference to Professor C. J. Rawson.

# Notes on Contributors

W. B. CARNOCHAN: Professor of English and Dean of Graduate Studies, Stanford University, California. Author of various articles on Swift, Pope, Johnson, satire and literary theory, and of *Lemuel Gulliver's Mirror for Man* (1968). His edition of Sir George Etherege's *The Man of Mode* was published in 1966, and the second edition in 1975. His most recent book is *Confinement and Flight: An Essay on English Literature of the Eighteenth Century* (1977).

DAVID NOKES: Lecturer in English at King's College, University of London, spent six years at Christ's College, Cambridge. His research interest concerns the Scriblerus Club, and he has published articles on Swift, and on Pope's manuscripts.

CLIVE T. PROBYN: Lecturer and Chairman of the School of English, University of Lancaster. British Editor of *The Scriblerian*, and author of several articles on Swift, Pope, the Earl of Burlington, Johnson, and of the Introduction to the Everyman *Gulliver's Travels* (1974). His reviews have appeared in the *Times Literary Supplement* and *Plays and Players*. His book *Jonathan Swift: the Contemporary Background* is to be published by Manchester University Press early in 1978.

ANGUS ROSS: Reader in English and Dean of the Graduate School in Arts and Social Studies, University of Sussex. Author of a critical study of *Gulliver's Travels* (1968), and an edition of *Gulliver* (1972). He has also edited *Robinson Crusoe, Humphry Clinker*, and *Poetry of the Augustan Age* (1970). (See also note on David Woolley below.)

J. A. DOWNIE: after a research fellowship in the University of Wales, Bangor, has recently been appointed to a lectureship at the University of Leeds. He has published articles on Robert Harley, Defoe, and Swift, and his forthcoming book is entitled *Robert Harley and the Press: Propaganda and Public Opinion in the Age of Swift and Defoe*.

DAVID WOOLLEY: since 1949 his appointments as principal or co-principal oboe have been with the Melbourne Symphony, London Philharmonic, Sydney Symphony, Royal Philharmonic, Royal Opera House Covent Garden, and guest principal with the London Symphony Orchestra, with all of which he has recorded and toured extensively. He has collected and studied Swift for thirty years, saw through the press Herbert Davis's edition of Swift's *Poetical Works* (1967), the corrected reprint (1972) of vols. IV and V of the *Correspondence*, ed. Harold Williams, and is re-editing Swift's complete prose for Oxford University Press, with Angus Ross.

PAT ROGERS: Professor of English, University of Bristol, has many and varied publications in the eighteenth-century field, and is best known for his important *Grub Street: Studies in a Subculture* (1972). Among his other books there are: *Defoe: the Critical Heritage* (1972); an edition of Defoe's *Tour Through the whole Island of Great Britain* (1971); *The Augustan Vision* (1974); and *An Introduction to Pope* (1975).

JENNY MEZCIEMS: Lecturer in English, University of Warwick, is currently writing a book about *Gulliver's Travels* and has published an essay on the third voyage and utopian fiction in the *Modern Language Review*. She is an assistant editor of the *Modern Language Review* and of the *Yearbook of English Studies*.

# Index